"Feelings Buried Alive

Never Die ..."

by

Karol K. Truman

PLEASE NOTE THAT "FEELINGS BURIED ALIVE NEVER DIE..."
IS A DOCUMENTARY AND REFLECTS ONLY
THE PERSONAL EXPERIENCE AND VIEWS OF THE AUTHOR

The ideas and suggestions herein are my own experiences. There may be some ideas in the book that may not agree with orthodox, allopathic medicine.

NOTE—IMPORTANT: The information contained in this book is for educational purposes only. The medical conditions discussed should only be cared for under the direction of a physician. Proper care from a physician should not be avoided, delayed, or discarded when there is reason to consult a physician. This book is not designed to diagnose, treat, or prescribe any disease. The author accepts no responsibility for such use. Conditions requiring proper medical attention should be referred to a physician.

— KAROL K. TRUMAN

"FEELINGS BURIED ALIVE NEVER DIE . . . "
Copyright © 1991, 2003 Olympus Distributing
Revised & Expanded 2003

Seventeenth Printing, 2014
Editor and word-processor: Joyce Hilton-Davis
Cover: Valerieann J. Giovanni
Illustration: Jerry T. Christopherson
Final Editor: Karen Pool

Published by Olympus Distributing
P.O. Box 4218
St. George, Utah 84771
All rights reserved. Printed in the U.S.A.

Library of Congress Cataloging-in-Publication Data

Truman, Karol Kuhn,
    Looking Good Feeling Great
    Feelings Buried Alive Never Die . . .
    Healing Feelings . . . From Your Heart
    1. Spiritual Healing   2. Adult Child   3. Inner Child
    4. BodyMind   5. Recovery   6. Personal Growth
    7. Self-Healing   8. Self-Discovery   9. Self-Help

ISBN 0911207-02-3   Price $17.95

Dedication

This book is dedicated to each of you who are seeking peace of mind and the gift of joy which intrinsically belongs to you by virtue of your Be-ing.

Acknowledgments

To my dear, departed Father ... for his gentle nature and his unconditional love and acceptance of me.

To my precious Mother for giving me the courage to look for the answers and the faith in myself necessary to keep going.

To my cherished husband, Delmont, for his role in working through many of my feelings . . . for his love and support, and for his patience.

To our beautiful children, Dan, Rhonda, Gina, Boyd and their spouses, for being the caring people they are, and for humoring me during the years spent searching for these truths and this understanding.

To Carolyn Lybbert, my eternal gratitude for sharing the original "Script" with me at such a crucial time in my life, and for always being there at the beginning, when I was processing, resolving, and healing so many of my feelings.

To my friend, Margot Bingham, for introducing me to Carolyn, and for her contribution as we learned about feelings, thoughts, and emotions, and how they impact our lives.

To Joyce Davis, for allowing me the use of her computer and her home while writing the original manuscript; for her untold hours and untiring efforts in the editing and word processing of this book. For her hospitality, for feeding me, and for all the other exhausting "extra miles" she went while working on this project. Without her, this book would not be. I cannot thank her enough!

To Don Davis, Joyce's husband, for sharing his home, his computer and sacrificing countless hours with his wife in order for this book to come about. (And, to Joyce's family—thanks for sharing her.)

To Marlene Yardley, for her love, support, encouragement and friendship. For her belief in me and the importance of disseminating this information. For the selfless sharing of her time in assisting me with ever so many things in order for this book to be completed.

And to the unnamed others who responded to my call and picked up the pieces during the completion stages of this book . . . my deepest gratitude.

To Nancy Peterson for her patience and unending effort in helping conceptualize the book cover. And . . . for being such a great sounding board.

To the many doctors and therapists who have experienced the value of the information contained herein and chosen to have this book available in their offices. Thank you for recommending it to your colleagues, patients, and clients.

To the countless people who have put the principles of this book to the test these several years, and validated the power of the "tool" in it's ability to change lives. You have taught me much! Your e-mail, phone calls, and letters are very much appreciated.

Further, and most importantly, to God the Father, for allowing me the particular "pain" I needed on my life's journey to cause me to go inward for solutions. This journey has taught me, and continues to teach me, deeper understanding and greater love; bringing me more happiness and joy than I could ever have experienced any other way. I rejoice in His love for you and me, and praise His name forever!

Table of Contents

Introduction

Everywhere I turn, people from all walks of life are experiencing what seems to be insurmountable challenges in their lives. Those who are striving to alleviate the pain created by these challenges have undoubtedly searched for relief. Many have found or are finding help to minimize the pain they are experiencing as they continue to add knowledge and understanding to assist them on their journey through life.

Yes, I too, have had my share of challenges. In 1984, however, I was given the gift of a wonderful "tool" that began instantly to impact my life in a very positive manner. Those family members, friends and clients who have had benefit of this "tool" and who have used it on a consistent basis have also made significant alterations in their lives.

I would be the last one to tell you or lead you to believe that this "tool" will solve all your problems, or that you won't need to know anything else after you learn to use this "tool"— the journey is on-going. I only know that by using this "tool" I have been able to alleviate about 90% of the negativity and erroneous programming in my life, the result of which has brought me the sweet gifts of serenity, love, contentment, peace, and joy. I am compelled to share it with you. This "tool" has the potential of revealing you to yourself, IF . . . you are prepared to be accountable for your feelings, your thoughts, and your beliefs.

My sincere intent is that you will have a strong desire and the motivation to incorporate this "tool" into your life and come to a better understanding of who you really are.

May your journey be as exciting and fulfilling as mine. May you be able to alleviate those significant negative feelings, thoughts, and beliefs in your life that have caused or are causing you to experience pain of any kind.

Chapter 1

The Language of Feelings

Of all the languages in the world, the most difficult language to communicate is the language of feelings. One of our greatest challenges as human beings is to effectively communicate with other people what we truly feel. Perhaps the most significant and consequential challenge we face, however, is acquiring the ability to communicate congruently with ourselves.

Have you ever felt as if there was a time bomb inside you ready to explode at any second, yet you were unable to identify the source of this feeling? Have you experienced one day where an ordinary task was easy and then the next day it was an impossible, gigantic mountain to climb?

Have you ever had the feeling of being two (or more) separate individuals or of being someone totally different than yourself—wondering who the REAL you was or where the real you had gone?

Perhaps for some unexplainable reason you have been touchy or agitated for longer periods of time than you would like—maybe even unleashing verbiage or exhibiting behavior that was unworthy of you.

Have you ever had the feeling that you were two enemies (or more) who were constantly fighting each other—as if there was a war going on inside you? Or perhaps you've experienced sleeplessness night after night for no apparent reason.

Have you ever felt that no one understood you? Or, even, and perhaps worse, that you didn't understand yourself? What causes these disquieting moments—these uncomfortable feelings and this internal conflict?

If you recognize yourself in the above examples or have experienced similar frustrations, I would suggest to you the possibility that you could be suffering from unresolved, repressed and suppressed negative feelings you thought you had taken care of—feelings you thought were dead and gone. What you may not realize is that when negative feelings are not resolved as they occur, these feelings remain very much alive in your physical energy field (body) and these feelings affect each day of your life. In other words, unresolved "FEELINGS BURIED ALIVE, NEVER DIE!"

These buried feelings are very real. They are energies in and of themselves. They are alive, living, and constantly affecting you. These buried feelings have a personality, and these feelings that have been buried alive will, of necessity, have to manifest themselves sooner or later.

Somehow, somewhere, in some aspect of your life the effect of these negative feelings WILL be realized. They will make themselves known when you least expect it. These buried feelings may suddenly—after smoldering or fermenting for who knows how long—become apparent in your physical well-being. How? Through dis-ease. Or, the effects of these buried feelings could be exhibited in your relationships. Perhaps these feelings will become evident in your mental, emotional or financial well-being. Take your pick . . . one or all!

Often, however, we do not get to "pick or choose" which feelings will manifest in our life. Nor do we consciously choose how or when they will manifest. Suffice it to say, these feelings trigger our everyday, minute to minute choices and behavior whether we recognize it or not. Feelings that we have buried and are completely unaware of are what create the challenges, the uneasiness, the dis-ease, the pain and the crises situations in our lives.

Thus, it is possible to experience one or more of these negative states at the same time, whether in our relationships, our physical, our financial, or the mental/emotional areas of our life. In other words, DIS-EASE in any form is the natural consequence of unresolved negative feelings that have seemingly been forgotten, ignored or buried.

According to Prevention Magazin:,

> It is estimated that 90 percent of all physical problems have psychological roots. That may sound like a gross exaggeration. In fact, it's probably a conservative estimate. A growing body of evidence indicates that virtually every ill that can befall the body—from acne to arthritis, headaches to heart disease, cold sores to cancer—is influenced, for better or worse, by our emotions. (Quoted from *The Complete Guide To Your Emotions And Your Health* p.563 by Emrika Padus and the editors of Prevention magazine.)

This subject is, and has been the focus of research projects, human behavior studies, TV programs, and many books. Much emphasis has been placed on this topic in recent months and years.

The world population is looking for answers to the whys of varied problems and negative experiences. People look to their peers, to professionals, to educators, to education, to religious authority, to books, or to self-awareness seminars for answers. What are they seeking? What is the bottom line? Observation from my counseling experience is that most people have a deep desire and are searching for peace of mind and the ability to truly love and be loved unconditionally.

It seems that part of us—our Higher Intelligence—is crying out to be liberated from untold years of suppression and denial. What is more, this cry for liberation comes from every corner of the globe. The cry comes seeking relief from pain, hate, anger, fear, war, suffering, hurt, sickness, resentment, loneliness, depression, failure, misery, prejudice, guilt and many other undesirable conditions that afflict mankind today.

The decade of the 80's established an impetus for bringing the physical body back into order and balance. One has only to consider the explosion that work-out books and tapes initiated during the 80's to recognize the impact of that new awareness—the need for physical fitness and well-being. And the impetus continues.

In the 90's self-examination of feelings and emotions began receiving a focus that is contributing to an emotional cleansing and healing of major proportions. At long last, humankind's willingness to retreat from denial, to own the source of their problems, accept responsibility for them and become accountable for the feelings and thoughts which created them, is establishing an energy that is opening the channels for bringing the inner peace people are so desperately seeking.

People everywhere are questioning, seeking, and striving to understand what makes them tick. They want to find the cause of their suffering, their pain, and their problems. They also want to learn how to alleviate these problems and heal themselves. Perhaps what we have not comprehended before, is that our experiences in life are actually our own state of mind being projected outward. When we have a state of mind that indicates inner peace, joy, love and well-being—then peace, joy, love and well-being is what we naturally project outward and, consequently, these positive states of mind bring us positive experiences.

On the contrary, when our state of mind is one that is occupied with fears, doubts, troubles and concerns—then fears, doubts, troubles and concerns are what we naturally project outward. Consequently, we will experience that which we fear, doubt, are troubled by and concerned with as our reality.

Put another way:

> Whatever we choose to focus our attention on will automatically multiply in our lives. If our attention is on our troubles or

the injustice of the past, they will become our trials of the present also. If instead our minds are focused on the blessings we have received or the love of God, family and fellowman, these will grow stronger. (*Bring Forth Your Light*, Frederick W. Babbel)

Most of us recognize that we are not just a piece of flesh. We are at least five-dimensional. By this I mean: spiritual, emotional, mental, physical, and social. And, in order to be in tune or in balance and work in harmony and realize fulfillment, these five dimensions serve us much more efficiently and effectively if they are attended to equally.

In our younger years, many of us were taught to shut off or close down the emotional facet of our Be-ing. We were programmed to deny feelings, to bury them. If our feelings were hurt or we didn't like something the way it was, we were taught to "forget it;" "ignore it;" "it doesn't matter;" "don't think about it;" or "be quiet and it might go away."

Well, guess what? "It"—those feelings—didn't go away! Denying them didn't make them disappear. Those feelings were repressed, suppressed, stuffed, or buried. However, that doesn't mean they went away. On the contrary, they registered somewhere inside us. And the less-than-desirable circumstances we may find ourselves in today, in any aspect of our life, are the manifestation of those so-called buried feelings.

Those feelings did not leave. Just because we buried them alive doesn't mean they are dead. Those feelings are NOT dead unless they are resolved. They remain the source of our unresolved conflicts. Subconsciously, they are not forgotten nor will they be forgotten. Those feelings from long ago have been and are still being registered at and in the cellular level of our Being. They are the feelings which govern our thought patterns, our beliefs, and our attitudes. Those feelings determine our emotional reactions and our experiences in life. They are unconscious, hidden and have been denied. Nevertheless, they are a definite part of our intra-cellular and subconscious programming. The experiences we are having in our lives today are the effects caused by those unresolved feelings we denied; those feelings we stuffed and then buried alive! The problem is, once again, THOSE FEELINGS DID NOT DIE!

The purpose of this book is to share with you how to return to, or perhaps attain for the first time in your life, the forgiveness, peace, love, joy, success, happiness and tranquility you are desiring and seeking.

The principles contained in this book will aid you in re-focusing your life and eliminating negative feelings, beliefs or states of mind you are or have been harboring, protecting and nurturing. In turn, this will allow you a much more fulfilling, self-validating (positive) day-to-day existence than you may have previously experienced and enjoyed.

Using the principles and the *tool* contained in this book on a daily basis enhances your ability to bring the physical, mental, emotional, spiritual, and social aspects of your Be-ing into alignment and balance. This alignment then provides the internal environment that makes it possible for you to achieve an inner harmony and peace—contributing greatly to any desirable changes you wish to make.

Your life can realize a cohesiveness it has never known.

How do we accomplish this?

> Let us open the eyes of our eyes so that we can see.
> Let us open the ears of our ears so that we can hear.
> Let us open the heart of our hearts so that we can listen and hearken to truth and light.

First, it is imperative that we learn to identify negative feelings and thoughts. This is necessary before we can avoid or resolve them. It doesn't take long for this to become automatic, and we are able to be happier, more cheerful, more appreciative and more caring much of the time. "We can dispel discord among those around us by becoming conduits [of] peace and love." (*Bring Forth Your Light*, Frederick W. Babbel)

As words and their meanings are crucial to a clear communication of the material contained in this book, it is vitally important that you have a clear and correct concept of the following four words as they are used in this book: (Taken from *Webster's 1828 American Dictionary of the English Language*, and *The Reader's Digest Great Encyclopedia Dictionary*.)

Feelings

1. To perceive or to be aware of through thought, bodily or emotional reactions, instinct, etc.
2. To produce an indicated overall condition, impression, or reaction.
3. An impression produced upon a person; having sensation.
4. Marked by or indicating emotion.

Thoughts

1. That which the mind thinks.
2. The act or process of using the mind actively and deliberately.
3. The product of thinking; an idea, concept, judgment, etc.
4. Inward reasoning; the workings of conscience.

Emotions

1. A strong surge of feeling marked by an impulse to outward expressions, and often accompanied by complex bodily reactions; any strong feeling as love, hate, or joy.
2. Any agitation of mind or excitement of sensibility.
3. A moving of the mind or soul.

Beliefs

1. Acceptance of the truth or actuality of anything without certain proof; mental conviction.
2. That which is believed; something held to be true or valid. BELIEF denotes acceptance with or without proof or strong emotional feelings.

Allow yourself to flow with these words. There is such a fine line of distinction between the definition of FEELINGS and EMOTIONS that it may be easy to become confused.

Let me give you a simple illustration of how I use these two words: If you became very angry at someone but held the anger inside—this is a FEELING. However, if you became angry and let yourself explode, either verbally or physically, the feeling of anger would then be manifesting itself as an EMOTION. In other words, the EMOTION is the outward expression or reaction of the FEELING. Or . . . the EMOTION is the result of an intense feeling and a thought coming together.

BELIEFS are established in our psyche as a result of the conclusions we unknowingly establish from the experiences our feelings and thoughts bring to us.

Chapter 2

Energy Vibrations

In this exciting, magnificent, electro-magnetic Universe of ours, everything found in, on, under and above the Universe has an energy vibration. Literally *EVERYTHING* has unique energy! Anything that is "matter" has energy vibrations. When energy is discussed, however, most people think of energy in relation to our bodies, such as "I ran out of energy before the day was half over." Or, they relate energy to an energy crisis—gas, gasoline, oil, fuel or electricity.

These are definite sources of energy, but not energy in the true sense of the word. Real energy is an unknown force. It is used by each of us every day of our existence, and yet we still don't know exactly what it is. We can't see it. We can't smell it, taste it, hear it, or hold it in our hands. We do experience manifestations of it everyday in many ways, although it is still a mystery to the majority of the population. Light is energy, water is energy and electricity is energy. But, how do we explain it?

Energy is a force that takes many forms and can be manifested in many ways. Rocks have energy. Likewise, trees, plants, soil and insects have energy. The carpet on your floor has an energy. So does the material in your sofa, the wood your piano is made of, and the ivory keys. The glass in windows has energy vibrations as well as the brick in the fireplace, the frame around the painting and the paint in the painting.

The food you eat, the clothes you wear, your hair, your nails, your glands, and your organs all have energy. Everything about you is energy. Most importantly though, for the purposes of this book, it is imperative to understand that your FEELINGS and your THOUGHTS are energy. Your feelings and your thoughts are matter. And, according to what physics has taught us, matter cannot be destroyed. The form of matter CAN be altered, but matter itself is indestructible.

Scientist and author, Edward W. Russell postulates the actuality of thought-fields. In the book, *Vibrations*, we are told that a thought is an independent force all it's own . . . that it can produce effects which form a field.

So, if thoughts are matter and have their own thought-field, why can't they be destroyed? Because thought consists of atoms and atoms are composed of tiny amounts of pure energy—waves of energy solidified or frozen into the non-movement recognized as matter. Matter is a form of energy that is in very slow or stopped motion (or frequency).

Therefore, thought as matter is impossible to destroy. Feelings as energy, or matter, are also impossible to destroy. Nevertheless, MATTER CAN BE ALTERED. Consequently, the energy of feelings and of thoughts can be changed. If the feeling or the thought is negative matter (energy) it can be changed to positive matter (energy).

What criteria determines whether a feeling or a thought is negative? When the energy of a particular feeling or thought obscures the truth of our Be-ing, obscures our perfect blueprint, negativity is created. According to Dr. Deepak Chopra, we all come here with a perfect blueprint, with a memory of perfection.

Negative energy of any kind covers over this memory of perfection to some degree and slowly obscures the truth of our Be-ing. As the negativity mounts in our Be-ing, little by little our memory of perfection becomes shrouded and obscured. Consequently, our negativity creates a false-Self.

If you wonder at the power of feelings and thoughts as an energy, the following information can assist you in comprehending it's ever present vibrational influence. Scientists used to believe that energy traveled at the rate of 186,000 miles per second. They have recently discovered, however, that it travels 700 times faster!! Thought being energy, therefore, means that thought travels at the same speed, which is 130,200,000 miles per second.

Energy vibrations move in pulses—like waves. The crest is the pulse of energy and the trough is the pause. How close together the waves are is called frequencies—how frequently the waves occur. This range of frequencies is called the electro-magnetic spectrum. What we see, feel and experience materially is but a tiny part of the entire electro-magnetic spectrum. Beyond this range lies the largest part of the spectrum, heretofore immeasurable and undetectable. Here lies the frequency rates of gravity, magnetism, and thought itself!

All elements of the earth have different energies. Some have energy vibrations whose frequencies are very close together and some have energy vibrations whose frequencies are very broad or far apart. In any given matter, the closer together the vibrational frequencies, the higher the vibration and the closer that matter is to its energy Source. Or, putting it another way, the more positive the energy of any given matter, the closer the frequencies, and thus, the closer that matter is to its Source. Likewise, the more broad the frequencies of any given matter, the further that energy is from its Source. In other words, the more negative the energy of any given matter, the wider the frequencies, and the further that matter (energy) is from its Source. (See illustration on the following page.)

A very vivid and profound illustration of the power of feeling and thought frequencies was told by Dr. W. Jerome Stowell. Here is his story:

> I was almost a devout atheist, I did not believe that God was any more than a conglomeration of everyone's mind put together, and the good that was there, that was God as far as I was concerned. As for the real, all-powerful God existing and loving us all, with power over everything, I did not believe that.
>
> Then one day I had an experience that really set me thinking. I was in a large pathological laboratory where we were attempting to find the wave length of the brain. We found a channel of wave lengths, and that channel has a mach room (unit of measure) in it wherein the different wave lengths of each individual's brain are further separated in identity more clearly than are the finger prints of each individual's hand. This is a

point we should remember: God can actually keep in heaven a record of our thoughts as individualals just as the FBI can keep a record of our fingerprints in Washington, D.C.

We wanted to make an experiment to discover what took place in the brain at the moment of transition from life to death. We chose first a lady whose family had sent her to a mental institution but who had been discharged. The doctors could find nothing wrong with her other than the fact she had cancer of the brain. This affected the balance of her body only. As far as her alertness of mind was concerned and in every other way, she was exceptionally brilliant. We knew she was on the verge of death and she was informed, in this research hospital, that she was going to die.

We arranged a tiny pick-up in her room to ascertain what would take place in the transition of her brain from life to death. We also put a very small microphone, about the size of a shilling, in the room so that we could hear what she said, if she had anything to say.

Five of us hardened scientists—perhaps I was the hardest of the group—were in an adjoining room with our instruments prepared to register and record what transpired. Our device had a needle pointing to "0" in the center of the scale. To the right the scale was calibrated to 500 points positive, to the left the scale was calibrated to 500 points negative. We previously had recorded on this identical instrument the power used by a fifty-kilowatt broadcasting station in sending a message around the world. The needle then registered 9 points of the positive side.

As the last moments of this woman's life arrived, she began to pray and praise the Lord. She asked the Lord to be merciful unto those who had despitefully used her, then she reaffirmed her faith in God, telling Him she knew He was the only power, and the only living power. He always had been and always would be. She praised God and thanked Him for His power and for her knowledge of His reality. She told Him how much she loved Him.

We scientists had been so engrossed with this woman's prayer that we had forgotten our experiment. We looked at each other and saw tears streaming down scientific faces.

Suddenly we heard a clicking sound on our forgotten instrument. We looked and the needle was registering a positive 500, desperately trying to go higher only to bounce against the 500 positive post in its attempt!

By actual instrumentation we had recorded that the brain of a woman alone and dying in communication with God had registered more than 55 times the power used by a fifty-kilowatt broadcasting station sending a message around the world.

After this we decided to try a case very unlike the first one. We chose a man lying in the research hospital stricken with a deadly social disease. His brain had become atrophied to the very point of death. He was practically a maniac.

After we had set up our instruments, we arranged for one of the nurses to antagonize the man. Through her wiles, she attracted his interest in her, and then suddenly told him she did not want to have anything more to do with him. He began to verbally abuse her, and the needle began to register on the negative side. Then he cursed her and took the name of God in vain. The needle then clicked back and forth against the 500 negative post.

By actual instrumentation we had registered what happened to the brain when that brain broke one of God's Ten Commandments, "Thou shalt not take the name of the Lord thy God in vain."

We had established by instrumentation the positive power of God and the negative power of the adversary. We had found that beneficial truth is positive, and non-beneficial things covered by the "Thou shalt nots" of the Ten Commandments are negative.

If we scientists can record these things, I believe with all my
heart that the Lord God can keep a record of our thoughts.

Do you think the vibrational frequencies of the positive feelings,
thoughts and words of the sick woman in this story drew her closer to
her Source? Likewise, that the vibrational frequencies of the negative
feelings, thoughts and words of the sick man repelled him from his
divine Source?

What is meant by Source? Source is what or who you consider to
be your Source . . . your Divine Source . . . whether that is God,
Universal Intelligence, Universal Mind, Buddha, Mohammed or
whomever or whatever you look to as a higher power or Supreme Being.

Most people have a reference as to their Infinite Source. And the
majority of us, either consciously or subconsciously, have a longing to
be able to better understand and eventually identify with that Source, if
at all possible. The closer your individual collective vibrational frequencies are, the more in tune or in harmony you are going to be with your
Source. The more in harmony you are, the closer you will draw to your
Source. The closer you are to your Source, the more peace of mind you
will experience; the more joy you will feel; the greater your capacity to
love; and the more content you will be.

It would be interesting and revealing if someone were to take a poll
to ascertain how many people truly experience the above characteristics
of well be-ing on an on-going, continuing basis NOW in their lives. I
seriously doubt we would find a very large percentage of the population
that does.

How did we get so far away? What happened to distance us from
our Source? Most of us are struggling daily just to maintain the status-
quo, let alone narrow the gap between us and our Source. Has the collective fear, anger, hate, pride, greed, blame, hurt, bitterness, discontent,
judgment, misery, sadness, hopelessness, and unhappiness in the world

today helped contribute to the conditions in which we presently find ourselves?

In the process of becoming civilized it seems man has repelled himself further and further away from that which creates positive vibrations—the vibrations with the more desirable, closer frequencies. In our quest for comfort, success, riches and gain we seem to have strayed far away from positive vibrations. Even though good intentions motivate most people, there is an increased inability to create and enjoy qualities of well be-ing in our lives—qualities which establish vibrations with the closer frequencies—on a permanent basis.

In an effort to fill our basic needs for love, acceptance and recognition, unfortunately we get caught up in what society seems to foster— the frame or game of seeing who can get the most, do the best and have the biggest. Anything to get gain seems to be a general rule with much of the human race today. Consequently, many themes on television, MTV, in movies, literature, magazines, and music appeal to our more base, sordid and depraved qualities.

If we add to all the items heretofore listed, liquor, tobacco and drugs, there is a further compounding of negative vibrational energy. This is all in consequence of the evils and designs which exist in the hearts of conspiring men in our time. These men do not care who has to suffer, or who dies . . . just as long as their objectives are met. "Anything to get gain," is the motto. And, the gain is called *greed* or *power*.

The theme continues: Anything to excite or satisfy my senses. Anything to satisfy my appetites. ANYTHING GOES! regardless of what it is. So, in accordance with natural laws, the disregard of others welfare (the "anything to get gain" syndrome) is contributing to the negativity which permeates our society today, and it is taking its toll on the human family.

Michael Wickett, in his audio tape program, *It's All Within Your Reach, Building Positive Self Concepts*, states that:

The Law of Control is an essential law in understanding how we function. Many psychologists, if not most psychologists today, have come to the conclusion that the degree of control that we feel we have is in direct proportion to the amount of mental health that we have.

The Law of Control simply says that we feel good about ourselves to the exact degree to which we feel we are in control of our own life. And that we feel bad about ourselves when we feel out of harmony with ourselves to the exact degree to which we feel we are controlled by outer circumstances, by other people—by things beyond our control.

Psychologists call this the difference between an internal locus (place) of control—a feeling that we're steering our own lives, and an external locus of control—a feeling that someone else is controlling our lives and taking us where they want us to go.

Control begins, first of all, with our feelings—what we feel, and what we feel controls our thoughts—what we think, and that leads to how we perform—to our actions. BUT ALL CONTROL BEGINS WITH TAKING CONTROL OF THE FEELINGS WE HOLD IN OUR HEART, because these feelings determine the thoughts we hold in our conscious mind.

The vast majority of us live our lives by the Law of Accident, that is, by failing to plan we are planning to fail. We have no goals beyond the short term. We make no plans. Consequently, we don't really feel we are in control of our own destiny. We just hope that somehow things will work out.

Mr. Wickett believes that one of the major reasons we have so much negativity, disharmony, unhappiness, misery and skepticism in our society is that most people feel like "bump cars" in a carnival. They go off in one direction or another, depending upon the next incident that happens to them. And, of course, people who live by the Law of Accident have no sense of control or mental well-being.

Wickett states:

> Opposed to the Law of Accident is what we call the Law of Cause and Effect. The Law of Cause and Effect is really the basic Law of the Universe. It is the reason that everything happens. And, the Law of Cause and Effect simply says this: that for every effect in our lives, there is a specific cause. If we do not like the effects that we are enjoying (or not enjoying) in our life, it is up to us to identify the causes, and change the causes. That, irrespective of whether or not we know what the causes are, there is a reason for everything that happens. There is in fact, no such thing as an accident. EVERYTHING THAT HAPPENS IN OUR LIFE HAPPENS BY LAW AND NOT BY CHANCE! It is our primary duty to understand the laws that control our destinies. By understanding the Laws we can control the causes and change the effects to anything that we want.
>
> You will recognize immediately that the Law of Cause and Effect is completely consistent with the Law of Control, because if we can identify the causes, we can control the effects and therefore control what happens to us in our lives. And people who live happy, fully functioning, harmonious lives are people who live by the Law of Control and understand the Law of Cause and Effect in their lives.

FEELINGS are CAUSES & CONDITIONS are their EFFECTS.

Our feelings are always the primary causes of the conditions or effects in our lives. Our lives are initially controlled by our feelings, which, in turn, create our thoughts. Everything we are today is the sum total of all the feelings we have had to this moment. If we wish our lives to be different in the future it is necessary to change our feelings, which then changes our thinking, in the present. By so doing, we change the direction of our lives!

Another author puts it this way:

> In all the universe there can be no such things as luck or fate; every action, every thought is governed by law. Behind every bit of good fortune lie the causes that we ourselves have sometime, somewhere set in motion. Behind all ill fortune we will find the energy, we ourselves, have generated. Every cause must have a certain definite effect, there is no dodging the results, we reap what we sow with exact mathematical precision. (Venice Bloodworth, *Key to Yourself*)

Any undesirable condition we find ourselves in today is telling us that natural laws have caught up with us and we are witnessing this Law of Cause and Effect reigning supreme on our parade. Our intelligence knows when we are not in harmony with the Laws of the Universe. We can only compromise for so long before the evidence is clearly obvious that natural laws have not been observed.

Breaking natural laws causes disharmony. The problems and challenges people are experiencing in their lives everywhere—as well as the undesirable conditions or events we may be experiencing in our own life—is a very clear indication that natural laws have been and are being, not only broken, but desecrated. Then let's combine all the factors of imbalance in our inharmonious environment with the individual negative feelings, thoughts, and emotions we have been burying—or were compelled to bury in order to survive. Could it be possible that the problems of disharmony and imbalance are further compounded? This disharmony has brought about a definite fragmentation of individuals, as well as families, cities, and nations. And the wide scale fragmentation it has created is the unfortunate effect all these collective negative energy vibrations are having on human lives on a global basis today.

Another sad commentary that results from breaking natural laws is the gross personal imbalance it causes, which subsequently undermines

an individual's ability to have or maintain peace of mind and a continual sense of well-Be-ing.

When we, as individuals, decelerate or halt this fragmentation by
fixing—making a shift or changing the energies in ourselves—we can
experience the harmony and balance that we are seeking, which is a natural by-product of our shift. At this point, OUR shift will have positive
and far reaching effects, not only on us, but in the lives of everyone
around us.

"So, what is it that needs fixing?" Our feelings and our thoughts
are what determined where we are today. If what is happening to us now,
both physically and emotionally, is undesirable, our feelings and our
thoughts are what need fixing.

Many people have a difficult time identifying their feelings and
their thoughts. (This was my problem, also.) Too many of us have not
been taught—or perhaps not allowed—to be cognizant of what's going
on inside our mind or our body. Perhaps, due to overwhelming pain or
abuse, our early conditioning kept us from being consciously aware of
our feelings and thoughts. Consequently, it's impossible for us to be sensitive or mindful of them today. Or, we could simply be so accustomed
to turning our pain and hurt over to something (i.e. drugs/food) or someone else to *fix*, that our ability to be consciously aware of what is taking
place inside ourselves has turned off. It's usually for these reasons we
haven't been schooled in how to resolve our feelings for ourselves.
Sadly, the majority of the human family's consciousness is either fragmented or missing entirely. Dr. Deepak Chopra tells us in his book,
Quantum Healing, "When consciousness is fragmented, it starts a war in
the mind-body system."

You may be asking, "So, what do I do about it?" Your first challenge will be to get in touch with your external and internal dialogue.
That is, what you are saying out loud and what you are saying to yourself. What you say—out loud and silently—leads you to what you are
thinking inside your head. This then leads you to what you are feeling

inside. One way to help yourself become more aware is to be sensitive to what is happening around you. Take yourself outside any situation and just be an observer . . . as if you were sitting in the audience and witnessing a play, with you as one of the actors.

The "Doing Something About It" formula:

1) Listen to your words—to your outer talk. By doing this you are training your Self for taking the next step, which is:

2) Listening to and hearing what you are saying to your Self—your self-talk. You then discover the passageway to your

3) Thoughts. By recognizing your thoughts you can begin tracing them back to

4) Feelings, which initially triggered the thoughts in the first place.

(See pages 39-45 in *Healing Feelings . . . From Your Heart* for a more in depth explanation.)

Many people ask me how they can begin to label their feelings; how they can become aware. My suggestion to them is to pay attention from every angle of their existence (seeing, hearing, smelling, sensing, feeling, even tasting) to what is going on in every situation they find themselves. Here are some simple examples: Have you ever walked into a room where two people have been engaged in a heated argument you didn't even hear? You can definitely feel that those negative vibes (vibrations) are still alive, resonating and bouncing around. "The air (vibes) was so thick you could have cut it with a knife." Notice the look on each person's face; the body language; your feelings; your thoughts; the awkward moments when everyone is at a loss for words; other people's reactions; what is said; how surface or how deep the conversation is, etc.

If you've ever been in love or been around two people who are in love, you can definitely feel those kinds of vibrations, too. There is a connective energy between these two people that is expressed through non-verbal body language inspired and motivated by the feelings which emanate from their hearts. How do they look at each other? How are other people acting by being around them? What are you feeling just being in their presence? In other words, what are you seeing, what are you hearing, what are you sensing, what are you feeling, what are you thinking?

Have you ever had someone say something to you that cut you to the quick? I'm sure most people have had this experience. WE know when our feelings have been hurt, whether the person who made the cutting remark does or not. Think about it . . . our FEELINGS have been hurt. What caused them to be hurt? Where do these feelings come from in the first place; and why would one person be hurt and another person not, in the same set of circumstances? What makes the difference? Where do these feelings begin?

Chapter 3

Where Feelings Begin

Where DO feelings begin? Many of our feelings were established before we were born. We entered this realm with some of them. We were sensitive to the feelings our parents were experiencing during our gestation period. These feelings often caused us to establish incorrect perceptions and beliefs at the time they were being experienced. How is this possible? The following information is from a collection of articles published in the 80's.

Until recently scientists believed that the infant was a virtual blank and, following Freud's dictum, that only at two or three years of age could personality begin to form. Gradually, however, over the last fifty years investigators have begun to break through the ignorance, preconceptions, and lack of data surrounding the prenatal and infant states to reveal a very different picture of these early stages of life. This emerging view gives a broader perspective on human consciousness and the intimate connections among human beings, as well as new insights into the meaning and responsibilities of parenthood.

Recent research on infants shows that even at birth the child has mastered many sophisticated physical and psychological skills. It is increasingly clear that the infant develops these skills in the prenatal period. In *The Secret Life of the Unborn Child*,

Dr. Thomas Verny tells us that the unborn child is not 'the passive, mindless creature of the traditional pediatrics texts.

'We now know that the unborn child is an aware, reacting
human being who from the sixth month on (and perhaps even
earlier) leads an active emotional life. Along with this startling
finding we have made these discoveries:

'The fetus can see, hear, experience, taste and, on a primi-
tive level, even learn inutero. . . . Most importantly, he can feel—
not with an adult's sophistication, but feel nonetheless.'
(*Mysteries of Pre-natal Consciousness*, by Sarah Belle
Dougherty, Sunrise Magazine, February/March 1990).

The article discusses the unborn's development and his sensitivity
to light at the sixteenth week of pregnancy. By the fourth month the
unborn baby has developed his basic reflexes which allow facial expressions. By the fifth or sixth month the unborn is as sensitive to touch as
a newborn.

From the 24th week on he hears all the time—listening to the
noises in his mother's body, and to voices, music, etc. Between
28 to 34 weeks his brain's neural circuits are as advanced as a
new born's and the cerebral cortex is mature enough to support
consciousness; a few weeks later brain waves . . . become dis-
tinct. Thus, throughout the third trimester he is equipped with
most of the physiological capability of a newborn.

Even more intriguing is evidence of the impact of the mother's and father's attitudes and feelings on their unborn child.
Based on the findings of many other researchers as well as his
own experience as a psychoanalyst, Dr. Verny presents evidence that the attitude of the mother toward the pregnancy and
the child, as well as toward her partner, have a profound effect
on the psychological development of the child and on the birth
experience. The mother, by her patterns of feeling and behavior, is the chief source of the stimuli which shape the fetus.

Communication between mother and her unborn child takes place in several ways: physically (through hormones, for example), in behavior (the child's kicking, the mother's job and environmental situation), and sympathetically or intuitively (through love, ambivalence, dreams). One of the main means for communication of maternal attitudes and feelings is the neuro-hormones the mother releases, which increase when she is under stress. These substances cross the placenta as easily as nutrients, alcohol, and other drugs do. In moderation these hormones cause physiological relations in the child which stimulate his neural and psychological systems beneficially, but in excess they can affect the developing body adversely. Because of the child's resilience, it is only extreme and generally, long lasting stress that leaves marked negative effects, not isolated thoughts or incidents. Moreover, the mother's love, acceptance, and positive thoughts for the unborn child act as a very strong protection, so he will continue to thrive even if her own situation is troubled. But if his needs for affection and attention are not met, 'his spirit and often his body, also, begin wilting.'

What the child experiences in the womb creates predispositions, expectations, and vulnerabilities rather than specific qualities: we are dealing with susceptibility, not predetermination. Increases in maternal neuro-hormones—such as adrenaline, noradrenaline, and oxytocin—do, however, heighten the child's biological susceptibility to emotional distress by altering the portion of the child's autonomic nervous system which controls physiological processes affecting personality structure. An excess of such maternal hormones has been related to low birth weight, reading difficulties, behavior problems, and gastric disorders. Cigarette smoking, by reducing the amount of oxygen in the mother's blood, has been linked to anxiety in infants traceable to the prenatal period. Most traumatic of all is when the mother, due to illness, a severe loss, or hostility to the pregnancy, withdraws her love and support from her unborn child. He then falls into a depression, is apt to emerge as an apathetic newborn, and may be plagued with depression throughout his life. In one case, a new-born girl refused to bond with, or nurse from her own mother, though she did not refuse other women. The mother, it turned out, had wanted to have an abortion and bore the child grudgingly at the father's insistence. With such mothers, the child lacks a feeling person to whom he can attach himself. His mother becomes absorbed in herself and has no resources left for the baby; nor can he bond with a woman over-burdened with anxiety or frustration.

The unborn child appears to distinguish very clearly between different types of maternal stress. He is affected most strongly by the mother's negative or ambivalent attitude toward the pregnancy, and also by a stressful relationship between the mother and her partner or by a habitual high level of anxiety and fear. As Dr. Verny puts it: 'If loving nurturing mothers bear more self-confident, secure children, it is because the self-aware "I" of each infant is carved out of warmth and love. Similarly, if unhappy, depressed or ambivalent mothers bear a higher rate of neurotic children, it is because their offsprings' egos were molded in moments of dread and anguish. Not surprisingly, without redirection, such children often grow into suspicious, anxious and emotionally fragile adults.'

He further informs us that,

The second most important pre-natal influence is the father's attitude toward the pregnancy and his commitment to the relationship with the mother. One investigator has estimated from his studies that women trapped in a stormy marriage run 'a 237% greater risk of bearing a psychologically or physically damaged child than a woman in a secure, nurturing relationship'—putting her child at greater risk than would many physical illnesses, smoking, or very heavy manual labor.

The article continues:

> The birth experience itself is influential; very detailed birth memories can be retrieved, and the more traumatic the birth experience, the higher the correlation with physiological and psychological problems, including serious disorders such as schizophrenia and psychosis. Again, the mother's attitude has been demonstrated to be the most important factor in determining the character of the birth. The vital factors in predicting the ease and speed of labor are the mother's attitudes toward motherhood, her relations to her own mother, and the presence of habitual worries, fears, and anxieties going beyond normal apprehension. Along with these, women trapped in an unsatisfying relationship fall into the high-risk category. Many problems associated with birth trauma can be prevented or reduced by increased understanding and sensitivity on the part of health professionals and by the parents' choice of who delivers the baby and of a humane and comfortable birth method and location.
>
> That prenatal experiences carry over after birth is beyond dispute, as case histories illustrate. In one, a man troubled with severe anxiety attacks accompanied by hot flushes was regressed by hypnosis to the prenatal period, and revealed that the underlying trauma had occurred in the seventh month of pregnancy. His mother subsequently admitted trying to abort him in the seventh month by taking hot baths. Such 'lost' memories form the record of prenatal consciousness and they can influence us powerfully all our lives.
>
> Why is it, however, that adults almost universally have no memory of these formative experiences without the aid of hypnosis, certain drugs, or various psychoanalytical techniques— memories retrieved from the sixth, and particularly the eighth month, showing that the brain is operating near adult levels? One of the hormones which induce labor, oxytocin, has been

found to wipe out memory. During labor the child's system is flooded with this chemical . . . . Another maternal hormone, ACTH (adrenocorticotropin hormone), which regulates the flow of stress hormones, has the opposite effect, helping to retain memory. Thus, each time the mother becomes frightened or stressed, 'large amounts of the hormone flood into the child's system, helping him to retain a clear, vivid mental picture of her upset and its effect on him.' [This is extremely significant.]

Interestingly, psychiatrists who regularly regress patients to birth and prebirth often report on experiences that appear to go as far back as conception. Dr. Verny hypothesizes another, intuitive form of memory which can be stored on a cellular level, allowing even an ovum or sperm to record and retain memories. [The memory is recorded in the DNA, which we will discuss further.]

The bonding between father and child also begins prenatally. When a man had spoken to his child before birth using short, soothing words, the child one or two hours old picked out and responded to his voice. With both parents, attention to the child is critical in the first four years of life. 'Next to genetic inheritance, in fact, quality of parenting is the single most important factor in shaping the depth and breadth of intellect.'

Empathy with the child and ability to see things from his perspective are key factors to parents' success in stimulating and interacting with their children. There is a marked correlation between rejecting or stressed mothers and traumatic births on the one hand, and later psychological problems and even violent criminal activity on the other. A more active, supportive attitude toward unborn children would have a positive impact on society as a whole by preventing or mitigating destructive personality tendencies, and by giving children a start which meets their need as human beings, not just as higher animals.

Parenthood, then, from its earliest stages is an inner as well as a physical responsibility. Although the influence of physical substances such as drugs (including alcohol and tobacco), viruses, and nutrients on the well-being of the unborn is generally recognized, we're only beginning to realize the parents' tremendous impact along psychological and spiritual lines. Dr. Verny points out several practical applications of this knowledge, such as providing psychological screening to locate emotionally high-risk mothers, so that counseling could be offered to them and steps taken to enhance the psychological and physical development of the child; and also increasing use of more humane, gentle birth practices on the part of medical professionals. His most insistent message, however, is that each individual parent can help by striving to provide a positive, loving psychological environment for the unborn child and infant.

Widespread recognition of the delicate and intimate connections between parent and child prenatally and in infancy will lead naturally to a more realistic idea of the far-reaching responsibility of parenthood, and new respect for the impact of our inner life on those around us. (Dr. Verny)

We are definitely influenced before we are born. We actually enter this realm with predispositions and vulnerabilities. We were sensitive to the feelings our parents were experiencing during our gestation period, often establishing perceptions as they occurred. How is this possible?

According to *The Incredible Machine*, published by the National Geographic Society, an adult human is an assemblage of some 100 trillion cells. In every cell there exists a Universal pattern of Intelligence. This Intelligence has been labeled DNA (deoxyribonucleic acid). There are a least six billion steps of DNA in a single cell that record one life's blueprint. *The Incredible Machine* tells us, "Through segments called genes, DNA determines the make-up of every cell and the hereditary traits of each one of us. DNA dictates the protein mix that fulfills our genetic inheritance." This book further instructs us that the DNA has two key roles: "to direct the creation of protein and to duplicate itself.

The DNA acts as a pattern for the formation of a chemical relative of DNA, messenger RNA (mRNA)" (ribonucleic acid). The RNA bears its coded message to its destination and transfers the message to a transfer tRNA to be decoded.

Dr. Deepak Chopra, M.D., in his wonderful book, *Quantum Healing*, puts it this way,

> RNA's mission is to travel away from the DNA in order to pro-duce the proteins, more than 2 million in number, that actually build and repair the body. RNA is like active knowledge, in com-parison to DNA's silent intelligence. This is how the cells know how and in what way to function, not only during times of devel-opment, but in times of sickness, trauma, emotional stress, accidents, healing and regenerating. In other words, the DNA is the blueprint and the RNA carries out the building instructions.
>
> There is a mind-body connection to the DNA. We can liken it unto a radio broadcast. The mind is sending out impulses of intelligence, DNA receives them.
>
> You may not think that you can 'talk' to your DNA, but in fact you do continually. Thinking happens at the level of DNA, because without the brain cell sending out a neuro-peptide or other messengers, there can be no thought. . . . . Everything in life pours out of DNA—flesh, bones, blood, heart, and nervous system; a baby's first word and a toddler's first step; the matur-ing of reason in the brain's cortex; the play of emotions, thoughts, and desires that flicker like summer lightning through every cell. All of this is DNA.

Every feeling, every thought—every emotion we experience sends a message to each cell in our body. Some messages are more intense and more deeply-seeded than others, but, each cell is nonetheless affected, either adversely or conversely (negatively or positively). It is not neces-sary for us to be consciously aware of the message that our cells are receiving. The cells are still being affected. Each DNA and subsequently, each cell is impacted by every feeling, every thought . . . every emotion we experience. The message response from these feelings/thoughts (emotions) that was sent to the cells of the body is registered in the DNA of the cell. The depth and the strength of the message each cell receives is determined by the intensity of the response to the message, and the intensity of the feeling that is connected with it. This message is then imprinted in the memory of each cell and creates an identity and an energy all it's own. This cell memory is automatically and unconsciously referred back to when the need arises. This same cell memory, thereby, governs our attitudes and beliefs which then directs our behavior from that point on throughout our life.

Barbara Ann Brennan, physicist, therapist, healer, research scientist for NASA and author of *Hands of Light*, tells us that we, as human beings, create according to our beliefs. She explains that the creation or manifestation of disease takes place when a concept or belief is transmitted (resonated or broadcast) from the mental, emotional, or other areas of our Be-ing, into the physical energy field.

This information will become more meaningful and you will gain a clearer understanding as you continue to read. But, for right now, how does this relate to the feelings or thoughts of the parents affecting an unborn child? To begin with, we all recognize that the sperm is a cell and the ova (egg) is a cell. Thousands of DNA steps make up a single gene housed in that cell, and tens of thousands of genes transmit instructions for that cell's existence. These genes have their own programming or genetic coding, which has already been established in the DNA.

When the sperm and the ova meet, they combine prior individual genetic coding and programming from two different people . . . *Mom* and *Dad*. This definite genetic programming is further affected by the feelings that Mom and Dad are individually and collectively experiencing at conception and during gestation, as shown at the beginning of the chapter. The fetus, then, senses what is taking place in the parents lives and is dramatically affected by the feelings and thoughts of the parents at this particular time. Wouldn't it be ideal and wonderful if the lives of everyone expecting a baby were going smoothly and brimming with happiness? Fortunate are those who had this experience. But, alas, often this is not the case. Let's look at some possible conditions that might exist during those nine months of gestation.

Many couples are confronted with stressful challenges during these nine months. Some may be having difficult marriage adjustments. There could be heartache from the loss of a loved one. Other parents might be experiencing serious problems or concerns with older children. Financial struggles are very often a major issue. Some have a great deal of family discord. Desertion or abandonment is not uncommon. There is the possibility of resentment when mother finds herself pregnant which could cause the baby to feel unloved, not wanted or rejected. (Think of the untold numbers of unwanted pregnancies.) I have even counseled people who picked up the feeling of rejection from one of their parents (or both) who wanted the opposite sex of what they were. As you can see, the factors influencing feelings in the unborn child are many and varied.

If you have had children, consider some of the feelings and thoughts (emotions) you went through while you were expecting these children. (Or would you rather forget?) Consider what your parents were experiencing during your gestation period. As you now know, these emotions DO have an affect on the unborn baby. And the effect can be an overwhelming motivator in the life of a person. For nine months there is an incubation period, not only for creating a child but, creating the feelings and predispositions which arrive with the child.

During these nine months, the baby is incapable of rational think-ing. But . . . it (the baby) FEELS. Then, add to this, the trauma of the birth!

According to Joseph Chilton Pearce in his book, *Magical Child*:

> . . . as the infant prepares for birth, it goes into an extreme stress state. This stimulates ACTH to flow from the adrenal glands, preparing the body for dramatic, drastic physical changes, alerting the body and brain of the infant for fight or flight to accomplish the fast work that is to be done. And the high-stress state the unborn infant body is in at this point, prepares the infant to be highly receptive and very desperate for nurturing stimuli that will reduce the stress.
>
> What is that particular stimulus they are needing, and where does it come from? The human mother is genetically programmed to nurture the newborn's body by a continual gentle massage and stimulation. This is what has been found in non-technological countries. Indeed, it creates a bonding. Holding, with a body-molding of the infant to one's self; prolonged and steady eye contact; smiling; and soothing sounds are other ways of bonding, according to Zaslow and Breger, in their brilliant study of infantile autism. Breast feeding, of course, furnishes all these at once. Body stimulus is what needs to be added to that vital body-molding contact.

Not only were most of these elements missing in birthing for a great many years, but during the process of birth the procedure of delivery was often seriously delayed and complicated.

> Drugs, particularly anesthetics, specifically slow up the synchronous movements by which the infant is expelled from the womb, and delivery gets extended to torturous lengths. Fear and anxiety build in the mother, and pain follows swift and sure. The pain calls for more medication, as does massive out-pouring of adrenal steroids preparatory to the great push and adaptation, but the movement does not come. The baby's . . . body continues its outpouring of hormones. Stress piles on stress; the

expected natural cycle of stress-relaxation is not forthcoming. After hours of this, both mother and infant are exhausted.

Then there are all the medical interferences, the carelessness, and the callousness. Coupled with the conditional reflex of fear and the operating amphitheater atmosphere, that deadly table, and being forced to lie down (or even be strapped down), which completely eliminates any last hope of muscular coordination. This is followed by drugs that incapacitate both mother and infant. (The average anesthetic passes through the placenta to the infant in 45 seconds.) Long before delivery (deliverance), mother and infant have been kept at a climactic point of tension, able to achieve no resolution.

After the natural expulsion process is thoroughly fouled up, Mr. Pearce explains,

Instrumentation like forceps and suction machines are casually used to claw or suck the infant out of the mother's body. That beautiful, very sensitive, fragile, precious little head is grabbed in order to expel it. And the mother undergoes an episiotomy which cuts the mother in a manner that would be considered major surgery at other times. This often causes permanent damage. [How sad, especially when, according to Pearce, only in a rare emergency could an episiotomy be justified.]

The semi-drugged, over-stressed, and exhausted infant is, of course, generally unable to get his breath, even if given ample time to do so. The many new, unused coordinates of muscles are confused and malfunctioning. His body is reacting only; all synchronous interactions have long since been destroyed. In addition to his prolonged body fear of oxygen deprivation, when he is finally sucked or clawed out of the mother, his entry is into a noisy, brilliantly lit arena of masked creatures and humming machines. (The hum of fluorescent lighting alone is an overload, much less fluorescence itself which, as the world's greatest authority on lighting, John Ott, makes perfectly clear, is disastrous to infants.)

Do you think the baby has any feelings during this process? Of course it does! What could some of these feelings be? The feeling could possibly be fear, due to the sensation of choking to death with the umbilical chord wrapped around its neck. Or the fear could be from being separated from its Source, and then its mother.

One of the more recent findings that sheds more light on the significant impact of a baby's birth is that the minute the baby's skin is exposed to the earth's atmosphere at birth, there is an automatic reflex that starts the breathing process. If a baby is born breech, naturally it would inhale before its head was out of the birth canal where fluid is possibly present. The baby may then have the sensation of drowning due to inhalation of fluid.

The baby can also feel anger—anger at any number of things; having to be separated from its Source, having to come here, having to go through the trauma of birth, having to leave its mother, etc. Suffice it to say, whatever feeling(s) baby is experiencing at birth, WITH THE FIRST BREATH THE BABY TAKES, THIS FEELING IS SEALED IN THE FLESH (body); ENCODED IN EVERY CELL OF THE BODY! This feeling that is established in the DNA initiates in the baby the core/root of a pre-supposition or belief system that becomes, forever after, the eye glasses through which he views his life. This feeling literally governs the road he travels for the rest of his life!

The beliefs or pre-suppositions that occur at birth, literally move us through life subconsciously creating situations that validate these core beliefs.

Example: I had a 44-year old client who was born two months premature. In the process of counseling Gayle, we found one of the behavior patterns that frustrated her the most about herself was that she could never see anything to completion. Gayle simply had a difficult time fin-

ishing things in all aspects of her life. We found the reason for this
behavior went right back to her birth. "It was as if I had been looking
out a dark window all my life, unable to see clearly." (Gayle's words in
describing it.) She literally was unable to envision herself completing
things. When she realized how her premature beginning had affected her
whole life's pattern—what her incorrect perception had done to her relationships (she was in the process of her second divorce), and other
aspects of her life—all of a sudden the "dark window was filled with
light," and she felt a great sense of relief. The light appeared because
Gayle finally came to an understanding of why she could not finish
commitments. She had not been able to see her gestation period to completion, so for some unknown reason the belief established internally—
the master program that kicked in at birth—was for her to not complete
important events, relationships or responsibilities. This behavior had
flourished throughout Gayle's entire life in everything she did. (The significance of this will become clearer later on.)

Now, back to Mr. Pearce:

> Suction devices are rammed into the mouth and nose, the
> eyelids peeled back to that blinding, painful light and far more
> painful chemicals dropped into the open eyes. He is held by the
> heels and beat on the back or subjected to a mechanical respi-
> rator: at this critical, oxygen-short period, the umbilical cord has
> been cut. He is cleaned up a bit from the blood of the episioto-
> my (which will knock his mother out of the picture for quite some
> time); placed on cold, hard scales to be weighed like any other
> piece of meat in a factory; bundled off to a nursery crib, scream-
> ing in pain and terror if he is lucky; or rushed semi-conscious
> and half dead to an incubator, far worse fate than a crib, if he is
> less lucky . . . . He has moved from a soft, warm dark, quiet, and
> totally nourishing place into a harsh sensory overload. He is
> physically abused, violated in a side variety of ways, subjected

to specific physical pain and insult, all of which could still be overcome, BUT HE IS THEN ISOLATED FROM HIS MOTHER.

During this process an important network of nerve cells called the reticular activating system is dramatically influenced in the baby. This system helps keep the brain awake and alert and helps regulate and coordinate many brain functions. It brings together information from different parts of the brain and from the sense organs, coordinating sensory messages and helping regulate the activity of the brain. Nerve fibers from the reticular system lead down the spinal cord to control the excitability of the spinal cord and the position and tension of muscles. This reticular activating system is the system that filters whether we come into the world with LOVE-based feelings/emotions or FEAR-based feeling/emotions during our birth.

And of course, the feeling/emotion that is unconsciously designated (selected) at this time is determined by our experiences during the birthing process and immediately thereafter. This is why it is of paramount importance for the baby to be held next to the mother's heart—the pulse/beat that he is so familiar with from the nine months gestation—and be comforted by the mother for a least 45 minutes after his birth. If this comfort takes place, the baby has a much better chance of embracing love-based feelings/emotions rather than fear-based feelings/emotions.

An example of a baby remembering what transpired during his beginnings on earth: Neighborhood friends of ours had a baby boy after having had three girls. Needless to say, they were ecstatic! However, this baby boy, whom we will call Kyle, had some problems at birth which made it necessary for him to remain in the hospital for an extended period of time, during which he was kept in an incubator.

Kyle was about 26 months old when his mother was showing him a collection of pictures in a scrapbook she had just completed, of those early days of his life in the hospital. When he looked at the very first page and saw the graphic pictures of himself in an incubator with life-support systems hooked up to him he started crying and blubbering, "Baby wants his Mommy, Baby wants his Mommy!" The buried feelings which he had experienced during those first few days of his life in the hospital were emerging with great intensity. The memory of Kyle's ordeal flooded through him with attending feelings, and he was extremely distraught over feeling those feelings again . . . the ones he had experienced in the hospital. His expression of, "Baby wants his Mommy" is a pretty good indication of the message he would have liked to communicate but couldn't, as he was going through those first few days of his life.

Back to Mr. Pearce:

> It is impossible to overstate the monstrousness of this final violation of a new life. No book can ever express the full ramifications of this crime against nature. This isolation neatly cancels every possible chance for bonding, for relaxation of the birth stress, for the activation of the sensory system for its extra-uterine function, and for the completion of the reticular formation for full mental-physical co-ordinates and learning.
>
> The failure to return to the known matrix (mother) sets into process a chain reaction from which that organism never fully recovers. ALL FUTURE LEARNING IS AFFECTED. (Emphasis added.) The infant body goes into shock. The absorbent mind shuts down. There will be little absorption again because there is only trauma and pain to be absorbed. The infant then surely exhibits only two states, fulfilling Spitz's expectations: 'quiescence,' which means semi to full unconsciousness, and 'unpleasure.' If awakened from his survival retreat from consciousness, he is propelled back into a state of unresolved high stress. He cries himself to sleep again. . . . Pleasure and smiling will surely be much later in appearing, just about two and half months later, because it will take that long for his unstimulated and iso-

lated body to compensate if it is to survive at all. The infant's body must manage slowly to bring its own sensory system to life.

During this period of shock, sensory closure, and retrenchment, there is virtually no development. How could there be? And all the other pre-programmed stage-specific developments are systematically missed, throwing the system farther behind.

We could go on and on. Some might say that Mr. Pearce is very extreme and over dramatic in his description of this process. There is, however, a large segment of the population that experienced birth the way he describes it. He does paint a graphic and vivid picture of those first few hours of life for the hospital born infant . . . at least, the way it used to be. Perhaps the emotion with which he describes it is an indication of the depth of his feeling as to the injustice of the situation and the damage it has done and can do.

With all of the foregoing in mind, try to imagine how this scenario impacts the feelings of the helpless infant. No wonder rebirthing centers have become so popular. No wonder countless people are striving to find the cause of their discomfort, their emptiness and their suffering. Undoubtedly they are looking for that comfort they never received at birth—the comfort and bonding they were never allowed to experience.

During our very earliest moments of life, whatever the situation was, our perception of life began. Our natural drive, however, was and is to return to the place of comfort and peace—to return to comfort, period! The place where we felt peace, love, tranquility and happiness, whether that realm was before the womb or in the womb.

While being hurled through those first few experiences in life, we naturally drew conclusions about our new sphere of existence, whether the comfort took place or whether it didn't. If this comfort did take place, or however it took place, has greatly determined the way we see our world. The feelings we experienced as we went through the birthing process and the events that immediately followed were the basis of our perceptions. These perceptions then contributed to the foundation of our beliefs. Our beliefs are established from the silent conclusions we draw about our perceptions of what we feel.

As we took our place on this earth, our daily experiences continued to validate or invalidate the beliefs established in those first hours of life. The perceptions that created our beliefs, and the degree to which they were validated, soon determined the pattern, or the road map, which we have followed throughout our life.

At this point you may be asking, "Is there something the matter with that?" Recall if you will, that feelings and thoughts have a definite energy; that your body's energy (electrical) system has a blueprint which requires it to be in balance and harmony if it is to function correctly. When negative/fear-based feelings or thoughts are registered in the body, the perfect operating energy patterns (circuits) of the body which keep it in balance, are adversely impacted. The electrical system is short-circuited, creating a block or mal-function in the system. These blocks obscure the memory of perfection in the DNA of the cells—the original blueprint can no longer be adhered to—all of which adversely influences our behavior and our health. Each time a negative feeling-thought-belief is re-experienced and re-validated, the energy surrounding the original block is reinforced and compounded. Consequently, these energy blocks grow, becoming larger and more powerful with time, unless the energy of that particular block is changed. These energy blocks are the cause of our illnesses, our problems, and our challenges in life.

How interesting—the detrimental effects of our fear-based feelings; that we could be continually thwarted by those earliest negative feelings and beliefs. Until we become consciously aware of these blocks and their causative feelings/thoughts and are willing to transform the energy around them, these feelings and their effects will be our constant companions.

Whatever you believe, with feeling, becomes your reality. You are the sum total result of all your belief systems to this moment. Your beliefs form a screen of logic or a screen of prejudices through which you see the entire world. You never allow in any information that is inconsistent with your beliefs, even if you have beliefs that are totally inconsistent with reality. To the degree to which you believe these things to be true, they become true for you. (Michael Wickett, *It's All Within Your Reach*)

Chapter 4

How Feelings Impact Our Lives

"I'm not important." This was the feeling that governed my beliefs and controlled my life. This cloud of negative feelings, "I'm not important, so I'm not worthy," created a hole that I could not find a way to fill. My existence was very frustrated, but I didn't know why. This belief of mine that "I am not important," was established because of the feelings I experienced at my birth. Then I traveled through most of my life setting up situations, subconsciously (of course), to prove that I was not important.

If the feelings we internalized during gestation or experienced at birth caused us to feel rejected, we have been going through life unconsciously setting up situations that cause us more feelings of rejection. Why? From those first feelings of rejection, our perception subconsciously established the belief in our mind-body that "Being Rejected" was the name of the road upon which we were to travel through life. So each time the opportunity presented itself, and in order to stay on our road, we unknowingly validated this erroneous belief through our behavior. Because, you remember, our mind—our ego—HAS to be right! So, subconsciously, our mind is just doing its job by helping us carry out this belief.

Even though a significant number of our feelings originate during gestation or at birth, not all of them do. Nevertheless, whatever or whenever our mind established a belief (subconsciously), the mind then lets us help prove *it* right, for this allows *it* to be *justified* in that belief. The mind directs and creates situations whereby it can fulfill whatever the belief is. Consequently, most of us go through life continually driven to prove our beliefs—without even knowing what they are most of the time. Going unchecked, these beliefs become our self-fulfilling prophecies. And if we don't experience validation of them, we don't feel comfortable. Having that validation makes us comfortable at some level— like we're on the right track, even though it may hurt like hell. How many of us have been going through life with incorrect perceptions and beliefs about ourselves without realizing it?

For some reason, when the mind is validated as being right and justified it is interpreted on the inside that we are in our place of *Comfort* and *Peace* (from the discussion in Chapter Two), that place which first provided us with warmth and security—where we yearn to return. Being validated also gives a quasi-feeling of being in control (and remember, we all want to be in control). This state of Be-ing—finding and enjoying our place of *Comfort* and *Peace*—is only momentary and very short-lived, however. Why? Because it is based on an incorrect perception, an untruth. Many of us are continually frustrated (subconsciously) due to the inner conflict of not really enjoying the situations we've been driven to create—the situations we unknowingly orchestrated (when we proved our belief was right). The inability to hang on to that feeling of being in control, or of being *Comfortable* and *Peaceful*, is frustrating. In reality it is NOT a place of *Comfort* and *Peace* at all! Talk about a war going on inside!

Deep, deep inside (subconsciously), all of us desire feeling the same quality we knew inutero or before we were born. Consequently, we are generally ill at ease or frustrated by our inability to find it. Regardless of how diligently we strive to find and experience our comfort and peace, we are unknowingly driven to create disorder or dysfunction in our lives. We do this by having to be right about something which the mind perceives incorrectly—based on those erroneous beliefs embraced at birth. And so, this becomes a lose-lose situation for us more often than we know.

For some of us it seems the more we strive, the more comfort and peace eludes us. Our innate drive to arrive at this place and take up residence creates inconsistencies in our life's experiences with no rhyme or reason. And for some of us, the more we strive, the more chaos we experience. Others of us never seem to achieve the results (on an on-going basis) we are seeking in various areas of our lives. Therefore, we may experience more and more frustration—which could eventually lead to our giving up.

When we reach this point we may presume that we have no control over our lives. "Complete helplessness or hopelessness" could be the feeling we experience, which, in turn, can lead to the feeling of, "Oh, what's the use?" And then we "throw in the towel" and fold up.

An example of this happened with a client whom I'll call Sarah. Sarah just recently divorced for the second time. She is extremely desirous of having a loving, caring, companionable man in her life. Sarah is very attractive and fun to be around. It's not a challenge for her to attract men to her. Her challenge comes in having them show appreciation for her and take her seriously. She finds herself being the aggressor, which she doesn't want to be. Sarah has a real NEED FOR APPROVAL, but when she doesn't seem to be receiving the approval she needs so desperately, she worries and frets beyond reason . . . to the point of almost giving up. However, Sarah has now come to realize that when she approves of herself, she will then be able to attract that quality in others with whom she would like to associate. After using the *tool* to process her feelings involved with this predicament, her situation improved greatly and she started feeling better about herself. As I write this, Sarah is on a journey to healing using the *tool* I will share with you later in the book. The improvements she has experienced in her life from using the *tool* are becoming apparent. Each day she gains more confidence in her ability to deal with her own feelings. With consistent use of this *tool* Sarah will be able to significantly change the feelings and beliefs that cause her any discomfort in this area of her life.

Let's look at some of the characteristic qualities we, as human beings, create in our lives as we are striving to return to our place of Comfort and Peace. Have you ever known anyone who seems to purposely (subconsciously, of course), and continually experience chaos in their relationships with other people? They are unable to keep friends for long periods of time—constantly looking for new friends that will accept them, relate to them, identify with them and be loyal to them.

Perhaps you've known someone who is always manipulating or trying to control others. Those who try to control, characteristically, need to be *right*. If they are right, then they feel they are in control. They won't let down their veneer or facade for fear of letting someone see they might not have it "all together." If you ask them how things are going, they will always tell you, "Everything is great." But, in reality they may be hurting deeply or feeling very inadequate or insecure because of some of their unresolved feelings. They never want you to see or perceive them as lacking in any area of their life. That would be too much for them.

People who feel inferior are often the ones who allow others to control them . . . use them for a door mat, time after time. Their motto is, "Keep peace at all costs." (And it usually costs them their inner peace or their peace of mind.)

Then there are other people who seem to take advantage of family, friends and associates. They use everyone to their advantage with little regard for anyone else's welfare. They are forever insensitive as to what is going on outside themselves.

Have you ever known a person who always has to have things done their way? (Sometimes they could be considered perfectionists, and sometimes they may not.) This is someone who never allows anyone else to be in charge, whether it has to do with something around the house, around the office, at a party or on an outing. And when they insist on doing everything their way—not letting anyone else help—they often act like martyrs, seeming to want to make others feel guilty because of all the work they are doing. When the event is over and they are exhausted, they characteristically gasp, moan and sigh, "I'm all right—don't pay any attention to me."

Then there are the *rescuers* and the *pleasers*. These are those people who feel they must make everything *right* or solve everyone's problems, so they keep their antenna poised, always looking for people to help. They seemingly feel responsible for each person's ills and want to have the solutions for everyone else, but are usually unable to see the root of their own problems. Generally, the rescuer or pleaser is suffering from deep-seeded feelings of rejection (which they don't realize). It is this type of person who often has numerous health problems.

Some people may be unable to adequately communicate and express their feelings to their loved ones, or anyone else for that matter. Often this type person, because of an inability to communicate, experiences a total lack of coping skills and eventually withdraws from society, hibernating in their own little world.

Then there are those at the other end of the spectrum who seem to talk just to hear themselves talk. What they have to say is usually irrelevant or mindless chatter. They want to be included in what's going on around them, but lack the confidence or social skills to be able to be part of the group, so they always seem to be on the outside looking in, just hoping that what they have to say will be accepted or appreciated and help them be part of the group. Often, these people are their own worst enemy. Instead of being included, they repel themselves from others, no matter how much they want acceptance, to be liked and to have friends.

Most of us have known people who have one health problem after another, or someone who has a major health problem that has stayed with them most of their life. And there are others who have less significant challenges with their health, but seem to have something the matter with them all the time. These people can be found in the doctor's office every other week, looking unsuccessfully for the answers to their problems. I know one woman who judges how alive she is by how sick she is. That is, by how many aches and pains she can count. She then keeps the aches and pains alive and well by continually talking about them to whomever she converses with. What she doesn't understand is that the more she talks about her aches and pains, the more energy she gives them and the more she reinforces her illness. (This holds true with any kind of problem.)

Whatever the case may be, whether the illness is serious or insignificant, these people never seem to get to the core of their predicament no matter how long or how hard they look.

Then there are those who have a difficult time getting ahead financially in this life. No matter how conscientious they are, it's a real challenge for them to obtain permanent employment. They may go from job to job without much success at all. Or, they may have a good job, but never seem to have enough money to cover their financial obligations. They are never able to buy or afford a decent car, and they can rarely buy new clothes. They seem forever deprived, which appears to be their plight in life. Yet, other people with a similar set of circumstances make it fine on a comparable income. What makes the difference? (We'll come back to this later.)

You may have known someone who seems to have a combination of the above examples working against them much of the time. What's their story? Some people have one sort of tragedy after another. Is it their fate in life, or is it something they sadly, but unconsciously created? Applying the Law of Cause and Effect (Chapter Two), we begin to understand the reason for all these kinds of conditions in peoples lives.

Any or several of the above described characteristics (as well as those unmentioned) are indicators of being out of harmony with natural laws. When our Be-ing is subconsciously seeking to return to Comfort and Peace, in order for *It* (our Be-ing) to get our attention, often it is necessary for *It* to create pain or discomfort. For, if we experience pain or discomfort long enough, we usually start looking for the answers . . . answers that will lead us back to *real* comfort and peace.

What we don't realize is that our ultimate unconscious goal is to come to understand who we really are. How else would we be driven to know our truth? Isn't it by desiring to understand why life isn't working for us that we begin searching for answers? What else would motivate us to start looking for the causes of our effects—for what makes us "tick"? It is for the purpose of searching, understanding, and finally discovering our Real Self.

So, take a REAL GOOD LOOK at what is going on inside if you identify with any of these characteristics. What are your thoughts? What are your feelings? If the negative conditions in your life are on-going and the patterns are repeated over and over again, this is telling you— screaming at you—that you are definitely out of harmony with natural Laws—God's laws—the laws of the Universe. It's time to wake up! Elevate your consciousness and locate the cause of your effects.

One of the more obvious indications that your feelings and thoughts are inharmonious or out of sync with natural laws is when health problems appear. Illness reminds you of your purpose in life—to return to the original pattern of balance—the memory of perfection. Pain of any kind lets you know that you are out of tune with natural laws. God is trying to communicate to you through your body, and pain is one sure way He gets your attention. It is most unfortunate, however, that very often a person doesn't listen or won't listen to this communication. Consequently, the message does not get through.

Barbara Ann Brennan, in her book *Hands of Light*, puts it another way:

> Illness is the result of imbalance. Imbalance is a result of for-getting who you are. Forgetting who you are creates thoughts and actions that lead to an unhealthy life-style and eventually to

illness. The illness itself is a signal that you are imbalanced because you have forgotten who you are.

Illness can thus be understood as a lesson you have given yourself to help you remember who you are.

Still another author, Dr. David Frawley, O.M.D., who penned *Ayurvedic Healing* tells us that disease is, at the least, a spiritual opportunity, if not a sign of spiritual crisis or change. And, according to the main spiritual teaching of ancient India, disease is a vehicle whereby the truth of life and the truth of one's own self can be revealed. Could disease be a sign of wrong action in life? Could it also be an indication that the soul is directing its energy within? Either way disease requires a spiritual reexamination of our lives, particularly if the disease is severe. Hence, in order to understand and resolve any disease, self-examination is the first step and fundamental basis in accomplishing this.

Dr. Bernie Siegel, in his wonderful book, *Love, Medicine & Miracles*, says, "I suggest that patients think of illness not as God's will but as our deviation from God's will."

Dr. Siegel goes on to tell us,

> I feel that all disease is ultimately related to a lack of love, or to love that is only conditional, for the exhaustion and depression of the immune system thus created leads to physical vulnerability. I also feel that all healing is related to the ability to give and accept unconditional love. I am convinced that unconditional love is the most powerful known stimulant of the immune system. If I told patients to raise their blood levels of immune globulins or killer T cells, no one would know how. But if I can teach them to love themselves and others fully, the same changes happen automatically. The truth is: love heals.

The most important law of the universe is LOVE. Love of self and love of others. We cannot wait to be loved before we love. We just need to love! I heard Dr. Gerald Jampolsky speak at a meeting and his words were to this effect: "Whatever the problem, love is the answer. Whatever the fear, love is the answer. Love is all there is. Whatever the question, love is the answer."

If we truly love, that love casts out all fear. The King James version of the Bible tells us: "There is no fear in love; but perfect love casteth out fear; because FEAR HATH TORMENT" (Emphasis added).

He that feareth is not made perfect in love." (1 John 4:18)

How many and what are the conditions, situations, people and experiences you fear? Think about it.

How does love cast out fear? Real love is unconditional. Real love accepts the perfection of all . . . accepts that EVERYTHING is perfect just the way it is, and EVERYONE is perfect just the way they are! When we accept everything and everyone just the way they are, there is no reason to find fault or judge. When we are able to accept the perfection in everything and everyone, the ego doesn't get bogged down with it's fears—fear of not being equal; fear of being rejected; fear of not being good enough; fear of failure; fear of success; fear of the future; fear of being unworthy; or whatever the fears may be.

Unconditional love accepts the perfection of all people and all situations just the way they are. This statement can be confusing because most people want to be better. Too often we look at our incorrectly perceived problems and our incorrect perception of others' faults and we think they are not perfect—that the perfection is to change—that we can't be perfect until we are changed, or someone else is changed. The problem is, too many of us are so emotionally involved in trying to get others to change that we fail to realize that the *only* person we can really change is numero uno—number one, OURSELF! Someone said to me recently, "We're always trying to get the tree out of the other persons' eye." What a graphic way to refer to the mote and the beam in the eye.

In her book, *Minding the Body, Mending the Mind*, Dr. Joan Borysenko invites us to:

> See people for who they are instead of who you want them to be. Then accept them as they are rather than judging them for who they are not. The more accepting you become of yourself, the more you can see others in the same light. The core of every human being is the same—unconditioned consciousness—the Self. See the Self in others. If you are religious or spiritual, you can think in terms of seeing the divine in one another. Honor your own Self and honor the Self in others. The Eastern greeting Namaste is similar in meaning to Hebrew and Hawaiian greetings. It means, 'The Self in me honors and salutes the Self in you.' (My Self salutes Your Self.)
>
> Ponder during your daily activities and interactions how much energy is used up in defending various positions that make you feel 'right,' worthy, okay. When you begin to realize your own precious, unique self-worth, the need to define yourself will diminish, and your body will naturally relax.

When we are finally able to release the need to be *right* and can accept everything and everyone as being perfect, a shift of major proportions takes place in us. In *Love, Medicine & Miracles*, Dr. Siegel states, "You can't change your shortcomings until you accept yourself despite them. I emphasize this because many people, especially those at high risk of cancer, are prone to forgive others and crucify themselves."

There is no reason to feel that you or someone else must change before you can be happy. YOU are the only one you can change . . . and it's necessary to accept yourself despite your shortcomings, before you *can* change. YOU are the only one who can make YOU happy! When we accept ourselves the way we are, we increase our ability to change. and when we start to change, those around us do likewise.

We may still recognize when someone would be happier if they chose to change, but, we also understand that it's much easier for us to allow them to change in their own way and at their own speed without our help—as we are not the one responsible for making that change in them. When we arrive at this place in our knowledge and understanding, we naturally move forward in life with more ease. We are more open, more receptive and more able to gain further understanding and knowledge. We are more tolerant and accepting of the experiences that challenge us and teach us those things which are necessary for our learning and growth. These growth experiences will no longer be a *hard* procedure we feel we HAVE to go through, but rather one of anticipation that we GET to go through.

The wonderful prospect and attitude of accepting everything and everyone as being perfect, is, that change is also perfect! What you are going through is perfect. It will cause you to move toward the growth you are to experience, gaining the understanding or learning the lessons that are necessary for you to learn in this life. With this frame of mind, your life becomes more fluid—more flowing without you feeling the need to always run things your way, thereby blocking God's way.

There is a purpose for every challenge and every situation in which we find ourselves. THE PURPOSE IS FOR LEARNING AND GROWTH—and FOR GETTING TO KNOW WHO WE REALLY ARE. After attaining this frame of mind, we get to consciously choose how we will react, how we will manage, and what we will do with these challenges. The depth and width of the growth we experience will be determined by these choices. Sometimes our choices may not result in growth instantly, at the moment, because we may have made a negative choice. By that, I mean a choice that brings negative results. But even in the negative choice, we still experience consequences that will eventually bring us around to positive choices . . . or choices that bring positive results.

When we are mindfully conscious of what is taking place in our lives, and are willing to make a shift from the *victim* role to the role of *master* (explained in Chapter Two), our mindfulness will motivate us to make wiser choices on a daily basis. This can eventually lead us to the kind of growth and development that will ultimately bring the Comfort and Peace to our Be-ing for which we have been seeking and longing.

The more we avoid or resist what we may consider in our mind to be an undesirable person or an undesirable situation, the more we block the flow of energy that facilitates change. When we are able to view the less-than-desirable occurrences in our lives as learning experiences, or minor inconveniences on our road towards growth and fulfillment—knowing that is is perfect for the time—these undesirable experiences won't seem nearly as terrible, as awful or as lengthy while we are moving through them.

And how does this work? It all comes back to love. Love is accepting what is. Put another way, unconditional love is understanding, accepting and letting go of any disagreement or issue. Whatever the condition or situation is, let it go—let it be. Oliver Wendell Holmes once said, "Love is the master key that opens the gates of happiness." And what is the key that opens the gates of love? Forgiveness. Forgiveness of self and forgiveness of others. Forgiveness also opens the gates to peace of mind. (See Chapters 15 & 16 in *Healing Feelings . . . From Your Heart* for the "how to.")

> When you DO NOT see yourself and the situations in your life as being perfect, there is no energy for anything to change. You stop the flow of energy. We all know women who desperately want a child and cannot conceive. They adopt and months later they find themselves pregnant. I know a woman who in her late thirties finally adopted a baby. Due to a long history of female problems she was scheduled for a hysterectomy. At her pre-operative exam, she found out that she was pregnant! SHE HAD GIVEN UP RESISTING—SHE HAD ACCEPTED THE

PERFECTION OF HER SITUATION. We all have that power. We give up that power when we do not accept WHAT IS. We stop the flow of energy surrounding it.

If we want our mate to change, first WE must love them the way they are. Then the space for change is created. We need to love our illnesses because love heals . . . it allows wellness (wholeness) to move in (to take place). Trying to change things without first accepting them as they are is like wearing Chinese handcuffs . . . the harder you try, the more resistance you create. Relax. Let the energy flow. Accept the perfection. Feel the love. Now you can manifest anything. (Jackie Pratt)

Discomfort does not last unless we resist it. "That which we resist, persists." If we stop and think about it, most of us will agree that this is certainly true. When we resist a pain or a situation, sometimes that very thing we want to eliminate or ignore becomes more glaring. As you will recall, everything has an energy, and when we try to force or manipulate a situation (problem or energy) to our pleasing, we are forcing or pushing to make it happen. When we do this, it's just like a child trying to put a square peg in a round hole. No matter how strong his will, or how hard he works, or how good his intention, he will never be successful in accomplishing this task. It will never happen!

Having money worries is another example of how this principle functions. The more we worry about where enough money will come from to pay our bills or buy what we need or want, the tighter our grip becomes on that energy. We could safely say, "The more we squeeze, the tighter it gets." So, when we continually worry, we squeeze the money energy so tightly that it literally dies—we choke it to death! Let go of the choking, the forcing, the pushing, the worry. Do your best to establish the faith that when you are doing your part, you know the necessary finances will always be available to you. Worry is negative and faith is positive. Faith and worry cannot occupy the same space at the same time. So, which one would you rather have working in your life for you, the negative or the positive? You can't afford the luxury of a negative thought! Let go of the "have to" and allow the natural flow of things to occur. Then life flows *much* easier and is more enjoyable.

I'm not suggesting you do away with goals or other plans for your life. I'm suggesting that you be flexible. Then if situations or opportunities seem to take you in a different direction than planned, you will be more willing to flow with it. You might find it much more exciting and beneficial than the original plan. Keep in mind that everything happens to us for our own good, for a reason . . . for our experience and growth.

When we heighten our awareness to the point of recognizing that the pain, the challenges and the changing of plans could be an indication of another opportunity to grow—really stop and look at it—then life can become a game, a party, and it will be a lot more fun! Heighten your awareness . . . pay attention. Or, as Dr. Borysenko suggests, be mindful of every aspect of your life.

Ellen J. Langer suggests in her book, *Mindfulness*, that we are like programmed automatons when we are mindless, treating information in a rigid and narrow-minded way, as though the information were true regardless of the circumstances. Whereas, we are open to surprise when we are mindful-oriented in the present moment, being sensitive to context, and above all, we are liberated from the tyranny of old mindsets.

Wake up! Open your consciousness. Be enthused about becoming more aware of what you are feeling, of what you are thinking, of every word you speak and of how you act or react in everything you do! Pay attention! Awareness causes results. When you become more aware of the challenges as they occur and see them for the opportunities they are, opportunities for growth—give thanks for what you are experiencing.

Miracles happen when you express gratitude to God. Praise Him and give thanks in all things! JOY is preceeded by gratitude. And doesn't it say in the scriptures, "Man is that he might have joy?"

You are now at the beginning of the return road back to that place of Comfort and Peace, and to the memory of your perfection.

Chapter 5

The Importance of Becoming Single-Minded

In your search for the answers to life's problems—with a desire to effect a social-physical-mental-emotional or spiritual healing; to experience a higher degree of joy, success and happiness—you may have tried achieving your goals by incorporating various methods of self-improvement. Positive affirmations is one method lauded by many who have experienced significant results. Positive self-talk (Shad Helmstetter wrote two books that contain superlative guidance on this subject) is another approach incorporated by numerous individuals with much success. Perhaps you've had results working with one or more of these principles, because they *are* correct principles and they *can* be effective.

Innumerable people through eons of time have attained emotional healing and peace with the age-old, tried and proven tool of meditation. In my opinion, meditation is one of the best and most effective tools we can use. Visualization is also an excellent tool. I use them both on a daily basis, recognizing the definite difference they make in my life. Motivational tapes have their place in helping us gain understanding and insight as to what makes us tick. There is an abundance of viable, effective procedures available to assist change, if a person is looking. To talk to someone who has experienced desirable results in their life from using these various methods is very enlightening. Undoubtedly, many lives have been affected as a result of applying some of these principles. How fortunate we are to have so many avenues available to us when we are ready to move forward on our journey toward obtaining the peace and joy we are seeking.

Getting our lives back in balance, in alignment, in harmony is what it's all about. We need to learn how to put our Intelligence, Higher Self, Spirit, Super-Conscious, Creative Source—or whichever we choose to call it—back in charge of our Be-ing. Whatever we use to attain this balance, will come together faster, more solidly and be longer lasting and more effective IF we are single-minded in the process. Until that time, for many of us, confusion will reign supreme, and the peace and joy that we seek in life will be evasive. Until we learn to achieve balance we will have our up days (real good days), but we will also have many down days (not so good days). A measure of how we are doing will be obvious by the state of our health, our finances, our relationships; or, in other words, by our success in each area of our life.

Do you ever ask yourself the question, "Why isn't my life going the way I want it to?" Are you experiencing desired results? If the answer is "no" it could be due to your very earliest programming. What were the erroneous beliefs you or someone else unknowingly programmed? What were the incorrect perceptions you established? What cell memories are stifling your progress? You probably don't know at this point. You just realize you could certainly benefit from being able to do *something* different.

If you desire better results on a day-to-day basis, it is necessary to realize that "you create your own reality." Some of you may have heard this before, others may not. So, you might ask, "What do you mean by, I create my own reality?"

On a subconscious level you create your own reality with your feelings and your thoughts regardless of when, where or how they were established! After reading Chapter Three you can undoubtedly understand how your very earliest feelings determine your beliefs. And in turn, your beliefs determine your thoughts. Your thoughts are seeds and you plant them in very fertile soil (feelings) that has been prepared from conception and infancy. When you plant your seeds (thoughts), you nourish (water) them by continually holding onto the thought with deep intensity. When a thought (seed) and a feeling (soil) are harbored, germination takes place and an energy is naturally released into the forces of creation. An emotion is created and the synergy of what has been created grows a crop. It creates your reality—is the cause of your effect—whether that crop is good or bad, desirable or undesirable. This is all done on a subconscious level.

In other words, when a strong feeling connects with a thought (or vice-versa) an emotion is created. The point where feeling and thought meet is also the place where vibration is released, and vibration is life! Thus, your reality is created by your feelings and your thoughts.

Many books have been written on this subject, so I won't go into more detail here. It could be the basis of a complete book in and of itself. Suffice it to say, OUR VERY OWN FEELINGS AND THOUGHTS ARE WHAT CREATE THE CIRCUMSTANCES THAT BRING OUR LIFE TO US!

What usually precedes or follows a thought? A feeling. And the feeling is what rules our mind-heart. Another way of saying it is, we always get the prayer of our heart. What does that mean? We do feel with or in our heart, don't we.

Interestingly enough, Dr. Christian Bernard is reported to have made the statement that a person would not be able to live for a very long period of time on an artificial heart as it does not have brain cells. In order for a person's heart to function on a continual basis, it must have brain cells.

Why is this? It has to do with the DNA and the RNA. In order for the harmonious flow of life to continue in a human being, the part of the cell that contains the blueprint or intelligence (DNA) and the part of the cell that carries out the instructions (RNA) has to have directions. An artificial heart is void of this intelligence (DNA). In my opinion, the mind is too intricately connected with the heart for the body to be without this organ for an extended period of time and be able to function as a normal human being.

Points of interest are references the Bible makes to the mind-heart connection, indicating clearly that the DNA is involved in this process. Following are just some of these Biblical references regarding heart and mind:

Genesis 6:5

And God saw that the wickedness of man was great in the earth, and that every imagination of the thoughts of his heart was only evil continually.

Proverbs 23:7

For as he thinketh in his heart, so is he . . .

Matthew 9:4

And Jesus knowing their thoughts said, Wherefore think ye evil in your hearts?

Acts 8:22

Repent therefore of this thy wickedness, and pray God, if perhaps the thought of thine heart may be forgiven thee.

These scriptures give us clear indication and appreciation that the heart and the mind are inseparable. And whatever goes on in our heart or mind definitely affects our actions and therefore, our whole Be-ing. "But how does this work?" you may ask. It has to do with our brain, which has two sides.

The left brain is the thinking and the conscious side. The right brain is the feeling and the subconscious side. If we THINK in our brain that we want something in our life, but, we unknowingly FEEL in our heart that we are not worthy of it, we will generally not receive it. You see—our FEELING will win, rather than our THINKING. When the two sides of the brain are not in agreement, there is inner conflict or war, and that conflict will remain in place until agreement is reached—until both sides of the brain come together.

In order for us to experience in life what we THINK we desire, the THINKING and the FEELING have to be in unison. If the FEELING is not the same as the THINKING, then we need to change the FEELING so that it becomes the same as the THINKING. After we align the THINKING and the FEELING so they are the same, we become single-minded. Until we accomplish this, we are double-minded and life works against us. When we are single-minded about what we desire in life, life works for us because, the FEELING, or heart, always wins. What we FEEL is literally the "prayer of our heart," and we always receive the "prayer of our heart!"

Do you recognize the importance, now, of being single-minded?

James 1:8
    A double minded man is unstable in all his ways.

If we want to locate what we feel and think in regards to a particular belief, we can perform a muscle response test (kinesiology). As an example, we could ask a person who would like a greater income if he THINKS he desires an income of $100,000 a year and the test arm will hold strong. Now, let's ask that same person if he FEELS he desires an income of $100,000 a year. Unless his thinking and feeling are in unison, his arm will go weak on the muscle response test when asked this question. Perhaps it goes weak because he FEELS he doesn't deserve $100,000, or he can't be a good person if he earns $100,000, or he does not have the capability of earning $100,000 in a year. The point is, the thinking and feeling are not together. THE FEELINGS, WHICH ARE

IN THE MIND-HEART, ALWAYS WIN. THE PRAYER OF THE HEART IS ALWAYS ANSWERED!!

Did you ever wonder why positive affirmations work for some people and not for others? For those who do not experience results it's because the feeling and the thinking are not together. And for those who *do* experience results, it's usually because their feeling and thinking *are* together. When the feeling and thinking are not together it will usually take a long time, but if a person continues saying affirmations long enough, it *is* possible for the feeling and thinking to come together and effect a change. It's called, once again, becoming SINGLE-MINDED. Another way to describe this phenomena is that we become integrated—bringing together the thinking-conscious left brain with the feeling-sub-conscious right brain—so that the two sides of the brain are no longer separate, but have become a whole, compatible unit. When we establish this unity, real power is created.

Answers often come immediately when we are single-minded in our requests. This explains why some people receive answers to prayer and others do not. The people who receive answers are single-minded. They not only THINK God will answer, they FEEL He will answer, which adds up to KNOWING. Everyone who asks with the heart receives answers. Being able to do this unlocks an unlimited force in our life! However, in order to bring this about it is essential that we be willing to own our negative feelings and thoughts without blaming or shaming ourselves or anyone else, and honestly look at the issues in our life. If we can't do this we are not being true to ourselves. We are laboring in self-deception or shame. And there is no place for self-deception or shame in this process.

Are you able to identify your feelings? Most feelings are registered on a subconscious level, so when you get in touch with your feelings, you are also in touch with your subconscious. The conscious mind only functions in the past and its illusion of the future, whereas, the subconscious mind functions in the NOW. In what seems to be the nonknowing, non-factual mind (the subconscious) is, in reality, the all-knowing mind. All the answers to your challenges are contained therein.

When you can communicate with your own feelings, you are able to communicate more positively with others. This is the key to successful, healthy relationships as well as to vibrant physical, mental and spiritual health.

GET RID OF GARBAGE—THE COVER UP—IN ORDER TO TAP INTO THE REAL YOU!

M I N D F U L N E S S
* MINDFUL OF THOUGHTS
* MINDFUL OF WORDS
* IDENTIFIES FEELINGS

Brain Hemisphere Functions

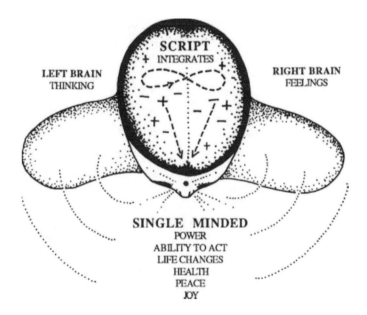

For those of you who are not familiar with the functions of the Left-Right hemispheres of the brain, the following will contribute to a clearer understanding. This illustration does not exemplify all the aspects of the Left-brain, Right-brain functions. To keep this as simple as possible, the characteristics listed here most closely typify the qualities of the brain that are significant for our purposes.

Left Brain (CONSCIOUS)	*Right Brain* (SUBCONSCIOUS)
THINKER	CREATIVE
LOGICAL	FEELING
ANALYTICAL	INTUITIVE
PRACTICAL	ARTISTIC
MOVER	NURTURER
SEQUENTIAL	EMOTIONAL
DUALITY	UNITY
WORDS	IMAGES
WILL	POWER
MATERIAL	SPIRITUAL
CELEBRATION	REVERENCE
EXPRESS	SILENT

Remember, when we FEEL one thing and we THINK the same one thing, we are functioning from our whole brain. We are no longer at war inside (where that one feeling/thought is concerned). We no longer experience inner turmoil. We are no longer double-minded. We are then single-minded in that one area . . . on that one particular issue. The internal conflict is over and life responds by offering us peace of mind.

Chapter 6

Erasing Illusions

Illusions represent unreal or incorrect perceptions They are fantasies, imaginings, false notions, misbeliefs and mis-conceptions.

In the exciting process of learning to communicate with yourself, (and it is a process), you develop an increased sensitivity as to how your thinking and feeling processes operate. As your awareness and sensitivity become more finely tuned regarding what and how you are thinking, you will become more astute in recognizing each thought, whether negative or positive, as it enters your mind. Thoughts are an indication of what you are feeling at the moment . . . feelings of which you may be totally unaware. So, the more often you recognize and can identify the underlying feeling behind each thought as it pops into your mind—the more proficient you will become at *getting in touch* with what you are actually feeling.

This whole process—the thinking/feeling process—is SO subtle that you will want to develop this heightened awareness on a consistent basis in order to experience the results you are seeking.

When a feeling is aroused, it is usually triggered by a belief or a system of beliefs previously established within you. When this happens, the feeling will be followed by a flood of thoughts or by more feelings. This concept may seem complicated, and perhaps you are wondering why I am putting such emphasis here. Unless you learn where the focal point begins, the effectiveness of what you can accomplish will be limited.

Even though we don't consciously think about what we are thinking (most of the time), our thinking occurs in the conscious part of us. Whereas, the feeling is in the subconscious part of us. The challenge is in getting *to* the subconscious.

Your prime responsibility is to *tune in* to your *inner dialogue.* Discover those thoughts in your mind that keep looking for a home. Learn to recognize mindless chatter, prattle or self-talk. As you listen to your inner dialogue, focus on what it is you are saying to yourself. This is where the transfer point, or the shift to awareness begins.

To illustrate this concept let's look at a hypothetical situation: One day at work you unexpectedly receive a notice that the boss wants to talk to you later in the day. This is thoroughly unexpected and you are naturally curious as to what the boss wants. Depending on the type of person you are, you may start wondering what it was you could have done *wrong*, and you frantically begin reliving the past few days or weeks in an attempt to locate the reason for the boss's request. You imagine every reason he could have to, perhaps, *call you on the carpet.* The longer you have to wait for your appointment with him, the more nervous you become. Your vivid imagination works overtime and you become paralyzed with thoughts of horrible consequences you may have to suffer for whatever you did wrong. In other words, your thoughts go wild as you anticipate meeting with the boss. Now, where did those thoughts come from, and why did they become so blown out of proportion? How did these thoughts cause you to feel inside as you were anticipating this meeting?

On the other hand, you may be the type of person who sees this situation as a positive indication of your boss's appreciation for your superb performance as an employee. It all has to do with your prior internal programming. You could be having thoughts of what the boss may say to commend you for your dedicated contribution, and how he wants to reward you.

My point is this: be mindful of your *inner* dialogue! YOU have a choice of what that dialogue will be. If your dialogue is negative rather than positive, you will want to start processing with the "Script" I will share with you in the next chapter, in order to change your *inner* dialogue. To experience rewarding and peaceful results instead of living with the conflict of jangled, frazzled, disrupted nerves, it is necessary to change this *inner* dialogue—this *inner* self-talk.

In the foregoing example, you begin to see how thoughts start very innocently and with the passing of the day, become runaway. Unruly feelings and emotions are a definite side effect. Look at the illusion these negative thoughts created . . . the illusion of being a failure or possibly losing your job.

Sometimes you may encounter unexplainable feelings that get your attention before thoughts enter the scene. One example of feelings coming first instead of thoughts is on a morning when you get out of bed and suddenly realize that you are feeling something you don't enjoy feeling, but you are unable to identify the feeling. Just ask yourself, "What am I feeling, and where do I feel it?" If an answer does not come to you, and it is impossible to identify what you are feeling, see how the word *blah*! fits. This happened to a friend of mine. She immediately became sensitive to the fact that she was having a new experience. She was willing to be further sensitive, aware, and to listen, accept and own what she was experiencing. She then went through the "Script" literally describing her feeling as *blah* in the "Script" (as explained in the next chapter). When she replaced the *blah* feeling with, "I feel excited, I feel happy, I feel energetic and enthused about life!" her *blah* feeling shifted immediately.

The more you *get in touch* with and identify what you are really feeling, the more capacity and ability you have to change your negative internal programming, self-talk, or inner dialogue. As you continue to be *Response-able* and *Account-able* for your thoughts and feelings, processing them to resolve them with the *tool* as explained in the next chapter, you WILL eventually become the person you really CHOOSE Being instead of remaining the person your incorrect perceptions have created.

We create illusions from our incorrect perceptions and our belief systems on a daily basis. (Belief systems are also created by perceptions. Sometimes these perceptions are correct but most of the time they are incorrect.) And, many of us already have long-standing illusion/belief systems created by incorrect perceptions, either about life or about ourselves. These illusions often cause us to become stuck in a rut. For instance, you've heard of or known someone who is very thin, but their reality, their internal dialogue is that they need to lose weight. They constantly feel they are too fat. No matter what anyone says to convince them they look great, they will not accept it. Their reality perceives that they are overweight. Your reality perceives that they are just right. Most of us maintain these same kinds of illusions in different areas of our lives. Our own illusions can be just as erroneous or incorrect as in the foregoing example.

It has been my experience that as our awareness, or our *mindfulness* of what we are feeling and thinking sharpens and expands, we can begin to eliminate these illusions by substituting undesirable feelings and thoughts with positive, sound, constructive feelings and thoughts. Thus, we enable ourselves to correct our mis-perceptions, incorrect beliefs and illusions.

After we strip ourselves of our old, worn out, tattered illusions, we will scarcely recognize ourselves as the same person. This is exciting to witness, as the majority of us would like to improve ourselves. As we learn to shift the negative to positive in our emotional patterns, we *can* reap peace of mind, *more* joy and *more* happiness.

Instead of allowing your feelings and thoughts to run away with you (creating all kinds of excuses or blocks to keep you from moving forward on your journey to self-improvement), view this process of shifting/altering your feelings/thoughts as you would if you were practicing a musical instrument or learning to read words. When you first learn to read musical notes or words it takes concentrated effort and you have to name the notes or say the words one by one. It doesn't take long, however, before you are able to look at a measure or a line and read all the notes or words in one or two glances. The only difference you are experiencing in *this* process, is that *you* are practicing monitoring, ruling, managing, or governing your feelings and thoughts.

Your ability to accomplish this goal will depend upon the intensity of your desire. A half-hearted effort won't *cut it*. When your desire to become the master of your feelings and thoughts—instead of them being the master of you—is foremost in your heart, accomplishing this feat will become simple with practice. Look at it as *effortless effort* and know that, "that which we persist in doing becomes easier."

Let us review the definition of Feelings and Emotions.

Feelings
1. To perceive or to be aware of through thought, bodily or emotional reactions, instinct, etc.
2. To produce an indicated overall condition, impression, or reaction.
3. An impression produced upon a person; having sensation.
4. Marked by or indicating emotion.

Emotions
1. A strong surge of feeling marked by an impulse to outward expressions, and often accompanied by complex bodily reactions; any strong feeling, as love, hate, or joy.
2. The power of feeling; sensibility.
3. A moving of the mind or soul.

It is imperative and essential that we understand the fine line of distinction between the definition of feelings and emotions as they apply in our lives.

Any word or data chosen by our conscious mind establishes images within our subconscious mind. REPEAT: Any word or data chosen by our conscious mind establishes images within our subconscious mind.

Let's go back to the concept of the thought being a seed (spoken of in Chapter Five) and review it because it is imperative to clearly understand the importance of what actually transpires: Every thought is a seed at the conceptual level. When a seed (thought) is planted in fertile soil (feelings already established), this seed and soil (thought/feeling) will then—depending upon prior programming and the intensity of the feelings—create a reaction to that thought/feeling, or . . . create the physical expression of that thought/feeling. At this moment, something new is brought into existence. Now we have what is commonly known as energy in motion—E-motion. This emotion then becomes a living vibration which *fertilizes* that seed/soil (thought/feeling), and we begin to grow our *crop* of *effects* (conditions in our life). In other words, thoughts and feelings create emotions that cause effects.

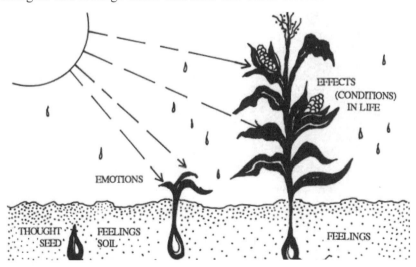

Are we planting the seeds that will produce the crops we wish to harvest?

If we are looking for desirable effects in our lives that are productive and rewarding we will naturally want to resolve and release any undesirable thoughts or undesirable feelings . . . the ones that cause undesirable emotions and effects. We will want to choose the most positive, mature, best seeds (thoughts) available and plant them in the same kind of cultivated soil (feelings) so that any emotions resulting from this planting will grow and yield a crop of the most desirable effects (emotions and conditions). Canadian Government and religious leader, Nathan E. Tanner, once said, "You cannot live right and think wrong anymore than you can plant weeds and harvest grain." We cannot think *weed* thoughts and expect to harvest *grain* effects. Another way to put it is . . . you will reap from the Law of the Harvest that which you sow. What are you sowing? What is your harvest yielding?

If you want to change your harvest to a different crop than you are now yielding, it is essential that your goal be singular: to recognize and *own* the negative aspects of both your thoughts and your feelings. Simple.

Dr. Joan Borysenko's book, *Minding the Body, Mending the Mind*, offers an insightful guideline to assist a person in identifying emotions.

> Positive emotions create bodily sensations of openness and expansiveness. They invite the world in. The body feels relaxed, even though some emotions such as joy are very energizing. In contrast, negative emotions create a tight, contracted feeling. Everything pulls inward. The world is pushed away. Positive feelings invite unity. Negative feelings invite isolation.
>
> Becoming a skilled observer of your own emotions allows you to make a conscious choice between love and unity or fear and isolation.

From the time of conception until we are adults we are strongly influenced by the feelings, thoughts, and attitudes of others. These feelings and attitudes are supplied to us by those who love us, by those who teach us, and by those who interact with us on a daily basis. Those who interact with us include parents, other family members, playmates, school companions, friends, relatives, teachers and other authority figures, as well as what we may ingest from observing the media.

When a thought (in this case, something someone said) is fed to us, and this thought connects with an established feeling that becomes energized by an emotional response, we unconsciously *buy into* what the person said as though it were an authentic, actual, valid truth. Sometimes the thought fed to us may even be a further validation of our already established, false, or incorrect feelings and beliefs. Or, that particular thought may start a new system of beliefs. These beliefs which we see or think of as truth, may be correct or incorrect.

Perhaps some of you can recall being taught not to make a mistake. Maybe as a child you were playing with something interesting—some possession of one of the big people. In your efforts to find out more about it, you broke it. You learned that grown-ups' playthings were considerably more fragile than your blocks—and there was also a chance that you were punished. In other words, your efforts to learn were rewarded with a spanking—and the association between mistake-making and pain was set up.

In some cases it is not even necessary for actual pain to occur: The threat of pain is often sufficient to alter the child's conduct. If you were told, 'Don't do that—you'll hurt yourself!' you certainly weren't encouraged to learn.

We suspect that this business of learning followed by punishment (or threat of punishment) has something to do with the creation of the so-called 'inferiority complex.' The person who feels constantly inferior to everyone else, who insists that everyone else is superior to him, has been taught to think and feel that way. And what better way could he be taught such a self-deprecating attitude than by being constantly corrected? He tries to do something and a fond parent says, 'No, darling, you're making a mistake—that's wrong. You should do it this way.'

The parent is sincerely trying to help—but a constant repetition of such help will also teach the child that he's wrong, that someone else is right. And after a few years of this, the child comes to the conclusion that he's just not very smart, and another case of inferiority begins to bloom.

It is characteristic of the inferiority complex that the person who carries this mental burden is hesitant about taking action. He'd rather sit back and let somebody else do it first—for that is the lesson which he has been taught. By being led to be uncertain about his actions, he grows to fear action. Action, to him, is the equivalent of making a mistake—and he doesn't want to do that. (*The Origins of Illness and Anxiety*, by J.A. Winter, M.D.)

The person who is made to feel that he is continually making mistakes will then automatically embrace the feeling of guilt for being, as he sees it, so dumb and stupid. The feeling of guilt is then added to his negative beliefs about himself and thus becomes further validation of his inadequacies and a sad, depreciating and motivating factor in his life. One incorrect perception can lead to another, and another, and another, until the majority of the perceptions he has about himself are so distorted that he feels absolutely worthless.

Remember, even if the perception is distorted and untrue, the mind-body still believes it to be true. When a feeling or a thought validates what we already believe to be true, the emotion accompanying the validation gathers energy and becomes more and more indelibly fixed, rooted and ingrained in us. And this, in turn, is what profoundly governs our daily beliefs, attitudes and actions from then on.

Like a magnet draws iron filings to it, our belief systems draw situations to us that automatically validate those beliefs, regardless of what they are. When any feeling is aroused, it is generally triggered by our already established beliefs. We naturally have experiences in life that continue to prove our belief systems are *right*, as we see it. However, often we are the only one who perceives our self as being *right*.

Said another way—situations are drawn to us that validate what our mind believes, correct or incorrect as the belief may be. Remember, the mind always has to be *right*. When it is *right* it thinks it is in control—and it always wants to be in control.

Remember, too, all of this happens on a subconscious level. So, once again, in order to get what we THINK we desire, it is necessary that we change the FEELING so that the FEELING corresponds with the THINKING, resulting in single-mindedness.

At this point, you may ask the question, "How can I really know if I am single-minded?" One of the best ways to know is by observing how your life is going. Do you enjoy loving and satisfying relationships with family and friends? Are you enjoying your work or role in life? Do you feel fulfilled? Are you experiencing desired results? Are you happy and peaceful most of the time? Do you enjoy optimum health? If the answer to these questions is yes, there's a strong indication that you are already single-minded in most areas of your life. If the answer is *no*, this indicates mixed messages are being communicated between your thoughts and your feelings.

If you are continually disappointed in your relationships, in your business affairs, or in the circumstances of your life, and nothing seems to work—everything seems to go wrong—if you are not experiencing desired results and frustration plagues you, then you are undoubtedly being double-minded in particular areas of your life. The soil of your feelings would truly benefit by having some cultivation work done on it in order to create a different and better environment . . . in order to bring you to single-mindedness. When you weed and cultivate your feelings you are able to plant more suitable, more desirable and more productive seeds (thoughts). In other words, double-mindedness can be overcome. You *can* bring your THINKING and FEELING into unison. These two factions—the thinking which is in the head and the feeling which is in the heart—NEED TO GET TOGETHER. You *can* eliminate the conflict between the two. You *can* win the war that is going on inside. You can then reap a harvest more to your liking.

Mainstream thinking has purported that to become single-minded a person needs to change the way he FEELS by changing the way he THINKS. It *is* possible to change the way we FEEL by changing the way we THINK. However, before we can do this, our perception of a situation, our feeling or our belief must change before our thinking can change. To illustrate this point:

> Four-year old Victor, a very active, precocious child loved to visit his grandparents because there were so many fun things to see and do. Victor's grandparents had a basement in their home with several rooms, one of which was a large dark storeroom. Victor had only glanced into this room on one occasion because grandpa always kept the door closed and locked.
>
> One day as Victor was playing in the basement, he wandered beyond his usual play area and noticed that the storeroom door was ajar. Being the curious four year old that he was, he decided to venture into the storeroom and see what was in this mysterious sanctuary of interesting forms and objects. As he opened the door and peered into the room, the angle of the dim light coming through the basement window created an even more eerie scene than usual. He glanced around the room. Suddenly he saw the form of something that looked like a person.
>
> This was so frightening to him that he abruptly turned and fled upstairs to the safety of his grandmother's arms. From then on, his grandparents could not persuade him to even go down-

stairs, let alone to play there. Finally, after months of observing Victor's apprehension and anxiety over his experience and his flat refusal to go back downstairs, grandpa very lovingly took Victor in his arms and coaxed him into going downstairs with all the lights on in the middle of the day.

Victor was very tense as his grandfather carried him down the stairs, but when grandpa turned on the light in the dark storeroom and showed him that the *scary thing* was only an old upright vacuum cleaner with a sheet over it, Victor slowly started to relax, and the corners of his mouth began turning into a smile. A big smile covered his face as he finally saw how harmless the big storeroom was.

The point of this story is to illustrate that Victor's perception was changed when he looked into the storeroom with the lights on, and in the protection of grandfather's arms. In an instant, all of his feelings of fright, fear, anxiety and terror melted away. All the fear energy stored in his little body from the original scary incident quickly changed. Victor was able to slide down out of grandpa's arms and start playing in the basement once again.

Altering our perception can happen in an instant . . . or it may take time. We CAN change our feelings by changing our thinking. But this is difficult because, we MUST change our perception of the situation first. As adults, our perceptions may be more complicated than Victor's, but the principle is still the same. The older we are, however, the more challenging it may be for us to change our perception without the help of a psychiatrist, or a professional counselor who is knowledgeable and understands these principles. Becoming better educated on the subject might also help, but this takes considerable amounts of time. Consequently, the change generally takes longer when going this route.

Conversely, changing the way we THINK by changing the way we FEEL is faster, much more effective, and further reaching. In our beginnings as a baby, FEELINGS came first when we had no way of expressing what we needed or wanted through words. The feelings we experienced during infancy and throughout our childhood which we were unable to express, are well established, longstanding feelings which naturally registered in the DNA and the subconscious part of our mind/body. These feelings are what now cause us to think and react in life the way we do. In other words, these feelings have helped create the beliefs and attitudes that motivate our everyday behavior and give us the effects in life that we experience. Bottom line—*feelings* are what make us tick!

If we choose to change the effects these undesirable feelings have created in our life, it will be necessary to simply resolve the feelings. Resolving the old feelings will also change the energy these feelings brought with them.

We, in our subconscious, can go back to where undesirable feelings began and change the vibration—change the energy of these negative feelings. This process re-programs the subconscious and literally changes the undesirable programming. This process will be explained in Chapter Seven.

But, what about thoughts?

As children, we function primarily from the right brain—from the feeling and intuitive side—because we have not developed the conscious thinking/analyzing process. When we start venturing out as we become more mobile, we explore, learning by what we experience. Sooner or later we start getting hurt or are told NO! NO!, over and over again. We are punished for doing something *wrong* when we don't mind. As we hurt ourselves or receive punishment for something we did, we soon learn that choices have to be made every time we turn around, literally. We also learn that if we make *wrong* choices we usually get hurt or are punished for it. So, we eventually reason out in our little mind, if we don't want to get hurt or invite displeasure or punishment from others, what we need to do or not do in order to forego pain. We start putting two and two together, and little by little we begin to shift . . . to move over into the left brain where the logical thinking and analyzing takes place.

Then, when we start going to school we are bombarded with left brain activities—rules, regulations, reading, writing, math, etc. Yes, this is all a necessary part of life, but isn't it sad how we lose our spontaneity, our enthusiasm, our desire to explore and reach out.

Eventually, we go from functioning and responding to our feelings, to functioning and responding to our thoughts. The reason our child-like perception takes over, is that we always seem to get in trouble when we function from our feelings. So—we begin stuffing them and sooner or later shift into thinking and analyzing our daily situations, rather than respond to our feelings. Therefore, there does come a time when the thoughts or thinking cause our actions. But, remember, the thoughts are still based on our feeling nature—on our feelings being triggered at some level.

We *can* change our thoughts and this *can* change our feelings and our actions. However . . . if the thoughts are caused by unresolved, deep-seeded feelings that are governing our existence, the thoughts will reoccur time and time again until we resolve the *core* feeling.

A thought remains only a thought until a feeling joins it and causes a response or sensation within us . . . the emotion. Each emotion has a personality all its own. It is an entity. Most of the time the emotion we experience is a reaction to *an illusion* that is already in our belief systems. This emotion may cause us comfort or discomfort. If it causes us discomfort, our *inner child*—that aspect of us that usually perceives things incorrectly—that aspect of us that still has a lot of hurts and unresolved feelings—is being challenged and we immediately move into a defensive or survival mode. At this point, the emotion may be a new emotion, validating an established belief. Or, what we are feeling could be a tired, old shop-worn extension of something that is already resonating within us—something that has been lying dormant but is now being revived and regenerated—registering in every cell of our body. Or, what we are feeling could be old feelings that we don't want to accept or allow in ourselves, so we repress, suppress or stuff them and pretend they don't exist . . . thinking they might go away. These feelings and emotions are, nevertheless, registered in our subconscious and in every one of our cells' intelligence (DNA), thereby propagating our belief systems which affect our whole electrical system . . . our body, for good or for not so good.

I would like to share a graphic illustration of this principle as related by my friend Sharon. Here in her own words is her story:

> I remember the time, the hour, almost to the second, where I was, where I was sitting, what I was thinking and feeling, just like it was yesterday, even though it's been over two years. It was midnight, and I was working feverishly to finish preparations to leave at three o'clock that morning to drive to San Francisco.
>
> I was in the basement, at the desk, typing on the computer, attempting to finish an important document. I had an extremely busy and frustrating day, and at that late hour, I still had fourteen things to finish.
>
> I was tired, on edge, worn out, and stressed (actually bent out of shape) from not only the day, but from the mental exertion of being a pro se litigant (we couldn't afford an attorney). And, to make matters worse, (in my mind) my husband had left for a 20 minute errand that had lasted already ONLY three hours. Where was he? Dead? Hurt? Why didn't he call? Why wouldn't he think of what was going on inside of me and know that I would be worried sick about him?
>
> We were going to leave for San Francisco for a very important court appearance where we were defending our rights of claim in a bankruptcy case with a very large corporation. We had a relatively large sum of money involved (large to us) and the outcome of the decision meant a lot to us.

The longer I sat there, the madder I got. I fumed, I fussed. I fretted, I stewed, agonized and thought of all the things I was mad at him for. I thought mean, hateful, bitter thoughts about my husband.

My husband had a weakness or tendency (in my mind) to waste time, putter around and procrastinate; put off, dawdle, dilly and dally with things until we managed most of the time to be late to functions, and seemed to be always on the late and cutting, rushing edge of *behind the time curve*. He would always find (or, would they find him?) someone to talk to and visit with no matter where we went or what we were doing. He drove me "nuts" with what I thought was *wasting my time*! Certainly HIS time wasn't important to HIM (in my mind)!

As I sat at the desk, raging and ranting, foaming at the mouth, (inside myself), I felt surging waves of resentment, billowing currents of suppressed anger, red-hot anger. Yes, even hate. These emotions welled-up, soaked, drenched, swept and immersed me with such force I was almost overcome by the intensity of the fury I was witnessing within myself. It was almost as though I *relished and regaled* in those feelings that I was entertaining. I was right and HE was WRONG! My husband was such an inconsiderate and insensitive oaf (I thought). Why couldn't HE see that HE caused me such pain, suffering and consternation?

I thought thoughts of ugly things and was shocked at the power, force and energy that those thoughts elicited and produced within me. Just at the moment my husband walked through the door, I was at the height (in my mind) of ugliness, and I locked onto the idea of resentment and anger so profoundly that I decided (in my mind) to not even speak to him.

Certainly, HE would know that I was upset because he had been gone so long. Certainly, HE KNEW the errand was only a 20 minute project. Certainly, HE KNEW that I would be hostile! My self-talk went on and on, justifying to myself my rage, my anger and resentment . . . yes, I was feeling pretty *high* knowing that I WAS RIGHT, and HE was miserably, undeniably, WRONG!

Through clenched teeth, I impolitely asked where in the world he had been (not that I cared a whit!). He apologized, saying he knew he had been gone a long time, but he had met an old Air Force friend and they visited and talked for awhile. The time had gotten away from them and then he had gone to wash the car and when he looked under the hood he saw that he needed to change all the hoses on the car. He is a master mechanic and is very fussy and caring about the vehicle and its road-worthiness, and while I knew that what he was saying was only for our well-being and safety, when one is on a negative emotional high, logic and reason counts for nothing! And, you certainly don't want to hear reasonable, safety-minded reasons now! He was innocent, I knew that down deep in my heart, but I couldn't unlock the hold that the powerful, fiery emotions had on me.

'Well,' I screeched, ready to blow apart, 'do you know what time it is and that we have to leave here in less than three hours, and all the things are not done that need to be done, (those things that HE SAID HE would take care of doing) and I'M under terrible pressure and stress. WHY couldn't you call me and let me know that you're not dead!' (Never mind that HE is under pressure and stress, and he will have to drive because I'M so exhausted I need to sleep before court THIS morning.)

As the feelings and emotions swept over me and settled, I mentally remember thinking the thought, 'I'll take care of this *crap* and handle this myself.' At that point, I actually locked and internalized all these emotions (literally felt it lock) into the front, left side of my body.

These feelings of annoyance, resentment, aggravation, etc., had been festering for many years. This was finally the 'straw that broke the camel's back!' Critical mass—an explosion of immense proportions—had now been invoked, and the exponential factor (an avalanche) was now in place. Those molding, festering feelings, charged by the powerful forces of negative emotions became irreversible! The environment in my body had been waiting for a 'match to light the fuse!'

That incident took place around the first part of October, 1987. I started having constipation problems, but just thought that was because we had been traveling, and I was reacting to sitting. Not to worry, it was no problem.

Two days before Thanksgiving, I noticed little red specks that looked like rust in my stools. 'Hummmmmmm,' thought I. That's interesting. I've never seen anything like that before. I decided to make an appointment with the doctor. I saw him the day after Thanksgiving and he diagnosed diverticulitis. He gave me some antibiotics and sent me home.

The symptoms seemed to clear up, except that I still had a problem with constipation but, I knew that it would go away. Then I started feeling very tired. I wanted to sleep. I didn't seem to have any energy and my stools became very odorous and noxious. Believe it or not, I could not smell it. I began to sleep more and more. I couldn't move. There was no energy. Soon, I was unable to think clearly.

On April 30, I woke up early in the morning, sat up on the side of the bed and heard a *clunk, swish, slosh*, on the left side of my abdomen. I thought to myself, 'Hummm, that's interesting. I've never heard anything like that before. So, I went to the bathroom and I was dumfounded and astonished. The bowl was filled with blood.

The doctors that day were very solicitous. By three o'clock that afternoon I was in the hospital undergoing tests to find where the bleeding came from. I was dumb-struck and shocked when I was told it was cancer. 'NO, NO, not me,' I said. 'It is NOT possible! This could NEVER happen to me!'

After the surgery to remove the tumor, I started thinking and wondering, 'WHY? HOW? How in the world could/did this happen to ME?' As I pondered the situation, slowly, ever so slowly and painfully, I came to the FULL and awful truth staring me full in the face—ugly and monstrous. The realization that I had been on a 'do-it-yourself project.' I HAD, with no equivocations, no excuses, no blame of anyone else, done this to myself and there was no other person in the whole world I could point the finger at and blame. I, MYSELF, HAD set in motion that set of circumstances that allowed my body to internalize destructive feelings and emotions that created a dis-ease in a section of my body just above the Sigmoid colon, a tumor that had to be surgically removed. A tumor that had perforated the colon wall and spilled into the abdominal area. A tumor that was the result of anger, resentment, suppressed hurts, hate, meanness, and unforgiveness. In a word . . . ugly, black, negative feelings.

'Now,' said I, 'What am I going to do about it?' In my mind I kept trying to weasel out of, side-step, turn away from the awful, terrible, realization that I—ME—that person of whom I thought was so untouchable to disease, had initiated—clearly and forcefully—the manifestation of such a dread, ugly, awful, frightening disease!

All of a sudden, in a flash, I knew what to do! In an instant I knew what I had to do and how to do it! I had been studying about illness and their emotional causes, and my husband and I had taken a seminar where we were taught to access the part of us that knows all things. I had created the tumor . . . I could heal it! I had allowed and entertained those terrible, ugly thoughts, feelings and emotions to putrefy, to torment, to mature, to corrupt and erupt.

Of course! Of course! Thank you, God. Thank you. I now see the lesson I must learn. I will love the cancer! I will love it. I looked at the cancer. I put my hands (in my mind) on the cancer and I told the cancer, 'Thank you for this great gift of knowledge!

Thank you for allowing me to see what I have done. Thank you for giving me this chance to know myself better. Thank you for supplying me with this opportunity to live life to the fullest and to learn to love unconditionally. Thank you for this great blessing and opportunity!'

My attitude and demeanor changed instantly! I felt alive and vital! I was now ready, willing and able to accept what I needed to learn, and understand what was necessary from this experience to grow and develop and expand my reason for existence on this earth. I decided right there and then, and from that moment forward, I would NOT *shift* down. I would not allow those negative thoughts to be entertained one more second! I would not allow the luxury of a negative thought! And, I would not allow my family to shift down and feel sorry for me and speak of MY CANCER. The cancer was not me! I am not a cancer any more than I am a cold or a flu! It would be known as, 'The tumor with a message.'

No. NO! NO! Absolutely NOT! There would be no self-fulfilling prophecies come to pass in my life like that! No, NO! NO! I was going to do what had to be done to change, shift, alter, renew, build, create new realities! I was in charge of my life and destiny! I would allow no quarter! I would be unmerciful! YES! YES! NOTHING would deter me from the new road I would travel and the journey I would begin! YES! YES! I AM health! I AM happiness! I AM JOY! I AM UNCONDITIONAL LOVE! I would, for the rest of my wonderful, exciting life BE that fulfillment of unconditional love!

I had been given a second chance. This gift of new life and expanded view offers and bestows gratitude for fullness and thankfulness that I am now able to understand a new dimension and fullness in my life.

From now on, those memories of the hate, resentment, anger, and rage that I waged and wrought upon myself would only be remembered and used in a positive manner. From this day forward, and forever, this experience would be registered and considered as a, 'minor inconvenience in my life!' And, that's the way it continues to be!

God merely uses coincidence as a way of remaining anonymous. Karol and I had been friends for years, but hadn't seen each other since 1976. She called me when she moved to Las Vegas in 1989. As we were visiting that morning, she shared with me the concept of the "Script." Now, I'm one who says, 'Will you share? Your words strike a responsive chord.'

This knowledge I felt was vitally important to me, as I knew there were still many unresolved feelings I needed to work through. Karol did share the "Script" and I immediately began to work with it and use it. I noticed and felt an immediate healing shift occur. The "Script," I feel, has wrought and worked wonders. I have, and do experience, an unqualified peace, happiness, contentment, and healing release as I continue to process deep-seeded and deep-seated negative emotional feelings dumped, stored and *buried* for many years. The "Script" has allowed an emotional stability and maturity to enter my life.

As I explained in Chapter Two, every feeling, every thought, every emotion and every belief that we have, has its own vibration! Everything you have ever felt, everything you have ever thought, everything you have ever believed, said, done, heard, or experienced has been recorded and registered in the body somewhere. If your feelings, thoughts, emotions or beliefs have been negative or positive—regardless of the intensity—it makes no difference. They have all registered in every fiber, nook and cranny of your Be-ing! Yes, all of it has been recorded in the DNA of the cells of your glands, your blood, your lymph system, your organs and your muscles . . . in your flesh.

Negative vibrations (fear based) create a heaviness in you, while the positive vibrations (love based) create a lightness. If you have experienced more negative vibrations than positive vibrations throughout your life, you will feel an imbalance somewhere in your Be-ing. When the negative becomes so overbalanced, something finally has to happen to make you aware of this overbalance/imbalance . . . whether the imbalance be physical, mental, emotional, spiritual or financial.

Many people will experience a crisis of some kind before they truly recognize that, as Dr. Bernie Siegel says, "one needs to take another road in life." Some of us have to get to the point of crisis before we are open to the possibility that we would really benefit by changing or shifting to a new awareness.

What is it that we need to change? We need to change negative feelings (vibrations) we have buried for untold years to positive feelings (vibrations) . . . negative feelings that pertain to any area of our life where challenges occur and keep reoccurring.

We learn the lessons in life we are to learn two ways; either through obedience to natural laws or through suffering the consequences of not observing those laws—through adversity. None of us consciously create the suffering we experience. Any suffering we may go through is due to natural consequences—the Law of Cause and Effect being manifest in our lives.

Are you learning through obedience or through suffering adversity? When you look around at others, you will probably agree that most of us are reaping the natural consequences of not observing the laws. Many of us are having to learn through adversity. "The Lord often allows us to wallow in mindless confusion before the teacher within us follows the path that lightens our way." (Patricia T. Holland)

If we experience suffering long enough, being sufficiently miserable while we are going through it, we usually become more teachable and are ready to eliminate the misery, no matter what effort it takes or how much dedication it requires. There are people, however, who are very teachable and willing to travel a better road without experiencing misery and heartache. They hear truth and are ready to incorporate it into their lives without being tried and tested . . . without being miserable and having to undergo the suffering.

At the turn in one's road where a person is miserable and ready for relief, he usually begins listening and looking for answers. He becomes more mindful of what he is feeling and thinking . . . of what makes him *tick*. He begins asking questions. He reads articles on the subject, or attends classes and seminars. He searches for self-help books or tapes that give him insights that assist with answers which will help him ease and understand the pain he is experiencing.

It is at this particular time a person is generally ready for change—for the quantum shift. He wants his life to be full and he wants to feel fulfilled. He is tired of nothing working, tired of ill health, tired of disastrous relationships, or tired of financial ineptness. Now his mind has opened. He is more aware and is wanting and looking for answers. He is ready for a great adventure! But, how does he go about making a change? Where does he start?

Chapter 7

Let's Get Started

The place to start is to become mindful or conscious of *what* you are feeling, *what* you are thinking, *what* you are saying and *what* you are doing. The minute you awaken in the morning, access your first feeling and your first thought. That first feeling or thought of the day commonly sets the stage and the tone for the rest of the day. So, if that first feeling/thought is not to your liking, the choice is yours. Right then and there is the best time to change it with feelings/thoughts that *are* of your liking.

Become aware of any incident, comment, situation or person that triggers in you some kind of discomfort response . . . when you feel something you don't enjoy feeling, or think something you don't enjoy thinking.

For instance: You're stopped at a stop light when it is red; it turns green, but the person in front of you fails to see the green light and doesn't move forward. Do you impatiently honk your horn, get mad or upset and start calling that person all kinds of names? At the very moment this happens, what are you feeling?

What feelings are generated in the following situations: 1) Your neighbor down the street drives by in the brand new car that you would give anything to be able to own, but can't afford. 2) Standing in a long line at the supermarket, movie, bank or restaurant, someone comes and breaks into the line. 3) The group of friends you associate with attend some activity and don't include you. 4) Someone makes a cutting remark about your abilities or your looks. 5) Someone else takes the credit for one of your original ideas. How do these situations cause you to feel?

As we sharpen our awareness we gather strong clues from the little daily incidents in our lives that will help us learn to identify what we are feeling and what we are thinking. Do you become disgusted with yourself for feeling a particular way whenever the same situation presents itself over and over again, and wish you didn't feel that way? This could be a definite indicator to you that the feeling involved with this situation is a good one to start working on and resolve.

For example: Between the ages of 16-48, I accompanied many fine musicians at various functions. Very often my name would *inadvertently* be left off the printed program, or I would somehow be overlooked in spite of hours of rehearsal. There could be as few as three on the program or as many as 50, yet, often every participant but myself would be listed on the printed program. This caused me to feel slighted, left out, hurt, and overlooked. But what I felt most of all was, "I'm not important." (As you read on you will understand the significance of my feeling "I'm not important.")

This all happened before I understood the principles I have learned and am sharing with you in this book. I didn't understand why this was a continual scenario for me. With every similar incident, I would experience hurt feelings no matter how many times I told myself, "It doesn't matter. It's okay. The important thing is that you did a good job." I thought of everything I could to talk myself out of the hurt feelings. And each time it happened I would tell myself, "Next time, I won't allow it to bother me." Even so, the next time the experience was repeated, those same feelings would *hit me in the face.*

In any situation, become conscious of what you are feeling, of what you are thinking, and whether it's comfortable or not. Be conscious of yourself and what you are experiencing in the moment. We all go through peaks and valleys with our feelings and emotions. Be aware of the peaks as well as the valleys and learn to recognize where the difference BEGINS. When you can identify where the shift occurs soon enough and often enough, the valleys won't be so low and your inbetweens (when you feel peace) will be of longer duration until you finally enjoy smooth sailing.

All too often our conditioning has forced us to turn our feelings and emotions off. Social restrictions often made it inappropriate to say what we truly felt or thought. Rather than learning how to appropriately address our true feelings/emotions we were led to believe that if we turned them off, somehow we wouldn't hurt inside. Or, sometimes we were forced to turn them off because the pain of feeling was overwhelming. Consequently, we have paid a high price by supposedly turning them off—by always conforming. The price was that we lost touch with our true feelings. If and when we reconnect with those feelings—we face them head on—our growth and progress will be much better served.

In order to remedy the negative effects any feelings/emotions have had in our lives, it is necessary for us to take responsibility for them and become accountable to ourselves for them. If our conditioning continues to cause us denial of our feelings as they happen, and we are unable to be accountable for them, there is NO growth. Even though we may deny our feelings, we can't sweep them under the rug. They don't, and they won't go away.

To deny feelings doesn't mean they are dead or no longer exist, that the energies of those feelings are no longer present in your energy field. On the contrary, if feelings are not resolved, their energy remains stored inside you, and, like a yeast, this energy continues growing and expanding, gathering more and more energy—resonating and joining forces with all similar feeling vibrations that are still inside your body. These energies create blocks like a dam in a ditch of water and short-circuit your system in more ways than you can imagine. If the feelings remain unresolved, this process continues to compound, and you could experience any number of disturbing effects. When you recognize these disturbing effects, be aware that alterations are now in order.

As I stated earlier, these unresolved feeling vibrations can never be considered dead and buried because they are energies that are still alive —resonating at some level. And these feelings *will* manifest themselves somewhere, sometime. Their vibrations are on-going. How liberating it is to know that any negative on-going vibrations you are storing inside you can be transformed into permanent, positive, healing energy vibrations.

Since energy matter is indestructible but possible to change, so, likewise, feelings are energy matter and possible to change. You *can* change their vibrations from negative to positive. These negative feelings can be *permanently resolved*. And it is an exciting, fun, therapeutic, healing and rewarding endeavor—an endeavor which enables you to tap the yet dormant, unrealized, and full potential innate within you. How do you accomplish this resolution?

When you *tune* into your feelings and recognize what you are feeling, you are ready to use the *tool* dialogue, the "Script," as I call it, that transforms those feelings. This dialogue has helped me and many others come to a better understanding of ourselves as well as those around us. It works most effectively when you use it during or after each situation in which you find yourself experiencing negative feelings. In order to fill a container with new material, first, you must eliminate the old garbage. In other words, to replace the negative with the positive, it is first necessary to identify and process the negative so a resolution is possible. Even though it takes time and effort to accomplish your desired goals, when you are ready for changes in your life, you will be motivated to make a commitment to yourself and apply yourself to achieving an "inner healing." Just remember, what's going on inside you didn't happen overnight. Therefore, it's unrealistic to expect the impact of years of negative feelings to disappear overnight.

Where Did This "Script" Come From?

At the *perfect* time in my life, I was introduced to Carolyn Lybbert, who is a hypno-therapist. After using hypno-therapy for a period of time in her practice, she came to realize and understand that a person does not really have to be hypnotized in order to trace back an emotional problem. She also realized that our Intelligence, Spirit, Higher Self, Subconscious remembers or knows everything that concerns us as individuals. Carolyn prayed for direction to know how she could help her clients help themselves. Little by little the original "Script" evolved for her, and as she used it in her practice more and more of her clients were able to process and change negative feelings to positive feelings by themselves at any time. They became responsible, accountable individuals who no longer needed to lean on her.

That's the beautiful part about the "Script" . . . you can do it all by yourself once you have the understanding. You don't have to depend on anyone else to help you. This gives you true FREEDOM.

Your personal strength and direction can then develop from the inside, and that's where you want strength and direction to come from— inside. A great ecclesiastic leader once said words to this effect: God works on a person from the inside out. The world works on a person from the outside in. The world would take people out of the slums. But, God takes the slums out of people, and then they take themselves out of the slums. The world would mold men by changing their environment. God changes men, who then change their environment.

Using the "Script" as a processing tool enables you to know and understand yourself better. It can literally take the *slums* out of you and then you can change your environment.

Another beautiful aspect of this process is that you do NOT have to remember or recall where or when the feelings started, because your Spirit/Intelligence/Subconscious knows. Can it be that simple? My husband continues asking that question because it is hard for him to believe it is simply that simple, and yet the results are so unquestionably astounding!

This dialogue, or "Script", has become a powerful tool for thousands of people. They have been able to significantly change negative feelings they believed were dead and buried . . . those feelings that choked, smothered and stifled their progress in many areas of their lives or caused health problems. This process of changing the vibrations in a persons energy field has been an exciting, marvelous schooling and journey. In my counseling it has been extremely gratifying to see so many lives literally transformed through the use of this powerful process.

Using the "Script" has contributed to exceptional (mine and others) emotional growth and development. It has assisted in restoring health, in healing relationships, and in establishing or re-establishing financial success. The "Script" has helped women who have experienced sexual abuse in their youth gain a peace of mind they heretofore had never known. It has even been credited for keeping several people from committing suicide. The "Script" has assisted people in removing the beliefs that blocked them and kept them from attaining their goals. They are now moving forward and achieving their goals. It has helped bring forgiveness, love, peace, joy and happiness to those who have made it a part of their daily routine.

I know that with your consistent application of the "Script," you too, will be able to realize the results you are seeking.

Let me explain the actual vernacular of the "Script." There is an aspect of our Be-ing that remembers and knows everything about us there is to know. This part of us has forgotten *nothing*. Some people would call this aspect of us *Intelligence*. Others may call it *Higher Self* or we may refer to it as *Super Conscious, Subconscious* or our *Spirit*. I choose to call this aspect of my Be-ing, Spirit. When I say *Spirit*, this refers to MY *Spirit* . . . no one else's, when I am using it for me. And when you use it for you and say *Spirit*, you are referring to YOUR *Spirit* . . . no one else's.

My Soul is comprised of my Spirit and my Body. Having been schooled by my senses from birth, my human nature is to listen to the needs and the wants of my Body. So, naturally, the desires of my body seem to receive the most attention, thereby governing my actions and my existence. Because of this, my Spirit is often neglected—much to the detriment of both my Body and my Spirit. My desire is to function as a whole—a whole Be-ing—to be at peace in my Body and in my Spirit (Soul). In order to do this, my Body cannot be in charge and allowed to overrule my Spirit. Both Body and Spirit need to be balanced, to be in harmony.

Because of my *human* nature and unruly will (my self-will), most of my life I have allowed my Body to "call the shots." But I experienced too much inner conflict and frustration functioning from the Body being the *master*. Life was not bringing me the peace and joy that I knew was possible. I definitely wanted to correct this, so, upon learning about the "Script," I decided to become aware, conscious and mindful of my feelings, thoughts and words so I could correct the disharmony, the conflict, the war going on between my Body and my Spirit that was causing fragmentation in my Soul.

As I recognize what I'm feeling or thinking that is bringing me any disharmony, I go through the "Script" stating that feeling or thought. I give MY Spirit instructions to correct the erroneous programming that is causing my discomfort.

Dr. Deepak Chopra, M.D., indicates in his book, *Perfect Health*, that the cells' memory of perfection contained in the DNA cannot be lost. It is only covered over, at which point the perfect blueprint of the cell is distorted. It is distorted by incorrect perceptions and erroneous programming, which alter the perfect blueprint and in turn distort the cells.

When I address my Spirit, I am talking to and instructing no one except my Higher Self, my Intelligence, my Spirit. My Spirit in turn goes to the feeling that has covered the memory of perfection in my DNA, knocks on the door, tells the feeling that answers the door that she (my Spirit) has been requested by her Body to make some corrections, to clean house, to uncover the memory of perfection contained in the cells original perfect blueprint; to eliminate the distortion and to restore the cells perfect function by re-programming them; to bring harmony and balance back to the DNA and RNA. When I do this, I am being response-able for myself. I am becoming account-able for what I feel and think. I am facilitating my own *shift*, my own transformation, uncovering the memory of perfection in the cells throughout my body. The cells then can begin functioning as they were designed to function. The cells can realign themselves to become balanced and more in tune with Universal Laws—with God's Laws. If you choose to use the word *Intelligence, Subconscious,* or *Higher Self* instead of *Spirit* in addressing that *All-knowing* aspect of yourself, the same principles apply and the "Script" still works effectively.

Please, do not allow any words contained within the "Script" to trigger discomfort in you. No offense is meant to anyone.

Processing with Updated Script

In the name of Jesus Christ . . . Spirit, Super-Conscious, Subconscious, Conscious, Higher Self, Heart, Mind, Will, Nervous System-Brain, Original Intelligence, RNA, DNA, & every genetic anomaly out of alignment with my pattern of perfection, please locate the origin of my conscious & sub-conscious destructive cellular memories which caused the incorrect perceptions that created feelings/thoughts/beliefs of

_____(feelings/thoughts/beliefs)_____

Take each & every level, layer, area, & aspect of my Being to these origins. Analyze & resolve them perfectly with God the Father's truth.

Come forward through all generations of time & eternity healing every event & its appendages based on the origins. Please do it according to God the Father's will, until I'm at the present—filled with light & truth, God's Immanence, peace & love, benevolence, forgiveness of my self for my imperfect perceptions, having compassion for every person, place, circumstance & event which contributed to any of these destructive cellular memories, feelings, thoughts, or beliefs.

With total forgiveness & unconditional love, I ask that my physical, mental, emotional, & spiritual memory of perfection resonate throughout my Being.

I choose Being_____(insert positive feeling/s, etc.)_____

I feel_____(same truth)_____

I AM_____(same truth)_____

(Replace previous feelings/thoughts/beliefs w/ the same desired truth on each line.)

It is done! It is healed! It is accomplished now!

Thank you all for coming to my aid & working together to help me rid my Being of stress, & attain the full measure of my creation. Thank you, thank you, thank you! I love you & praise God the Father from whom all blessings flow.

Now, all facets of my Being, please put this Scripting on automatic so it repeats itself throughout each & every cell & fiber of my Being every half hour of every day for the next 180 days, (or however long is best for me) thereby re-storing perfectly healthy frequencies throughout my Being & returning me to my original purpose, power & magnificence! And it is done!

A list of negative feelings and their positive opposites, are included in this book in Chapter 17. You will also find an in-depth section on health problems and their probable emotional causes in Chapter 18. If you have a health consideration you would like to work through with the "Script," see the probable feelings that are indicated under that health condition, (which is the negative aspect of your problem) then replace these feelings with appropriate positive opposite feelings.

Sometimes your positive replacements may be very short (one or two words) and at other times the replacement may be very long—depending on what you feel is appropriate at the time. It will vary according to the circumstances.

The more you use the "Script," the more readily the replacement words and feelings will come to you as you process. If you can't think of anything with which to replace the negative, you will always be very effective replacing it with *forgiveness* and *unconditional love.*

In fact, I always include *forgiveness* after "God's peace and love." Forgiveness opens the door for every kind of healing. Each time you go through the "Script", however, be sure to say "light and truth" and "God's peace and love" where indicated.

I believe that most of humankind, regardless of religious affiliation, desires to feel and experience peace and love in their hearts and lives. Using the "Script" is an appropriate way to accomplish this desire. Each time we process through it we are replacing negative vibrations with the positive vibrations of "light and truth" and "God's peace and love" (as well as whatever else we choose to say or use). Those powerful vibrations become stronger and stronger—automatically compounding with continual and consistent use.

Two reasons this "Script" is so powerful are: Number one—you are uncovering the memory of perfection in your DNA, which allows you to function more completely from your true *Self.* Number two—you become single-minded, bringing your Feeling and your Thinking together, thus integrating the mind and causing it to work as a whole unit. When you are single-minded, life works FOR you.

The emotional healing that occurred within me, took place in spite of my lack of understanding of these principles. It was marvelous and exciting beyond description. (The fact that a person's vibrations change each time one processes through the "Script" has been scientifically indicated—similar to the scientists' observation of the dying woman in Chapter Two—through subtle-energy instrumentation called an Intrinsic Data Field Analyzer.)

So, how do you get started?

In my counseling I have found that practically everyone (on a subconscious level), does NOT love themselves. They do not accept themselves nor trust themselves. Most of these same people don't even LIKE themselves. Interestingly enough, they all THINK they like, love, accept and trust themselves. But subconsciously, they do not FEEL it. Experience has shown that when using the Script you can proceed much faster in all areas when healing or changing negative feelings, if you first process and resolve: A) The feelings that keep me from liking myself; B) The feelings that keep me from loving myself; C) The feelings that keep me from accepting myself; D) The feelings that keep me from trusting myself. So, the first thing I would have you do is:

Find a comfortable, quiet place where you can sit, relax and close your eyes. Take a deep breath through your nose and let it out slowly through your mouth. Take another deep breath the same way, only this time hold your breath at the top of the full inhalation for three counts, then let it out slowly through your mouth. (This accesses both sides of the brain.) You are now ready to begin. The following is what I would say:

"Spirit/Intelligence/Super-Conscious (however you chose to address it), please locate the origin of the feelings that keep me from liking and loving myself. Take each and every level, layer, area, and aspect of my Be-ing to this/these origin/s. Analyze and resolve it/them perfectly with God's truth. Come through all generations of time and eternity healing every incident and it's appendages based on the origin. Do it according to God's will until I'm at the present, filled with light and truth, God's peace and love; forgiveness of myself for my incorrect perceptions; forgiveness of every person, place, circumstance and event which contributed to these feelings. With total forgiveness and unconditional love I allow every physical, mental, emotional, and spiritual problem and inappropriate behavior based on the negative origin recorded in my DNA, to transform. I choose liking myself. I feel to like myself. I am liking myself. I choose loving myself. I feel love for myself. I am loving myself. I give myself permission to like and love myself. I feel worthy of this love.

"It is done. It is healed. It is accomplished now!

"Thank you, Spirit, for coming to my aid and helping me attain the full measure of my creation. Thank you, thank you, thank you! I love you and praise God from whom all blessings flow."

After you finish the above, then repeat the Script for C) The feelings that keep me from accepting myself and D) The feelings that keep me from trusting myself. This time say, "Spirit, please locate the origin of the feelings that keep me from accepting myself and trusting myself." Continue on through the Script until you come to the next blank line, replacing the negative with words to this effect: "I choose accepting myself unconditionally. I feel acceptance of myself. I am accepting myself. I choose trusting myself implicitly! I feel total faith and trust in myself. I am trusting myself. I am my best supporter." Then finish the rest of the "Script."

It is essential that you mean what you say and say what you mean when you replace the negative with the positive, for the effectiveness of your processing will be in direct proportion to the sincerity and intent of your heart.

Another disturbing condition I've found with many people is that they have been subconsciously programmed for failure. If this is so for you, unless you change your programming it will continue to sabotage you and your progress will be impeded.

So, you may want to go through the "Script" on this one too. The following is how I would process to reprogram failure: "Spirit, please locate the origin of the feelings that cause me to continually fail." I would continue through the rest of the "Script" until I came to the next blank line, then I would replace "to continually fail" with, "I choose succeeding. I feel successful. I am succeeding. I now allow myself to succeed. I give myself permission to succeed. I choose reprograming myself for success. I am succeeding in all my endeavors. I am successful!" Then I would finish it on out with the balance of the "Script."

This does not necessarily mean that all of a sudden you are going to go out and succeed in everything you do. It is still necessary to observe and adhere to correct principles in your feelings and thoughts in order to succeed. However, reprogramming yourself to succeed opens up the channels to help eliminate the saboteurs that have been keeping you from meeting your desired goals. Be aware that you may also have other specific negative feelings you need to address where success is concerned.

When you are programmed to fail, it's like you have a brick wall standing in your way. Each brick of the wall represents a feeling that has contributed to validating your failure or lack of success. In order to move ahead in all areas of your life—after you've changed the master program from "failure" to one of "success"—it is necessary to disassemble that wall, brick by brick (feeling by feeling). You do this by taking each of your negative feelings encompassing the area of success, one or several at a time, and process them through the "Script" so you can change them to positive feelings. Processing further in depth contributes to a subsequent total shift of energies that will eventually produce the results you are seeking in that area of your life.

Imagine yourself as a computer. The master program is the "Memory of Perfection" in your DNA and could be considered the *hard-*

ware. The "Script," in this instance, is the *software* that you are using to change negative programs to positive programs. Uncovering the "Memory of Perfection" in your DNA enables the computer to function in the most productive and desirable manner.

As you begin processing your feelings, you may want to be more selective in choosing other influences that you bring into your life. While striving to change the negativity to positivity in your energy field, continually feed your mind positive information; view worth-while TV; watch uplifting movies; be more particular about the thoughts you choose and the words you speak; associate with positive people; listen to music with positive messages and beautiful melodies. In other words, create a more optimal environment for positive change.

Be certain you always replace your negative feelings with appropriate positive feelings. If a void or vacuum is left where negative feelings have been removed, more of the same can come back—multiplied—unless the void is filled with something positive. Also, you more easily pick up negativity from others around you if you leave a void. Remember, what you are doing is changing the programming. If the instructions to your Spirit are not specific and complete, the energy of the negative could be left in limbo—hanging and unresolved—and completion may not be realized.

After you have used the Script to process and resolve the initial feelings of like, love, acceptance, trust of self, etc., then continue on your transformational journey by:

1. Recognizing your uncomfortable feelings. The minute you feel them, if you are able to, take out your "Script" and state the negative feelings at the beginning, then change them to positive feelings at the appropriate place.

2. Doing this as many times a day as needed. If you are unable to resolve the feelings right at the moment they happen, make a mental or written note of them so you

won't forget what the feelings are. At an appropriate time, later in the day, process the feelings you were unable to address earlier with the "Script," changing the negative to appropriate positive feelings.

3. Doing a mental sweeping each night before you go to sleep. Think back over your day and remember negative incidents that caused you any hurt, pain or discomfort. Address and resolve them by taking them through the "Script."

4. Processing as many unresolved feelings as possible at this time. You may have quite a few to process by the time you go to bed. Nevertheless, your Spirit/Intelligence works on them very efficiently and effectively during the night.

5. Keeping in mind, that no matter when you are able to change the negative feelings to the positive, it will work.

6. Memorizing the "Script" as soon as possible so it is immediately available when you need it.

7. Saying the "Script" out loud or silently. (Either way works.) Ideally, a quiet place where you can be alone and are able to relax is best, but if that is not possible, do whatever is next best for you.

After the "Script" is memorized, you will find that you can go through it very quickly wherever you are.

One of the appealing things about the "Script" is that there are no limitations on ways to use it. A very healing and effective approach you may incorporate when dealing with your feelings towards other people is to write out all the negative feelings you have ever felt toward each member of your family. (It might surprise you what will come to your mind.) Then, do the same thing where any other person is concerned.

After you have listed these negative feelings, take all the feelings for one person at a time and go through the "Script," replacing the negative with *total forgiveness, unconditional love* and any other appropriate opposite positive feelings.

For example: If you have listed resentment as a negative feeling towards your brother, Jerry, ". . . please locate the origin of the resentment I feel towards my brother, Jerry." Or, ". . . the origin of the feelings that cause me to be ticked off when he always has to be right." Where the first blank line in the "Script" appears, just state that sentence. State it exactly the way it came to your mind. Then, replace it on the second blank line with something like, "I choose releasing all past resentments toward him. I feel to release all past resentments toward him. I AM releasing all past resentments toward him. He was only reacting to a lack within himself. I understand, I feel love for him and I forgive him," or whatever comes to your mind.

As was mentioned before, there is a list of negative feelings in Chapter 17—to assist you in identifying what you are feeling—and their opposite appropriate positive feelings for replacing the negative.

After you have worked through many of your feelings, sometimes you may come to an impasse where you simply don't know WHAT it is you are feeling. At this point, state it as such: "Spirit, please locate the origin of the feeling I'm feeling that is so uncomfortable." Your Spirit/ Super-Conscious/Intelligence will know what it is and process it for you.

Be prepared for a rewarding, ongoing process, because changing and eliminating layers of negative feelings does not happen overnight. Remember, you didn't acquire them overnight, so they're not going to disappear overnight! Also, keep in mind that you were born with some of those feelings (or vibrations), in which case, they have been there for a long time. They came with you in your genes at the cellular level—in the DNA. Sometimes these feelings can be very stubborn and don't readily release their hold on you. Nevertheless, you *can* accomplish what you desire to accomplish if you are committed to resolving those old, useless and sick feelings.

When you have made progress in processing your negative feelings with the "Script," do your best to keep from slipping back into the old, habitual grooves—the ones that became worn out from so much use, undermining your self-worth and self-esteem, or creating a dragon in you. If you find yourself slipping back, just know there are more layers to peel away. Focus on the feelings you wish to eliminate and continue processing them with the "Script," replacing them with appropriate positive feelings to resolve them.

After I had been using the "Script" for about four months, I began experiencing a feeling inside myself that was very disturbing, but I could not "put my finger on" what I was feeling. I just knew that emotionally I hurt inside . . . at my very core! Doing my best to identify what this feeling was, I kept asking myself the question, "What is it? What am I feeling?" I did that for about three days. Then, as I was reclined on my slant board after exercising one morning, I was just being with the feeling and asking, "What is it? What is it?" All of a sudden the words came to me loud and clear, "YOU'RE NOT IMPORTANT!" Immediately the impact of that feeling enveloped me and without even thinking about it I started crying. At that same moment, I instantly and automatically drew up into the fetal position. As these words were ringing in my ears I witnessed the circumstances of my birth in my mind's eye and felt the feelings that occurred during those first historical moments of my life. My mother and I were all alone during that event, with the exception of the hospital personnel. There was no one else from the family present to herald my entrance to earth. The absence of family members, especially my Father who was unable to be there, had told me, in effect, that "I wasn't important" . . . not important enough for anyone to be there awaiting my arrival. As the flood of feelings from my birth experience came rushing and gushing forward, I cried and cried. I couldn't stop for a long time, the hurt was so deep.

After this experience, I began to understand why I set things up throughout my life to happen the way they did. For instance, when my name was omitted from programs. Subconsciously, I felt I always had to validate this belief—I'M NOT IMPORTANT—in my social life, in opportunities of leadership, in my professional life, with my family, etc. I was sabotaging myself continually, not allowing myself to feel successful or important, regardless of my ability to achieve in all these areas.

The knowledge and awareness that came from this experience was: realizing in those first few moments that Mom and I were alone—in my heart I automatically concluded that "I wasn't important," because no one was there to welcome my arrival. I felt the feeling (incorrect perception) of abandonment, not only for myself but for what I thought my mother must have been going through. I felt sorry for her. And, wanting to soothe Mother's pain and make everything *better* or *all right* for her, I decided that I COULD be important by being her "champion," her "protector" so that she wouldn't ever have to experience this loneliness again. The feelings that were going on inside me caused me to perceive and say (to myself), "Well, Mom, it's just you and me against the world! I will protect you. I will take care of you and see that you are happy. It's my job to make this up to you. I will be strong for both of us!" And so, I carried that responsibility on my shoulders for over 48 years.

I am so grateful that a resolution of these incorrect perceptions and feelings was available to me through using the "Script."

Many times I wondered if going through the "Script" all the time was worth it. But, when a specific incident happens now, that used to bother me, and I recognize that I'm not affected or bothered by it in the least anymore, I know how valuable that persistence was, and continues to be.

Let me give you another example: I don't think anything made me more angry than being awakened from a sound sleep by someone or something. When this happened, I could never go back to sleep. It just infuriated me if the phone rang before I was awake, or if the toilet flushed and woke me up, or if someone was making too much noise either in the house or out of the house. When our children were growing up, their bathroom bordered our bedroom, so we trained them to not flush the toilet in the middle of the night so we wouldn't be awakened.

Once while staying in a motel with a group of family and friends in Jackson Hole, Wyoming, someone was having a loud party close by. It was very late at night and we were all quite tired from traveling. The noise from the party woke most of us and kept us awake. Much to the surprise of my friends and my children, I put my robe on, went to the room where the party was going on, knocked on the door and asked them if they realized that others may be trying to sleep! (Usually, I wasn't that nervy.) Yes, it was a real phobia with me.

Sound ridiculous? Well, at the time it didn't seem so to me. For some reason I was very possessive of my sleep. When I started using the "Script" to release that feeling of anger when I was awakened abruptly—guess what? It no longer bothered me. It's so wonderful to now feel peaceful and calm whenever I'm awakened from a deep sleep at (what I consider) an inappropriate time!

Using the "Script" accomplishes several significant things. As I have stated, it brings us to single-mindedness; it returns the cells to their perfect blueprint (when correct positive information replaces the negative); it brings us back into alignment and balance with the laws of the Universe; it changes and raises our vibrations, which brings us closer to our Source—to our place of *Comfort* and *Peace*; it eliminates the conflict between *Body* and *Spirit*, which then allows our Soul to be at peace and in charge; it creates a more favorable environment for social, physical, mental, emotional and spiritual healing. The "Script" is literally a vehicle for self-transformation. The "Script" assists us in changing our heart and in becoming more forgiving, loving, compassionate, merciful and accepting.

Chapter 8

The Major Feelings

How do you go about recognizing what you are feeling when there's such a maze of feelings and emotions running around out there? How in the world do you differentiate what's what?

My experience has been that all of the feelings and emotions in the world can basically be narrowed down to two . . . LOVE and FEAR. All positive feelings/emotions are LOVE-based. All negative feelings/emotions are FEAR-based. In other words, we are either coming from LOVE or we are coming from FEAR. It's as simple as that.

Gerald G. Jampolsky's book title, *Love is Letting Go of Fear*, is very meaningful and profound in regard to this principle; if all our feelings and emotions were love based there would be no reason to go through this process. Nevertheless, there are feelings that wreak havoc and turmoil in our lives, and these are fear based. Wouldn't it be wonderful if we were all coming from unconditional love? (That includes self-love.)

Let's broaden the principal feeling of FEAR into seven primary categories, then it won't be such a challenge to understand and to get started. There are seven primary categories of feelings. Most of us enter this earth with one of these primary feelings. Sadly, they are all appendages of FEAR. The major feelings are:

1. ANGER
2. HATE
3. GUILT
4. RESENTMENT
5. REJECTION/ABANDONMENT
6. NEED FOR APPROVAL
7. OVERWHELMED BURDEN

Countless other negative feelings related to these seven, are found listed in Chapter 17. As you tune into these principles and move with this process, you will come to understand that the negative feelings you feel—those feelings that take you out of a peaceful state; that bring discomfort and uneasiness into your life; the ones you would very much like to be rid of—can usually be traced back to one or more of the seven categories of fear, or an appendage to them.

At least one of the feelings from the fear category, or something very close to it, is usually internalized at birth by each one of us. This isn't to say that everyone embraced a negative *core* feeling at birth . . . only about 97% of us did. Those people who had very calm, happy, peaceful, pleasant and fulfilling birth experiences generally have internalized a love-based feeling. As a result, their experiences in life may be less challenging than those with fear-based feelings.

Once again, it is important to remember that the dominant pivotal feeling we experience at birth colors all our perceptions of life from that time on, and is therefore the ruling feeling through which we view life— the feeling that compels us to the behavior we exhibit each day.

You may or may not be sensitive to the feeling (know what it is) you embraced at birth. But, if you think you know, then process it with the Script to assist you in changing the negative core programming.

For example: Let's suppose your major feeling is a NEED FOR APPROVAL. Just say, "Spirit, please locate the origin of my feelings that created such a NEED FOR APPROVAL in me." After you say,

"With total forgiveness and unconditional love, I allow every physical, mental, emotional, and spiritual problem, and inappropriate behavior based on the negative origin recorded in my DNA, to transform," you may then like to continue with words to the effect of, "I choose approving of myself. I feel approval of myself. I am approving of myself. Everyone approves of me. I choose being cherished. I feel cherished. I am cherished. I choose being loved. I feel loved. I am loved. I feel valued. I am valued. I feel connected to all those I love. I am connected to all those I love." Then finish the Script.

Give yourself permission—allow yourself to feel whatever feelings you may feel. These feelings are much easier to change if you accept and *own* them rather than deny them and pretend they don't exist. When you feel negative feelings it does NOT make you a bad person! Who in the world can go through life without feeling negativity some of the time? I doubt that it's possible . . . even if you were on a desert island by yourself. Developing a consciousness of what you are feeling and thinking, then striving to overcome your destructive negative feelings and thoughts is part of the challenge of this life.

If obvious "less than glorious" feelings have caused a weakness in our character, by continually monitoring these feelings and processing them through the Script we can change our feelings and overcome any negative influence they bring to our behavior—thereby improving our character.

In the course of time, by transforming old unproductive feelings to productive positive feelings, the detrimental effects of the old feelings will lose their hold on us. This positive change will become a definite source of strength to us. This extraordinary remedial process all starts by us *owning* all our feelings and resolving the negative tendencies they create in our lives.

I had a client who processed the feeling of *rejection*. She had been unconsciously sabotaging herself in order to be rejected and create havoc in her relationship with her boyfriend. At this particular time, their relationship was on a down-hill slide about as fast as it could go! Consciously, she had no idea why she was doing what she was doing. She didn't even recognize she was creating havoc for herself. Finally, she dealt with the feelings of *rejection* and the *fear of being rejected* and replaced those feelings with "I choose accepting myself. I feel acceptance of my self and the acceptance of others. I am accepting of my self. People naturally love me. I claim the ability to be accepted and loved by others."

By going through the Script for those feelings, from that moment forward, her whole behavior pattern started to change and her relationships straightened out without any other conscious effort on her part. I was amazed and gratified to watch her relationship with her boyfriend change and become progressively better, until several months later they became engaged and were later married.

Several years ago, one of my friends became concerned about her sudden change of feelings toward her husband. Little by little everything her husband did started to annoy and bother her. She didn't like the way he ate; the way he talked; the way he smiled; the way he laughed; the way he walked. In short, she didn't like the way he did anything! She started wondering what on earth was happening to her. What was he doing differently that caused her to feel this way?

My friend feared she might have a difficult time continuing in the relationship having these feelings—even after 28 years of marriage. She was having a difficult time remembering her former feelings of affection for this man. In desperation, she started to process her feelings with the Script. She became responsible and accountable for what she was feeling towards her husband.

Much to her surprise, the feelings of annoyance, aggravation, distaste and disdain started to evaporate (as she described it). Slowly, the feelings of caring, concern, love and affection returned. She *squarely* looked at and addressed every negative feeling she felt where he was concerned. This friend replaced those negative feelings primarily with "forgiveness and unconditional love." Her marriage returned to the solid, fulfilling relationship it had formerly been. She is a happy, content woman today—17 years later—and is truly grateful for this tool she continues to use and share with others.

The foregoing examples talk about feelings that are comparatively simple to overcome. There is one feeling very prevalent in the world today that we haven't talked about, however. That feeling is HATE. With all the wars and rumors of war throughout the world, it makes a person wonder if there will ever be peace. When we see in the media the disdain, hatred and desire for revenge exhibited by people in many countries, it could make us wonder how this hatred got its root . . . how the retaliation that seems to go on year after year could ever be halted.

Then there is the world-wide racial prejudice. It reminds me of the song, *You've Got to Be Taught,* from SOUTH PACIFIC, which in essence says that we have to be taught to hate and fear, we have to be taught from year to year. We're taught to hate a person's race, the color of someone's skin, someone's culture, etc., etc. You get the picture.

Knowing how the feelings and thoughts of each parent can impact the prenatal period of their child's development—as well as the DNA— reminds us that our parents wouldn't even have to say one word against another race or people during our life. We would still be influenced by their unresolved feelings and thoughts towards those whom they consider undesirable. The tragedy of this commentary is that if we are prejudiced, we usually see the person, race or nationality we're prejudiced against as our mortal enemy. In reality, they are just as human as we are. They have the same needs, feelings, hopes, and desires that we do. How can they be our enemy? Have they declared themselves as such? So . . . what is the solution?

Let me share with you what John A. Sanford tells us in his book, *The Kingdom Within*:

The beginning of the solution to the problem of the enemy is to recognize him within ourselves. We carry the enemy in our own hearts. We hate him because he contradicts us. We fear that if we acknowledge him as our own he will take us over completely. The precise opposite is true. NOT to acknowledge him is to fall into the power of the inner enemy who mocks our futile efforts to get rid of him, by getting rid of those who carry the projected burden of our own darkness. To acknowledge him as our own is to begin to be released from his power and to find his constructive side.

In other words, if we are desirous of eliminating hatred of supposed enemies, we would do well to start by looking at the reflection of our *Self* in that enemy. If the quality that we hate is not in our *Self*, we can not see it—resonate with it—in another person. Or, saying it another way, we only see in others that which we see (subconsciously) in our *Self*. Until we own this truth, we will continue to carry the burden of our own darkness.

A beautiful illustration of a person eliminating feelings of hate towards his enemy is told by George G. Ritchie in his book, *Return from Tomorrow*:

When the war in Europe ended in May 1945, the 123rd Evac entered Germany with the occupying troops. I was part of a group assigned to a concentration camp near Wuppertal, charged with getting medical help to the newly liberated prisoners, many of them Jews from Holland, France, and Eastern Europe. This was the most shattering experience I had yet had; I had been exposed many times by then to sudden death and injury, but to see the effect of slow starvation, to walk through those barracks where thousands of men had died a little bit at a time over a period of years, was a new kind of horror. For many it was an irreversible process: we lost scores each day in spite of all the medicine and food we could rush to them.

And that's how I came to know Wild Bill Cody. That wasn't his real name. His real name was seven unpronounceable syllables in Polish, but he had long drooping handlebar mustaches like pictures of the old western hero, so the American soldiers called him Wild Bill. He was one of the inmates of the concentration camp, but obviously he hadn't been there long: his posture was erect, his eyes bright, his energy indefatigable. Since he was fluent in English, French, German and Russian, as well as Polish, he became a kind of unofficial camp translator.

We came to him with all sorts of problems; the paper work alone was staggering in attempting to relocate people whose families, even whole hometowns, might have disappeared. But though Wild Bill worked fifteen and sixteen hours a day, he showed no signs of weariness. While the rest of us were drooping with fatigue, he seemed to gain strength. 'We have time for this old fellow,' he'd say. 'He's been waiting to see us all day.' His compassion for his fellow-prisoners glowed on his face, and it was to this glow that I came when my own spirits were low.

So I was astonished to learn when Wild Bill's own papers came before us one day, that he had been in Wuppertal since 1939! For six years he had lived on the same starvation diet, slept in the same airless and disease-ridden barracks as everyone else, but without the least physical or mental deterioration.

Perhaps even more amazing, every group in the camp looked on him as a friend. He was the one to whom quarrels between inmates were brought for arbitration. Only after I'd been at Wuppertal a number of weeks did I realize what a rarity this was in a compound where the different nationalities of prisoners hated each other almost as much as they did the Germans.

As for Germans, feeling against them ran so high that in some of the camps liberated earlier, former prisoners had seized guns, run into the nearest village and simply shot the first Germans they saw. Part of our instructions were to prevent this kind of thing and again, Wild Bill was our greatest asset, reasoning with the different groups, counseling forgiveness.

'It's not easy for some of them to forgive,' I commented to him one day as we sat over mugs of tea in the processing center. 'So many of them have lost members of their families.'

Wild Bill leaned back in the upright chair and sipped at his drink. 'We lived in the Jewish section of Warsaw,' he began slowly, the first words I had heard him speak about himself, 'my wife, our two daughters, and our three little boys. When the Germans reached our street they lined everyone against a wall and opened up with machine guns. I begged to be allowed to die with my family, but because I spoke German they put me in a work group.'

He paused, perhaps seeing again his wife and five children. 'I had to decide right then,' he continued, 'whether to let myself hate the soldiers who had done this. It was an easy decision, really. I was a lawyer. In my practice I had seen too often what hate could do to people's minds and bodies. Hate had just killed the six people who mattered most to me in the world. I decided then that I would spend the rest of my life—whether it was a few days or many years—loving every person I came in contact with.

Loving every person . . . this was the power that had kept a man well in the face of every privation.

NOTE: Wild Bill lived on the same starvation diet, slept in the same airless and disease-ridden barracks as everyone else, BUT—without the least physical or mental deterioration! How amazing! Wild Bill's attitude—the feeling in his heart-mind—was one of pure and simple love. He loved every person with whom he came in contact. And in order to exhibit this kind of love he would have had to forgive. What a graphic example of the profound and magnificent power of forgiveness and love.

Negative feelings, thoughts and attitudes eat at our body. Positive feelings, thoughts and attitudes feed our body—nourish our body—sustain our body.

If you are sincere in your desire to overcome any prejudice or hatred you may be carrying around in your heart, but are having a difficult time accomplishing this, may I suggest that using the Script is one of the best avenues you could take to changing that negative energy inside you. The freedom and release you would receive by doing this is worth more than anything money can buy. Be specific in stating who or what you feel hatred toward. You may even want to make a list of them all, then take them through the Script one at a time, especially if the hate is old and deep-seeded.

Anger is another big stumbling block with many people. One young man, Kevin, was racked and possessed with terrible anger that seemed impossible to control or resolve. He had uncontrollable mood swings. Members of Kevin's family never knew what to expect where his feelings and emotions were concerned. After concentrating on what he was feeling, then processing these feelings through the Script for a period of time, Kevin became a much happier, self-fulfilled person. He is now more even-tempered, and has a job with important leadership responsibilities. Everyone he works with truly enjoys being under his supervision. But what is most gratifying to Kevin in his new found sense of true inner peace . . . knowing that whenever he shifts back into negativity he can use the Script to return to the coveted peace he enjoys.

There are many, many more Script experiences I could share with you (they would fill a book), including people who have had financial problems reversed; people who have improved their health; and people who had no desire to live anymore . . . who are now living happy, fulfilling, productive lives. There are those whose self-esteem was so low they could hardly look at anyone, let alone look them in the eye. Now their confidence is one of their greatest assets.

As you process your feelings, you may find the change you had hoped for is not forthcoming. Oftentimes you are dealing with unresolved generational (ancestral) feelings and trauma, as well as your own, and they can be many layers deep. You usually have no conscious awareness of what they are or from whence they came. Just keep digging by processing daily negative feelings and thoughts.

The body also has its own priority as to what needs processing next. Sometimes what YOU may consider a priority is not in agreement with the body. Consequently, you could experience "hit and miss" until you finally hit the mark and start realizing results. When dealing with major feelings (i.e. Fear) be aware of any appendages and be willing to look at them also, as shown in the illustration.

FEAR is the dark room where all the negatives are developed.

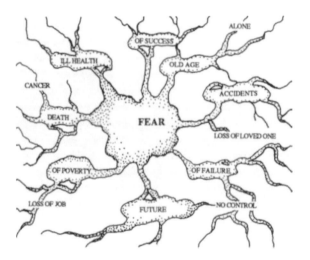

A man who had been Scripting for several months after attending one of my workshops in Washington, called me and told me that he had decided to Script for ANGER until it was gone. I said to him, "Wait a minute, Dan. You mean without being specific about who or what was causing the anger." He said, "Yes, I just Scripted anger." Then he said, "And in 30 days it was gone! It just left. Not only that, but Gary (his somewhat rebellious son who seemed to have been the recipient of Dan's unresolved anger through the DNA) did a complete flip-flop at the same time!" Needless to say, Dan was very excited.

Another man, after hearing Dan's story, Scripted FEAR for about the same amount of time and was finally free of that feeling which had plagued him for 60 years. Just remember, everyone is different. Consequently, the Script will have a unique effect with each individual.

Chapter 9

It Just "Is"

The question has been asked about the Script, "Does the Script take the place of prayer?" The answer to this question is an emphatic, absolute "NO!" The Script is not a prayer. With this Script you are addressing a part of your *Self*—your *Spirit, Higher Self, Intelligence* (or whatever fits your belief system), only in so doing you are directing your conscious thoughts and words rather than allowing unconscious, undirected, mindless thoughts and words. When using the Script your intent is to take accountability for what you are feeling and thinking. Consider it a poem or the words to a song, or a *tool* to correct the faulty wiring . . . to reprogram the distorted cells. In actuality, the Script is a vehicle of transformational healing in all aspects of your life.

In praying, you are talking to God. You are directing your thoughts and words to your Creator, or whatever your definition of Deity is. In my mind, one cannot compare the two. It may seem strange to some, to be conversing with their Spirit, or to be giving it instructions. Most people are not taught to do this, so it is quite a change . . . one that some may not want to make. However, we carry on a conversation, or are talking to ourselves all the time. It's called *self-talk*. Usually, we just don't pay any attention to our self-talk and what we are saying. Who is that inside our head we are talking to and making comments to, anyway?

If giving instructions to your Spirit takes you out of your comfort zone (like it did for me, at first), it will be more of a challenge to move forward in this process. Take a look at the discomfort you may feel at the thoughts of using the Script. It will be insightful and revealing and may create a new awareness in you. Be willing to experience discomfort in order to grow and move to a new level of maturity. Be willing to step out of your comfort zone . . . that's where growth takes place! Be willing to admit you may have an incorrect perception. Be willing to shift into a higher gear! The marvelous and rewarding by-product of improving ourselves is that others around us begin to improve also.

It has been said that when we lift ourselves we lift 30,000 other people with us. When we think of the far-reaching effects ONE life can have, as evidenced in the famous movie with Jimmy Stewart, *It's A Wonderful Life*, I'm sure there is a lot of truth in this statement.

Rather than accept the responsibility ourself, it's easier for us to blame our unhappiness or misfortune on someone else, saying, "If Bob would only do this, or if he'd only say this, then I would be happy." Or, "If it hadn't been for that person in front of me, this misfortune (or whatever) wouldn't have happened." YOU are the one that determines your happiness. It's only when you accept what "IS" and decide to make some improvements in YOUR SELF and not wait for others to improve or change, that you allow, make room for and create an atmosphere for others to improve also. Initially, the change has to come from within you before you will notice others changing.

The fun and enlightening part about working on yourself is that you forget about *helping* or wanting others to change. Because you are having such a good time, and are being rewarded in this new endeavor of discovering your own feelings and thoughts, it's easier to "live and let live." After all is said and done, YOU are NOT responsible for changing anyone but yourself, anyway!

It is exciting to observe the shift that occurs when a person is willing to take responsibility and start working on themselves instead of always looking OUT THERE (outside themselves) for their answers and their happiness. Unconditional acceptance of others becomes much easier for those who focus on themselves reforming, instead of always focusing on reforming someone else.

When we start looking to ourselves for the resolutions to our *own* problems, a definite shift takes place inside us. This shift creates and allows an environment of understanding and forgiveness of *Self* and others. When understanding abounds in us, it becomes much easier to "let go" of the blame and judgment that we have directed toward others. If we can honestly and maturely accept everyone, including ourselves, exactly where they are and the way they are—this very moment—great changes in ourselves, as well as others, will automatically occur.

To develop the maturity and compassion it requires to accept everyone just the way they are, it is necessary for us to embrace the internal conviction that it is IMPOSSIBLE for us to see a situation, problem, or challenge the same way another person sees it. In the first place, as we have learned from previous chapters, another person's conception and gestation period was totally different than ours. Their birth experience was unique unto themselves. We have NO IDEA what feeling(s) they embraced at birth . . . the feeling that has governed their whole lifes experiences. We have not had the same set of circumstances and experiences in our life that they have had. We have not been disciplined exactly the way they have been disciplined. We have not had the same heartaches and hurts they have had. We certainly don't have the same inner dialogue they have. Once again, there is NO WAY we can see things through another person's eyes! Who gave us license to judge or blame? Our only assignment is to NOT judge or blame, but to *FORGIVE*.

Where others are concerned, the attitude or situation just "IS." Attitudes are collective feelings and beliefs, and no two people have the same collection. We ALL have many of the same kinds of challenges and problems, but each one of us approaches their resolution from a different point of view. Who's to say which viewpoint is *right* or *wrong* or better than anyone else's?

During part of my life I was plagued with one of the worst diseases known to man. It is called, *automatic judging.* Indeed, it was one of my greatest shortcomings. I finally realized there was NO WAY I could accurately see things through someone else's eyes. There was NO WAY I could know what another person's experiences and upbringing had brought to his life. I have a whole different range of input, upbringing and experiences that make me who I am. What makes me think I can stand in another person's shoes and know what makes him tick?

Most people do the best they can according to their own perceptions. We have no license to find fault in their perceptions! We all have them.

It was such a relief for me to be able to allow every person their own life without feeling I had to pass judgment. I finally understood that I may not agree with another person's viewpoint, belief or behavior, but that doesn't make me *right* and them *wrong.* Even when I see immorality or crime where people break the laws of the land and the laws of God, I can't judge them because I wasn't there walking in their footsteps to understand what caused them to do what they did. I don't have to like what they are doing or condone it, but I have no business judging them. They will—sooner or later—suffer the natural consequences of their behavior. I can only say, "There, but for the grace of God, go I. Bless you."

How many times have we heard, "Only look for the good in others. If you can't say something nice, don't say anything at all." Someone forgot to tell us, though, "If you can't THINK anything nice, don't THINK anything at all." (Have you ever tried not thinking?)

Anyone can find the negative in others, but it's much more of a challenge to find the good . . . the positive. When we see the negative in another person, however, it is only a reflection of something we see in ourselves that we do not like. If it weren't in us we wouldn't be able to see it in someone else . . . we wouldn't resonate with it. This behooves us to look for the good in ourselves as well as in others. Accept what "IS."

In his fascinating book, *Return From Tomorrow*, George G. Ritchie asks: "Do you want to affiliate with the Christ in people or the Adversary in people? Which ever one you choose, it is necessary for you to find those characteristics—either Christ's or the Adversary's—in each person you meet" . . . and in, I might add, your *Self.*

Chapter 10

Early Up-Bringing

When we suggest to others that they may have an unresolved negative feeling toward some beloved member of their family, they could become defensive or offended, and respond by not wanting to continue the conversation. The important thing to understand is that there is no blame in these situations. It just "IS." Those people who influenced our early years usually did the best they knew how.

As a child, when we established a particular perception, we usually had an incorrect reference point because we were too young to understand and sort out the true picture. Our own lack of maturity—our own lack of wisdom—produced the incorrect perception. Therefore, our perception was usually an illusion.

Incorrect or not, that perception has been stored in our cells—in our DNA—covering over the memory of perfection in our original blueprint. These perceptions have been carried with us throughout our years, often creating enormous physical, emotional or mental pain in some area of our life. Our mind had to draw some conclusion for the discomfort (pain) we felt at the time the core incident occurred. Consequently, whatever data was available in our subconscious from previous experiences for us to reference, determined the belief we established, whether correct or incorrect. Then later, when similar incidents occurred in our lives, any old familiar feelings that were being resurrected responded once again by embracing the same incorrect perception—the same incorrect belief—thereby validating our illusion. Thus, a deeper and deeper endorsement of the discomfort was perpetuated (subconsciously).

Let us start with the factors described in the beginning of the book concerning our gestation and birth, and add to them the way we were treated by whomever was involved in our world as we grew up. Were we treated with love and acceptance or did we experience physical, mental or emotional abuse? Whatever happened to us . . . these experiences had a profound impact on our concept of Self.

When a child is abused, he is usually unable to express his feelings of fear, anger or rage. So, these feelings are stuffed inside him without a form of verbal expression. When feelings are continually stuffed inside, the child may lash out by being abusive to others, or he may be uncontrollable in different ways. He may become languid or non-communicative and withdrawn; or, he may become ill. The illness, at this point, will often affect the immune system, especially if the child views the situation as being unalterable, hopeless, or feels there is *no way out*.

Many children who come from an abusive background seem to always want to make things *right* for everyone. Their inner core has been so painfully violated that they want *peace at all costs*. They walk around in fear and trembling, hoping they will never be the focal point of anyone's verbal or physical disapproval.

A child's identity evolves around family members. In an abused child's pure intent to make things *right* for everyone around him as he is growing up, he finds himself taking care of others at the expense of his own feelings and needs. Consequently, the child has no identity of his own. This is what is known as co-dependency.

More often than not, the child does not approve of himself because he subconsciously feels somehow, that it was his fault he was abused. He always worries about other people's feelings rather than his own. He continually tries to make things *right* for everyone else, regardless of what he wants. Because it's impossible for him to make things *right* for everyone else, he then views himself as incapable, unimportant, as a failure. Because of his inability to change things for the better for others he particularly feels worthless. In his eyes, he is responsible for all the problems, regardless of what they are.

By always worrying about others and trying to meet everyone else's needs or expectations, the child shuts down his own feeling system to the point of not having any sense of who he is or where he is going. He thrives on constant outside approval. In fact, he NEEDS it! But, when outside approval is not forthcoming, this compounds his disapproval of himself. Ironically, in reality, it's this disapproval of Self that creates the lack of approval from others.

The co-dependent stays in a "Catch 22" situation, cycling through the same scenario over and over again. So, a person with these kinds of experiences will commonly end up a loner or go from one relationship to another continually looking for and seeking approval. These people frequently become involved with abusive people, and when their relationships don't work out they always feel responsible for its failure. This compounds the feeling of worthlessness, which is one of the most common co-dependent traits.

Sooner or later though, the erroneous programming with its resultant negative feelings which have been trapped inside since childhood—those feelings that are in the cell memory at the core—finally come to the point where they have to be recognized and acknowledged in order to correct or alter the behavior patterns. If this never happens, the co-dependent is very miserable emotionally, all his life.

In *Quantum Healing*, Dr. Chopra states, "This core is where healing begins. To go there and learn to promote the healing response, you must get past all the grosser levels of the body-cells, tissues, organs, and systems—and arrive at the junction point between mind and matter, the point where consciousness actually starts to have an effect."

Note the word *consciousness*. When a person is willing to be *conscious*, to recognize and OWN the negative feelings that have been buried alive, these feelings—these vibrations—can then be dramatically transformed by embracing positive opposite feelings. This, in turn, engenders a new and higher vibratory environment within that person. This now new, healthier, higher vibratory environment initiates a restructuring and reordering that begins the healing process.

One classic example of this sad state of negative emotions happened to a lady I knew. Brenda was in her forties. When I heard her story I could not believe that any one person could have experienced so much emotional pain as a child and still be alive and functioning! After hearing her account of sexual abuse by her father and other male members of her family, we processed with the Script many feelings she had bravely buried—feelings that definitely needed a resolution and healing in her life.

Sometimes it is necessary to process many feelings during one session, as in the case of Brenda, who lived in a different state than I. She expressed to me that she felt a definite emotional shift on the inside before we completed our initial time together. I later phoned Brenda to see how she was feeling. She indicated that the difference in her—the shift and change she was experiencing—was much greater than she ever anticipated. Although Brenda rarely confided in anyone, she had always yearned for love and understanding from others at a deep level of her soul, without having to reveal her abuse, her horrible emotional trauma as a girl. Most of her life she had felt an underlying desire to explain to people what she had been through so they would better understand her. Now, that desire to justify herself and what had happened to her earlier in life was totally eliminated. She no longer felt the need to explain her hurt, her distrust of men, her guilt or the shame she had carried inside her for years. She continued to use the Script on her own, and in a short time had made such progress that she felt a peaceful freedom and release she had never before experienced.

If you haven't encountered an emotional crisis or health crisis in your life and you identify with what you are reading, let me encourage you to make note of the feelings that may have been stored and stuffed for years, not at all dead and buried.

For example: There may be hidden anger toward one or both your parents. Have you been able to forgive your mother for letting your dad take advantage of her? And have you been able to forgive your dad for taking advantage of your mother? Have you forgiven your father for all the times he verbally humiliated you? Have you forgiven your sister for (as you perceive it) being prettier than you? Have you forgiven your brothers and sisters for not understanding you . . . for picking on you? Or does the resentment go much deeper?

Have you forgiven other family members for their "less than glorious" acts or actions (as you perceive them)? Have you forgiven your least favorite teacher in school for embarrassing you in front of the rest of the class when you were innocently talking instead of listening? These kinds of negative feelings can be so imbedded and at such great depth that they remain a subconscious, overwhelming, moving force in your life.

Remember, these feelings are powerful, living energies! And the examples mentioned are very minor compared to some of the more serious anger, hate and resentment people are carrying around inside them. Hate, anger, resentment and desire for revenge are energies that can eat you alive!

Tom was a client who was so filled with these feelings that he literally had a darkness about him when he came into my office. He had so much negativity inside that he was compelled to spout off . . . unleashing his anger and hate for almost two hours. He was conditioned to blame everyone he could for his problems. He was a very sick man, with all kinds of allergies and no physical energy whatsoever. Tom was in his early 40's, but seemed twenty years older. It was obvious to me why he was so ill. At this point in his life, however, he was so miserable that he was willing to try anything in order to feel better. However, Tom's unconscious didn't really want to *let go* of it's dark feelings. "It" seemed to thrive on them. He kept telling his wife there was no way he was going to forgive people and things of the past. But, his wife finally persuaded him to let his *spirit* help him change those feelings by going through the Script. After his second visit, Tom didn't appear so dark. He became more cheerful and amiable, and seemed to progressively improve. Soon, his pain and discomfort abated and was no longer there to remind him of the purpose and importance of the Script. When he no longer felt miserable he quit using the Script and his unconscious conditioning started slipping him back into his old patterns again. He had only scratched the surface of resolving the negative feelings at this point.

What I didn't tell you, is that as a child, Tom seemed to be the brunt of his mother's frustrations. For no apparent reason, she would often beat and scream at him unmercifully. He was the oldest of four, but was the only one who received this treatment.

We NEVER know what someone else has had to endure. Imagine how you would have felt had you been the recipient of Tom's treatment! You see, whatever you have been through could also cause you to be hanging on to negative feelings. Keep in mind, however, that the past is lost and gone forever. Your concern is with the NOW—with the present. You are fortunate, for you have the opportunity of choice at this juncture—whether things of the past keep you in bondage, or give you the key to open your door to freedom

At this writing, Tom is at a crossroads. He will be choosing whether to continue allowing his unconscious to keep him floundering in his negativity or whether to lift his head up out of the mire and become more aware and more accountable for his feelings—taking whatever steps are necessary to change these poisonous, destructive, negative feelings to positive, productive feelings. If Tom is capable, he does have a choice.

Having Tom's life touch mine served as an indelible reminder of how powerful hate, anger, resentment and a desire for revenge are in bringing someone down—physically and emotionally—in coloring the glasses entirely dark that they see through. How sad it is, especially when underneath all that anger is a real *gem* with great potential.

Even though all of these examples are just about one seemingly insignificant person at a time, when you compound their pain, their hurt, their hate, their fear, their sorrow, their anger, their guilt, their resentment, their feelings of worthlessness, and their need for approval, then let it resonate with all the other people in the world who have these same kinds of feelings, you end up with millions, or perhaps billions, of miserable, unhappy and hurting people. Even so, we have it within our power to do something about it. We CAN make a difference. How can we make a difference? We can start by creating a shift . . . by making a change within ourselves.

To some people, Colette's story may seem simple and unimportant. But, here is an example of a girl struggling for her own identity, for acceptance, for approval and for feelings of self-worth . . . qualities that everyone would like to enjoy. Colette was a college age client who constantly needed outside approval. Although she had not been labeled a "co-dependent" as such, she had a very strong co-dependent trait. Colette always needed outside approval to make her feel good about herself . . . to make her feel worthwhile. She had to be reassured constantly about the quality of her performance, whether it was her school work, her cheerleading, her ability to attract good-looking young men to her, or whatever. She was always seeking outside approval and acceptance.

When we finally got right down to the root of this problem, we found that as a child of five years, Colette had been singing with a group of children at a program. She didn't know the words to the songs and so she just mouthed the songs. Afterwards one of her aunts came up to her and mentioned that her sister was singing so nicely. What was the matter with her that she didn't know the words? The overwhelming feeling of disapproval and censure Colette felt from her aunt, whom she dearly loved, immediately caused her to establish a deep negative belief inside herself that she couldn't express. But the belief, nevertheless, was internalized. This new belief caused her to feel that she must make amends for her unpreparedness and forever after gain approval and acceptance in whatever she did.

However, the real *core* of Colette's problem became apparent at a later session. She was a twin, and since birth Colette had felt that her mother favored her twin over her. (Naturally, her mother was deeply hurt when she realized Colette felt this way.) Regardless, no matter what, Colette always felt she needed to prove she was especially worthy of her mother's approval as well as everyone else's. (This is what incorrect perceptions do to us.)

Now armed with the realization of what she was feeling, Colette went through the Script for, "the feelings that cause me to desperately want and need approval." After using the Script for those particular feelings and some appendages to the same feelings, she reported to me that she no longer felt the anxiety she had for so many years of her life. She became much more peaceful and relaxed and better able to flow with life. There were also other significant improvements in her day to day activities. Colette realizes that additional feelings with their incorrect perceptions and beliefs still need to be altered and conquered, so she continues to use this process in accomplishing her goals.

Most of us don't realize we're carrying all that *stuff* around with us. *Stuff* that determines our everyday decisions and actions; *stuff* that has caused us to be dysfunctional. All that *stuff* which has been affecting us has influenced us on a subconscious level.

There is something else appropriate to mention here. If a person was raised in a family with poor or inadequate communication skills, they often had to pretend that everything was fine. But, in reality, there was much awry and much hurting. Oh! How one longs for a healthy interchange of ideas and communication—sharing experiences and expressing feelings. Who could they talk to? Who could they tell their secrets to? Where could they go for release from the pain? Or did they think if they were quiet the pain might go away? Or, did they just turn their feelings off?

A person's mind-body can actually turn feelings off so the pain won't be felt. And their reality or method of coping becomes one of non-participation, i.e., "It happens to others, but not me." What is really happening, however, is that those painful (negative) feelings and thoughts are getting stuffed deeper and deeper inside because there is no release, no outlet, no resolution for them. How long can a person continue stuffing and storing before the "container" is full and there is no room left to stuff or store anymore?

When the psyche is no longer able to endure further stuffing and non-resolution of the pain and the hurting, the personality of the hurting person is often driven to split—to literally become another personality, another identity. At this point they retreat into their own make-believe world—which is totally apart from the real one—rather than suffering in their old painful world.

If we remember that we were totally innocent bystanders as we were growing up, and that these unresolved negative feelings are on a sub-conscious level, it will help us recognize and embrace the fact that there is no need to spend one more second feeling guilt, shame, or blame. The perceptions from which we viewed our experiences were created and validated in our immature minds before we were able to establish a conscious awareness. At this point—NOW—it is imperative that we be willing to leave *denial* behind, acknowledge our own *truth* and wipe the slate clean of negatives so we can go about healing our hurting Soul—rescuing our True-Self.

Many books have been written about co-dependency and dysfunctional families. Adult children, as they are called, come from these dysfunctional families where, as children, they have been abused either physically, sexually, emotionally, or spiritually. I have only touched on the subject here, so I would like to supply you with a list of incorrect perceptions, feelings, and subsequent beliefs about the Self. These all (incorrect perceptions, feelings, and beliefs) take root in children from dysfunctional homes during childhood.

The following are feelings and beliefs that cultivate and encourage dysfunction, co-dependency and/or addictions. Keep in mind that these characteristics are the natural by-product of a person's early conditioning. It just "IS". Therefore, there is no judgment, no blame—just awareness . . . and compassion.

1. Judges self harshly.
2. Fears criticism and judgment, but driven to be critical and judgmental of others.
3. Feels a sense of urgency; impulsive; impatient; compelled to seek immediate rather than delayed gratification.
4. Fears failure but unconsciously sabotages own success.
5. Fears disapproval and rejection, so unknowingly creates characteristics acceptable to others.
6. Fears commitment.
7. Feels inadequate/low self-esteem. Sometimes has to compensate by appearing superior.
8. Fears discovery of real self will cause rejection.
9. Fears intimacy. Unable to form close, loving, intimate relationships.
10. Fears loving and being loved.
11. Fears dependency on anyone or anything, yet are dependent personalities.
12. Fears abandonment but compelled to become involved with compulsive personalities that play out this fear.
13. Frightened of angry people.
14. Afraid to trust due to lack of trust in self.
15. Afraid to reveal inner secrets for fear of rejection or disapproval.

16. Afraid of people and authority figures.
17. Feels different/separated from others due to own feelings, which leads to depression. Isolates self.
18. Assumes responsibility for others' feelings and behavior.
19. Grieves for the *family* they never had.
20. Unable to identify or ask for own wants and needs. Unconsciously denies them, for experience has taught that they will not be met.
21. Feels guilty when standing up for self, therefore has to give in to others.
22. Unable to feel or express true feelings as adults, because to feel at all is unbearably painful. In "denial."
23. Unknowingly driven to build up barriers to protect self from own insecurities.
24. Unable or doesn't know how to let go, relax, play or have fun.
25. Learns to criticize and blame self and others.
26. Has to make excuses for others' weaknesses; has unreasonable expectations of self and others.
27. Tries to find own identity in doing things, but finds it difficult to accept honest praise.
28. Desperately wants control and yet over-reacts to changes they can't control.
29. Continually seeks outside approval by *doing*.
30. Takes things literally; it's either right or wrong, black or white.
31. Takes self very seriously.
32. Distorted sense of responsibility. Concerned more for others than self. (Keeps one from the pain of looking too closely at self and own problems.)
33. Tends to repeat relationship patterns.
34. Has a need to *help* and seeks people who are *victims*. Are attracted by that weakness in love and friendship relationships.
35. Doesn't know self or innate rights. Doesn't realize it's all right to make mistakes.

36. Craves validation of self-worth from others, not received as child.
37. Extremely loyal, even when loyalty is unjustified or even harmful.
38. Guesses at what *normal* or *appropriate* is.
39. Tends to be a perfectionist.
40. Unable to trust loved ones, authority figures or peers.

If you find yourself identifying with any of the foregoing feelings, attitudes, or beliefs, changing them can be achieved by going through the Script for them. Here is an example of how you can accomplish this:

Spirit, please locate the origin of my feeling guilty when I stand up for myself.

Take each and every level, layer, area and aspect of my Being to this origin. Analyze and resolve it perfectly, with God's truth. Come through all generations of time and eternity healing every incident and its appendages based on the origin. Do it according to God's will until I'm at the present, filled with light and truth, God's peace and love, forgiveness of myself for my incorrect perceptions; forgiveness of every person, place, circumstance and event which contributed to this feeling.

With total forgiveness and unconditional love I allow every physical, mental, emotional, and spiritual problem, and inappropriate behavior based on the negative origin recorded in my DNA, to transform. I choose standing up for myself. I feel perfectly within my rights when I stand up for myself. I am standing up for myself. I choose coming to my own defense. I feel to defend myself whenever necessary. I am defending myself. I feel confident that I am a worthwhile human Being and I deserve to come to my own defense. I feel peace of mind each time I do.

Then finish the Script on out.

When we look at the negative feelings we "buried" as a child, and participate in processing—by using the Script to resolve and heal those negative feelings—little by little we will be relieved of feelings, emotions, attitudes and beliefs that contribute to co-dependency, dysfunction, and addictions. Eventually the memory of perfection in our cells will be uncovered, reprogrammed and brought into harmony with our perfect blueprint, with our True-Self. We CAN gain our independency. And . . . after we have achieved our independence, we will victoriously experience the crowning touch—the *crowning touch* of rejuvenated, healthy, and rewarding inter-dependent relationships with all members of society.

Chapter 11

Becoming Accountable

What was your initial reaction the first time you were confronted with the possibility that YOU could be the cause—the creator of your own problems and your own illnesses? I remember how I felt when I first saw a list of probable emotions that caused dis-ease. (Meaning, that which takes one *out of ease*.) I felt like a ton of bricks had dropped on me!

My mind went into *SUPER DENIAL*! Though I wanted to forget about this new awareness, I couldn't. The concept kept popping up in my mind until it finally *ate* on me long enough. In order for me to be at peace, I had to concede and acknowledge that my buried feelings were causing several health problems. Now it is interesting for me to observe the *denial* that takes place in others when they are first confronted with the possibility that their own internal system may be responsible for their problems and illnesses.

It is definitely less painful and less threatening to think that someone or something *out there* is to blame for our health problems—or any other problems for that matter. When we blame someone else, however, it opens and creates a two-fold predicament.

First of all, blaming protects our unconscious survival system. It allows us to stay in our own comfort zone, where we assuredly feel safer. Regrettably, however, the growth needed for us to be free of our unconscious conditioning is diverted.

Secondly, and unfortunately, when we have been trained to put the blame or responsibility for our own feelings, thoughts and actions on someone else's shoulders, we avoid taking responsibility and becoming accountable for our own feelings, thoughts and actions.

"So what?" you may be saying. We cannot learn and grow from our experiences as intended when we blame others; we relinquish our agency, our will, our freedom of choice, and our personal power. And, we allow someone else to be responsible for what is happening in our life. We are left with NO input into our own growth and life when we do this. If we want to keep these greatest of great gifts—agency, will, choice, and personal power—we will take back responsibility from our unconscious for our own feelings, our own thoughts, and our own attitudes and actions. We will become accountable for what is happening in our own life.

When we overcome the need to blame, it allows us to let go of being a *victim* of life's circumstances. It eventually eliminates the *victim* pattern we've found ourselves in time after time. By recognizing that our plight and challenges are a result of the Universal Law of Cause and Effect, we are motivated to search for the "cause" so that we can change the "effect" of any undesirable circumstances in which we find ourselves.

If, as children in school, we had never been challenged to go from addition to subtraction, then to multiplication, and on to division, would we have completed it on our own? Most likely not. By being aware that each challenge in our life is an experience to learn from, then determining to do our best to confront and overcome the obstacle, we can move out of our "no growth", comfortable ruts. On the other hand, if we stay in those ruts we follow the path of least resistance, which stifles our progress, thereby causing it to be restricted or halted. Remember, staying within our comfort zone is equal to little or no growth.

Happy is the day when we are willing to step outside that zone of comfort, take a long hard look at our unwillingness to become accountable, and expand our horizons by risking a little effort, or a lot! When we are ready and willing to risk, to step outside that comfort zone, our growth expansion begins. Yes, often it is uncomfortable and perhaps even painful. And yet, it is necessary to acquire the willingness to experience discomfort in order to grow. As we do this, new experiences become less painful, less frightening and more comfortable. We may be surprised, however, and find that we can sail right through our growth experiences with little or no discomfort.

Another reason we may not be willing to become accountable for our feelings and thoughts (denial), is that if we admit, finally, that perhaps WE are the one who caused our own misery, illness, or problems, then we would be admitting we had been wrong all these years, about many things; especially *wrong* about the way we viewed our problems. We stay in *denial* because we feel attacked or that our very life's blood is threatened. *Owning* that we were *wrong* is more than some of us can deal with because our identity is wrapped up in our beliefs and they are what keep us going. If we own our wrongness many of these belief systems come under scrutiny and become extremely vulnerable and shaky. This can literally begin to strip us of our identity and throw us into total confusion, which may then cause us to lose our point of reference.

At this point, we may actually not know who we are or what we are about, the disorientation is so penetrating. So, rather than experience discomfort and vulnerability, some people will turn back to their old ways and refuse to face what is. These people are not able to tolerate or recognize that shifting into a more mature, and in reality, a safer *space* is what they were seeking all along.

What we don't understand is that it is permissible—it's okay to make a mistake, it's okay to be *wrong*, if that's what we choose to call it. We've grown up in a culture that has programmed us to be *right* for SO long that changing this mind-set may be a frightening and painful adjustment. The reason we may have a difficult adjustment is due to our mind thinking *it* always has to be *right and justified*.

Allow yourself to make a mistake. Give yourself permission to be *wrong*. That's how we all learn!

If we, as human beings, could just let go of the unconscious belief that we had to be *right* and replace that word right with the word *correct*, maybe the transition would be a little easier to live with. Perhaps the ego wouldn't be so traumatized at having to give up being *right and justified*.

"Does it really matter?" would be a good question to ask yourself when you feel the need to be *right* above all else. Most of the time if you answer the question, "Does it really matter?" honestly and truthfully, the answer will be, "No, it does not matter!" Or, another question to ask yourself is one that Dr. Jampolsky asks, "Would you rather be right or would you rather experience peace?" When you can truly say and mean, "It doesn't matter if I'm *wrong*. I would rather experience peace," or "I choose peace," many uncomfortable situations and explosive moments can and will be totally defused and you WILL experience peace . . . peace that is very sweet.

If you decide that you no longer care to be a victim—if this is one of your strongest desires—it is necessary to release blame from your Being. To further enhance and expand your ability and power to change, you will undoubtedly want to let go of judgment, also.

> If we feel we must judge—let's keep our judgments confined to the realm for which we are responsible, the immediate realm of (our own) mind, body and heart. And even when we do this, we must guard against judging ourself too harshly.
>
> A good goal would be to acknowledge our imbalances, adjust them and move on.

These are author Ken Carey's words of wisdom from his book, *Terra Christa*.

Once again, becoming account-able is what it's all about. Taking accountability allows a great shift of major proportions, one that allows you to become the master of your Self and your universe. All that is necessary is to be willing to be ACCOUNT-ABLE for:

1. Your own feelings
2. Your own thoughts
3. Your own words
4. Your own actions

How are you going to account for your feelings, thoughts, words, and actions? Health in every facet of your life is controlled by awareness. So, become consciously aware of what you are feeling, what you are thinking, what you are saying and what you are doing. If you have no consciousness in these four areas of your life, you could be likened unto a ship at sea with no compass or no rudder—you are tossed *to and fro* without benefit of direction and without the power to reach your destination.

"All human experiences can be evaluated in terms of consciousness and power. Without consciousness, power is sub-human in its manifestations." (Author unknown)

By choosing to let go of blame and judgment you start on your road to becoming a more responsible and accountable person. This—becoming *responsible* and *accountable*—is necessary if you choose to overcome the "victim" role in your life. Becoming responsible and accountable is necessary if you choose to change the causes that create undesirable effects to causes that create desirable effects; if you choose to claim your God-given power that allows you control of your life; and, if you choose to experience more desirable results in your life than you have previously experienced.

Just remember, things OUT THERE do not cause your problems. All the reasons for the problems in your life can be found WITHIN yourself.

When we quit looking for the answers outside ourselves, we will begin to gain control of what causes our challenges, problems and negative effects and turn from being victims to becoming masters of ourselves. "No man is free who is not master of himself." (Epictetus)

You can bring this about by:

1. LETTING GO
     of blame and judgment
2. LETTING GO
     of force and control
3. FORGIVING
     completely
4. LOVING
     unconditionally
5. ACCEPTING
     challenges with gratitude
6. ACCEPTING
     the perfection in everyone and everything
7. GIVING
     thanks in all things

By accepting responsibility for your own actions and behavior, and becoming 100% accountable for your feelings/thoughts(emotions), attitudes/beliefs and your words, you create your own joy and peace of mind. The choice is really yours. Do you choose going around feeling like a *victim* or are you the *master* of your destiny?

Always remember, when we recognize and accept with unconditional love the perfection in everything, it allows us to shift (change) and grow effortlessly.

Chapter 12

Getting Along With Others

Many people have real challenges in their relationships with others. Are you one of them? Whether your challenges are manifest by the way you interact or react to a spouse, a parent, a brother, a sister, a friend, an acquaintance, an employer, an employee, or a co-worker is determined by your past feelings and how they have registered inside you. One of the largest contributing factors to your ability to freely enjoy other people depends upon how much you enjoy your Self . . . how much you are able to accept your Self. Let me share with you what Dr. Joan Borysenko says:

> Accept yourself as you are. (Fat thighs, big nose, mistakes, health concerns, back pain, or other physical limitations notwithstanding.) This means more than a grudging realization that you'll never again be some way that you used to be or some way that you wish to be. Acceptance means actually honoring yourself as you are now. . . . This allows you to stop judging yourself negatively, which invariably brings forth feelings of blame, shame, guilt, or fear and escalates the cycle of anxiety and tension.

Getting along with others can be simple or complicated, depending on your internal programming. If someone annoys or irritates you, for what appears to be no apparent reason, it's usually an indication that you sense or feel something in this person that you also sense or feel (subconsciously) in your Self, that you don't like. In other words, the person annoying and irritating you is only a reflection of you—a mirror. This principle can be difficult to accept, especially if you or the person has a need to be in control. Nevertheless, the mirror principle is a true principle.

An example of this would be: You are a clerk in a retail store. Someone comes in to be waited on. From the very beginning of your encounter with this person, they demand your undivided attention. They act as if they are the only one in the store. Their behavior really "bugs" you, they are so demanding. You can hardly wait until they have completed their purchases so you won't have to put up with them and their attitude any longer. What you aren't aware of is that you may posses the same qualities—qualities of superiority or of being demanding in your attitude, or you would not be resonating with them . . . they would not be *bugging* you. Right here and now, as you complete your transaction with them, is a great opportunity to become aware of part of your Self that has been hidden from you; to take a look at the issue you may have where this particular characteristic is concerned. This is one of the best ways to find out what you don't know about your Self and—at an unconscious level—what you dislike about your Self.

This person is giving you a great gift by mirroring something that is in you. This person is there to teach you. When you have such an experience, a great opportunity for growth is presenting itself, and you may want to say to yourself, "Oh good, another chance to see a part of me I don't like." Take accountability for the unconscious distasteful part of you that you are recognizing in the other person. Process those feelings with the Script. You will be astonished and surprised at the change in your Self and your acceptance of others. All that is necessary in order for you to initiate this shift is:

1. Recognize the fact that a person is either irritating or annoying you, bugging you, causing you anger, or whatever the feeling.

2. Accept the possibility that you may have an undesirable attitude or characteristic in common with that person.

3. Be willing to let it be *all right*.

4. Have the desire to accept responsibility for a less than glorious trait.

5. Accept responsibility for the behavior. Process undesirable feelings through the Script and replace them with desirable feelings

Another example: You're at a party or a meeting with someone who enjoys making comments that you feel are totally irrelevant. You wish they would just be quiet and let the true order of business proceed without all their input. After awhile you can hardly enjoy anything that's going on because this person is so distracting.

If you haven't realized yet what is happening, perhaps at this point you'll begin to see that there is a part of this person's inappropriate (inappropriate, according to who?) behavior with which you identify. If you want it to cease bothering you, just quietly instruct your Spirit to "please locate the origin of the feelings causing Jane to bother you, irritate you," or whatever you choose to label it.

Go all the way through the Script until you come to " . . . recorded in my DNA, to transform. It doesn't matter, I choose seeing only the best in everyone. I feel like seeing only the best in everyone. I am seeing only the best in everyone. I choose accepting everyone just the way they are, including myself. I feel to accept everyone just the way they are. I am accepting everyone just the way they are." (or words to that effect) Then do your best to look at this person through eyes of acceptance and love. Not only will you feel better toward that person, but you will also be forgiving and accepting of those characteristics in yourself.

How does it cause you to feel when you have a strong disagreement or argument with someone? (It made me feel yucky! I always felt I had betrayed a vital part of myself.) Does it ever make anything better? (I never came away from an argument feeling I gained anything.) Is the issue ever resolved? And if so, in whose mind? Does it ever serve a purpose?

Can you imagine life without arguments or unpleasant confrontations with others? Wouldn't it be wonderful!

Have you ever wished that you could bring an unpleasant situation to a screeching halt by saying something appropriate yet uncontroversial, and keep your *cool* at the same time?

There IS one way that you can defuse an argument, disagreement or confrontation and remain true to your Higher Self. First of all, it's necessary to be willing to allow yourself to be *wrong*.

Let it be okay if the situation isn't resolved at that moment; let it be okay if no one wins; let it be okay if you don't get the best of the other person or make your point. You're only serving your ego when you feel you have to be *right* and win all the time.

I like what Joan Borysenko says in her book, *Minding the Body, Mending the Mind*, about the ego: "The ego expresses its insecurities by judging everything, trying to ensure happiness by keeping everything tightly controlled. For this reason I call the ego the Judge. It splits life into two rigid categories, good and bad."

"Blindly seeking good and avoiding bad, it is caught in the illusion that it must be good in order to ensure its own existence." And that is what we do when we feel we have to be right. In order to be good, we think we have to be right, thereby ensuring our ego's existence. (EGO has a wonderful acronym: Edging God Out). In the final analysis it usually doesn't matter whether we are *right* or *wrong*, anyway . . . unless our EGO is more important than peace.

If you can come from this posture—that it doesn't matter—keeping calm, just say to the other person as they start arguing with you, "Bless you, Jane or John (whatever their name is). Bless you."

The first time my 16 year old son said this to his 18 year old sister, she couldn't stay in the arguing mode, although she was poised and totally ready to go at it with him. When he said to her, "Bless you, Gina, bless you," it disarmed her so completely that she looked at him with shock registered all over her face, then she just started laughing. I've never seen anyone change their frame of reference *so* fast!

Saying, "Bless you," certainly works wonders when you become irritated at someone on the highway, in the supermarket, or wherever else you may be. Just bless them instead of cursing them as you go along. The words we speak have powerful vibrations just like our feelings and thoughts. Even though the person you have directed your thoughts or words to can't hear you, you have created a thought field with your thoughts. The vibrations of those words go out to the person, and that person is affected by the positive energy coming from you.

Another way to stop an unpleasant outpouring of negative words and feelings from someone you are with, is to stay centered, stay calm and collected, and just say to them, "Thank you for sharing." Then drop it. Don't say another word, or change the subject. Usually, a person doesn't know what to say to this, and it automatically ends the discussion. Saying "Thank you for sharing" changes your energy on the matter and keeps you from getting emotionally involved or becoming reactive. "Thank you for sharing," is also a good response to someone who continually complains about everything in life. Ordinarily these people are seeking sympathy, someone to agree with them, or idle discussion on the matter. They don't get any mileage out of their complaints when "Thank you for sharing" is your comment. And when you say, "Thank you for sharing," it's much easier for you to avoid involving yourself unpleasantly and lending your power to the negativity of the situation.

Direct love and caring to them from your heart by expressing in your heart/mind, "I BEHOLD YOU WITH EYES OF LOVE AND GLORY IN YOUR PERFECTION." This is a very powerful healing vibration for both parties involved. You CAN make the difference.

Chapter 13

When Feelings Remain Unresolved

Have you ever known an older person . . . anyone from 50 on up, (depending on your definition of old) with definite idiosyncrasies such as: living in the past—telling and retelling stories of by-gone years; feeling that everyone is taking advantage of them; that they never can *afford* anything; or that they always have to be *right*. Sometimes their idiosyncrasies are such a pronounced part of them it is challenging to find the person they really are or the person they used to be.

From where do these idiosyncrasies stem? They stem from a person's incorrect perceptions and their inability to communicate what they are truly feeling. Thus, their negative feelings remain unresolved. These unresolved feelings that have been buried in the older person for years, have caused their memory of perfection to be covered over. Because of these buried feelings, the negative vibrations created by them have become multiplied and magnified, producing blocks that cloud the older person's reasoning. As deeply buried negative feelings continue to be validated throughout a person's life, the covering over the memory of perfection becomes thicker and thicker with age, and further produces negative vibrations and blocks.

As time progresses, these negative vibrations and blocks gather more strength and power, eventually obscuring the truth of the cells' perfection. The person's light (truth) continues to diminish, thereby allowing more and more negative energy. This in turn causes gross confusion in the person. The negative energy finally becomes so pronounced that the person experiences fragmentation and overwhelm, as evidenced by their idiosyncrasies. Unknowingly they are literally being controlled by their unresolved, buried negative feelings.

If you desire helping someone you love alter their feeling or thinking patterns, you can talk until you are blue in the face, attempting to persuade or convince someone with these idiosyncrasies that they would be much happier and have more peace if they would change. However, no amount of talking or reasoning is able to change those negative, supercharged vibrations unless the older person wants to make a *quantum leap* and heal at the cell-level.

If there is to be a significant resolution of these quirks in an older persons life, this resolution has to come at the cell level—from within. This cell-level change can transpire by developing a conscious awareness of what feelings are bothering the person, and by using the Script to effect a change of these feelings. However, at a certain point in an older person's life they are usually unwilling to listen to suggestions that a change may be in order, or to put forth the effort required for change.

John Bradshaw tells us in his book, *Healing the Shame That Binds You*, that, "Underneath the mask of adult behavior there is a child who was neglected. This needy child is insatiable. What that means is that when the child becomes an adult, there is a 'hole in his soul'."

I firmly believe that the hole in the soul is due to a person's lack of success in returning to that place of Comfort and Peace (in Chapter Four). And also, an inability to resolve their negative feelings that were generated (called into existence) at birth or in their youth. These old feelings have subsequently remained unattended, hurting and crying. They still need to be resolved in order to heal the hole in the soul.

This child in the aging body has a difficult time producing the necessary mental or emotional shifts that would facilitate elimination of old behavioral patterns. Consequently, emotional healing becomes more of a challenge.

The old programming or conditioning that they grew up with was "ignore (deny), or bury your feelings." This conditioning created responses allowing the mind to support a wild imagination, thereby, undoubtedly developing a large range of *mountains* out of lots of little *molehills*.

Many older people with idiosyncrasies have a difficult time being realistic and mature in their view of life. They are conditioned to engage in endless, mindless, unconscious chatter and prattle. Thus, their long standing incorrect perceptions continue to be perpetuated. Very often they do not want to be bothered with what "IS," especially if what "IS," is challenging to their old mind-set or view of reality. They are tired of struggling, tired of disappointments, and tired of responsibility. Mindlessness, often for them, is the rule of the day and their ally. We are very fortunate indeed, if this is not the case with any of our loved ones.

Most older people rarely knew or understood what they were truly feeling through the years of their life, and many still do not know what they feel. So, it would be more difficult for them to effect a resolution in their lives unless they are able to identify their feelings and willingly use the Script to alter them. However, all is not lost. Just as members of one family have a similar genetic makeup, they also have a similar emotional makeup. The vibrational energies from feelings in a person are stored in the DNA and, therefore, can be passed from parents to children through the DNA. When you process YOUR feelings and change them, you are benefitting your parents and your children, as well.

For this reason it is imperative that you get in touch with your true feelings as early as possible in life . . . so the negative energy does not build up. When you become responsible for *your* feelings, will own them, then happily go about resolving them, chances for a smoother, less stressful and more peaceful life—now and in your later years—are much more predictable. You may be able to avoid those undesirable idiosyncrasies altogether.

Little children are very adept and piercing in the recognition of the feelings they are experiencing. When taught to utilize the Script they embrace the idea quickly and are very willing and enthusiastic about participating. The wonderful aspect of children sharing in this, is that they have fewer years of life's feelings to work through, therefore, everything about them responds much more readily to the Script. Whereas, an adult has many more years and layers upon layers of bottled-up feelings—a thicker covering over the memory of perfection—to process and uncover.

The key that either opens the door or closes the door to a child sharing and trusting their feelings is determined by the way we, as parents or adults, communicate with that child. By allowing expression of their feelings without shaming or criticizing them, then quietly discussing what they feel and helping them understand their feelings, we validate them as a worthwhile human being. They also learn that it's okay to feel—something many people have never been allowed, or have never allowed themselves.

Communication is the means whereby we acquire or impart information. When we receive information, we expect it to be accurate and that we can depend upon it—that we won't be hurt when we use it. We expect the information we receive to be unambiguous. If it isn't clear and concise, we become confused. We also seem to expect that the information communicated to us on the various levels should be consistent. But is it? And if information communicated to us is inconsistent or confusing, imagine how a child is affected by this same kind of communication.

The following illustration is taken from the book, *The Origins of Illness and Anxiety*, by J. A.. Winters, M.D.:

Take the case of Bobbie, a four-year-old boy. He asks his mother if he can go out and play. Mother is a little out of sorts that day, so she snaps, 'No—you stay in the house.'

'But why can't I?'

'I don't want you to. Now you be quiet—I'm not going to argue with you.'

Bobbie puckers up his face and starts to cry.

'Stop that crying!' his exasperated mother yells. 'You can't go out and that's all there is to it!'

Bobbie wails louder—and his mother slaps him. 'There—that'll teach you not to cry. Now sit down and behave yourself.'

Bobbie sits down, confused and bewildered. He's angry, fearful, sad and defiant, all at the same time. He scowls and thinks about what he's going to do when he grows up. He is tense, and he squirms around in the chair in an involuntary release of the pressure of his emotional energy.

His mother feels a little ashamed at losing her temper, yet tries to convince herself that her actions were justified. She sees her son's restlessness increasing and finally she relents.

'You can go out now, dear—but there's something I want to tell you first. You know that Mother loves you—but she doesn't want you to be a cry-baby. And you have to learn to do what I tell you—Mother knows what's best for you.'

This sounds like a rather common household tragedy, doesn't it? Let's look at it from the standpoint of communication, however, and see what Bobbie might have learned from the experience.

First, how consistent was the information which he got? He saw that Mother's face was flushed and heard her yell at him; previous experience told him that that meant she was angry. She also acted angry, in that she slapped him. That information is pretty consistent. But then he has to reconcile this with the words, 'Mother loves you,' 'Mother doesn't want you to be a cry-

baby,' 'Mother knows what's best,' and so on. At first wanting to
go out was dangerous; then suddenly it became safe.

If Bobbie were to take literally what his mother has said—
and we know that children are quite literal-minded—he might
learn from this experience that being loved is also being
slapped: that asking questions leads to punishments; that punishment is ('the best thing.') It's quite confusing—and the confusion could have been avoided if Mother had made her words
consistent with her deeds. . .

Dr. Winters goes on to talk about other misuses of communication.
He particularly refers to people who mislabel their own feelings.
Doctors see this very often.

The patient says, 'I feel just terrible—I ache all over, and I'd
give anything to feel better,' and the patient's actions during this
little speech indicate that he's proud of being ill, that this illness
is valuable and that he's going to hold on to it.

Or another example is the person who seems to enjoy mar-
tyrdom, who gasps, moans, then sighs, 'I'm all right—don't pay
any attention to me.'

Are these people faking? Does this sort of behavior mean
that the illness is unreal? No, definitely not. It indicates, rather,
that they haven't learned how to say with words the things they
are feeling in their bodies. The meanings of their communications are confused; they say things with one meaning, they do
things with another meaning. This very confusion leads to a
change in the way they feel—but they don't feel as they say
they are feeling. Doesn't this sound confusing?

It is this kind of confusion which compounds miscommunication.
A child becomes much more aware of what makes him/her tick when
parents are consistent in the messages they convey through their caring
love and discipline. When there is less conflict in the messages a child

receives from *Mom* and *Dad*, there is also less confusion as to his/her value in the family, and the child is much more receptive to learning, more sensitive to others, and more mindful of his/her feelings and thoughts at an early age. Parents who continually validate their child's feelings without judgment, help create an atmosphere where the child and all around him/her are permitted love and acceptance. Healthy emotional growth in the child is a natural by-product when parents validate their children. This healthy emotional climate allows further growth and development to occur in all areas of a child's life, and the memory of perfection in the cell doesn't become as clouded and distorted.

A very meaningful way to support a child in his willingness to *own* his feelings and to validate him as a human being, is to allow him to express his joys or frustrations when he comes home from school; how he feels when playing with friends; when having a *bad* day; when he is cross and mean to a friend or sibling.

When a child expresses anger, hate, disappointment, resentment, hurt or whatever, let him feel what he feels without making a judgment about it or shaming him. Validate him and what he is feeling by verbalizing back to him what you think he is saying. When a child is shamed he gets the message that he is defective, flawed, or always making mistakes. This creates unnecessary and unfounded guilt in the child. Unfounded guilt can truly sabotage a child's healthy emotional growth, undermine his sense of self-worth, and create scars that become deeply embedded in his soul, perhaps lasting a lifetime. His blueprint becomes sadly distorted, and aspects of his false-self emerge.

If you see where some improvement needs to take place with a child, all that is necessary to assist the child in responding positively to your suggestions is to talk WITH him in a calm, loving, supportive manner, validating what he is feeling. That is, explore with him what he is really feeling and the reasons he may be feeling it. Let the child know that it's all right to feel what he does. All feelings are permissible. Help him understand that it's what he DOES with these feelings that determines whether he experiences a negative (unhappy) or positive (happy) outcome. Teach him the Law of Cause and Effect.

One young client, Jim, was constantly made to feel guilty by his parents when he didn't perform exactly to their specifications or do things exactly the way his father would. Indeed, guilt was so well-programmed in him that he, after leaving home at college age, would subconsciously set up situations to create the guilt he had been so aptly programmed to feel at home. At the beginning of his college stay, Jim wasn't experiencing the familiar guilt he had grown accustomed to. He seemed to have a need to return to that old pattern in order to recognize and validate himself. And because Jim was not comfortable unless he was feeling guilty, his quiet master tape began to *set up* that which had been so well programmed in his mind. It was interesting to watch the behavior Jim exhibited in order to heap guilt onto himself . . . when it really wasn't necessary.

If a child is experiencing a negative feeling, suggest to him that perhaps he would like to look at the negative feeling in a new way. Ask him if he would like to substitute the way he is feeling now, at that moment, with a more comfortable, peaceful feeling? If the child responds affirmatively, then have him sit down, relax and close his eyes. Have him repeat in his mind what you say. At this point, go through the Script stating at the appropriate place the negative feeling he identified earlier. Then at the appropriate place toward the end of the Script, substitute the negative feeling with a positive feeling. It's very easy and they can do it in just a minute or two. You will be amazed at the calm, happy child they become.

Another aspect of a child's feelings that we need to consider here, is how he/she responds inwardly to what is taking place in his or her everyday life within the family unit and among friends or at school. Naturally, a child is being affected by the experiences of everyone around them. For instance, if Mom and Dad aren't getting along too well, the child is sensitive to this. The child may never refer to the situation but, nevertheless, they are feeling something—they are being emotionally affected by the vibrations created by Mom and Dad—and usually the affect is very devastating to them. The child may be too young to even talk. But, even if they are able to talk they often don't know or understand what they are feeling, or that they are even being affected.

An illustration of this point:

> Five year old Tracy was visiting his grandmother (a woman I know who uses the Script). Tracy had been experiencing adenoid problems which caused him to breathe through his mouth instead of effortlessly through his nose. His mother and father had been divorced for over a year. Before the divorce there was a lot of arguing and fighting. Tracy's mother, Sue, now has the sole responsibility of raising him and his two-year-old sister. It has been necessary for Sue to work full time, so Tracy and his sister are taken care of by baby sitters. Their time with their mother is rather limited so there's not a lot of *fun time* spent together. Sue has a boyfriend who doesn't seem to enjoy Tracy and his little sister very much.
>
> One day Tracy was visiting his grandmother. She was quite concerned with his inability to breathe through his nose. As they were sitting on the sofa reading a book, Grandma stopped reading to him and asked him to breathe through his nose. "I can't," he said. She asked him to let her see how he couldn't breathe through his nose. So, Tracy showed her. She then asked him if he would like to try something to see if it would help him so that he *could* breathe through his nose again. He readily agreed to try what Grandma wanted him to do. She looked up the emotional causes for adenoid problems, which are: Acute disharmony in the home; feels restricted in life; feels unacceptance or hostility from someone. Tracy's grandmother then asked him to close his eyes and repeat after her. She then led him through the Script. When they finished, Grandma was quiet for a few moments then asked Tracy to take a deep breath through his

nose, which he did. Much to his surprise and delight he was starting to be able to breathe through his nose. Before he left her home that evening, he was able to breathe normally.

Tracy didn't forget this experience. He left town and didn't get to see his grandmother for several months, but upon his return he was manifesting some hidden anger in his behavior. As Tracy's grandmother put him to bed one night, she really let him know that she did not appreciate his behavior. She talked to him as though he were an adult, hoping to indicate the depth of her concern about the way he was acting. Upon finishing what she had to say, Tracy asked her if they could go through that "talk," as he called it; the one that helped him breathe better. Grandma responded. As they completed going through the Script for some of the things at which Tracy seemed to be angry—his grandmother told me a calm and peace came over him that was very much like a transformation. Tracy seemed like a different child. He has since asked to use the Script several times, and each time this little five year-old can tell a difference in the way he feels.

Children learn very fast and are usually more willing to respond to true principles and change than adults. However, if they decline, don't push them. They deserve free choice in the matter.

When parents condemn or ridicule a child for his feelings, he becomes very confused. A child views his parents as knowing every-thing and always being *right*. So, he thinks something must be *wrong* with him—that he doesn't know what he is feeling. He may say or think to himself, "I must not know what I'm feeling because Mom or Dad said so." When this happens over and over, the child starts to doubt himself. When the self-doubt is consistently reinforced, eventually, he will turn his feelings off, because emotionally it is too painful to be unsure of himself and his feelings on a continual basis. At this point, he allows others to dictate his feelings to him. He does NOT understand what he

IS feeling, except that he is confused. He may turn to outside stimulus for comfort, or try to be validated by his peers, often succumbing to peer pressure. The child's feelings of valuable self-worth, self-respect and high self-esteem—which most human beings yearn to feel—are, sadly, a long time in coming, if ever.

The most tragic realization from counseling, for me, is how many people do not accept or love themselves! Most people even have an extremely difficult time forgiving themselves and are usually without a clue as to what and why they are not forgiving themselves. This is the result we witness when people mislabel their own feelings . . . that insidious misuse of communication. As incredible as it may seem, many adults don't even know what they feel on a daily basis. How many years have they been mis-communicating with themselves?

When parents accept each of their children the way they are, consistently validating their feelings—teaching them with love and patience, helping them understand what appropriate and inappropriate feelings are without judging, and then assist them in shifting their fear-based (inappropriate) feelings to love-based (appropriate) feelings by using the Script, these children will have a much better opportunity to progress through life with more confidence and higher self-esteem. These children will also be more mature and have a deeper sense of inner peace. They will be able to better identify with the world around them due to a healthier understanding of their feelings.

Perhaps in doing this, there will be a happier, healthier community of senior citizens by the time today's children reach that age. I know this is possible by just observing the major changes which have taken place in people who have already made the commitment to be accountable for their feelings and thoughts.

Many times upon learning new or different principles, we will nod our head in agreement as to their soundness and ring of truth. We may even say, "Yeah, yeah. I want to apply these principles and make them a part of my life!" But . . . in the next breath we continue in our old patterns, having the new concepts uppermost on our mind at first—but never quite making the internal commitment it takes to initiate a change. Our intentions may be good, but we never seem to get around to it. Let me just say, "It is necessary to do more than INTELLECTUALIZE these principles. Transformation can take place only when we INTERNAL-IZE these principles and ACT UPON THEM!"

Chapter 14

Discharge Your Stress

While watching TV talk shows from time to time, it became more and more obvious to me that there are many *hurting* people in our society today. I have been pleased to observe the resilience that is innately prevalent in a good number of the guests on these programs. Many of them have suffered unjustly through the thoughtless actions of others, but their indomitable spirits rose to meet the challenges caused by their suffering and they have overcome seemingly insurmountable obstacles on their road to recovery.

There are people who advocate that legislation be passed to eliminate the possibility of various bad things happening to them. These people would hope to save others from having to deal with negative conditions or challenges and suffering that they themselves have experienced. I can appreciate their concern. No one should have to suffer at the hands of someone who is totally insensitive to their feelings, their property, or their dreams and aspirations.

There also seems to be a prevailing attitude in this country today to "Let someone else take care of the problems." Of course, the large majority of us would like to feel that there *is* someone who has the power to remedy unfair or unjustified treatment.

Once again, how many of us seem to think the answers to the problems of life can come from outside ourselves? In reality each one of us has the answer to our own problems, and the answers are found INSIDE OUR *SELF*!

If each one of us would accept the plausibility that we DO have it within ourselves to heal our own life, to take responsibility for our *own* problems and misguided efforts, it is possible that much of the human misery (alcoholism, ill health, drug abuse, addictions, gang violence, etc.) in our society today could be minimized, if not eradicated.

When we were in school and we knew there would be exams, could we call upon someone else to come and take these exams for us? Not where I went we couldn't. I was the only one responsible for the scores and grades I received. In a like manner, I'm the only one who can design the causes that create the effects I desire in my life.

People talk about being under a great deal of stress, or of something that is stressful to them. Stress is blamed for problems and suffering by everyone. But, how could one identify your stress or my stress? What is stress to one person may not be at all stressful to another. In other words, what a *stressor* is to you may not be a *stressor* to me.

Have you ever experienced your heart pounding, a knot in your stomach, extreme nervousness, insomnia, impatience, anger, or anxiety? Many people have come to accept these conditions as a part of getting through the day and they label this STRESS. However, the effects of stress are much more insidious than many of us realize. According to Dr. Paul J. Rosch, former president of the non-profit American Institute of Stress in Yonkers, New York, the stress in the United States is taking a terrible toll on the nation's health and economy. Stress contributes heavily to heart disease, respiratory distress, cancer, lupus and numerous other life-threatening diseases. It is one of the major reasons for the astronomic health-care costs in the United States. And yet, stress is very difficult to define because it varies with each individual.

Stress and how you handle it can always be traced back to the early conditioning/training that contributed to your feelings and beliefs. While striving to overcome a particular stress, you will want to focus on what is happening inside you as you are going through it; determine what you feel each time you experience this stress—and change that feeling. This is necessary in order to eliminate the stress! How do you do it? By identifying exactly the way you feel as you are experiencing the stress or stressor, then taking these feelings through the Script.

Or, you may want to ask yourself, "What are the unresolved feelings or beliefs creating this stress?" If it is impossible for you to process the feeling at the time you are experiencing it, make a mental note of it so you can go back to it later in the day and resolve it.

Interestingly, an article in April, 1987 *Reader's Digest* entitled, "MIND OVER DISEASE: YOUR ATTITUDE CAN MAKE YOU WELL," reports:

> Many researchers are now investigating the effect of specific emotions on the immune system. Psychologist Margaret Kemeny of U.C.L.A. found recurrences of genital herpes correlated with feelings of depression. A husband-and-wife team at the Ohio State University School of Medicine documented vividly the injury the mental stress can do to the human immune system. Dr. Janice Kiecolt-Glaser, a clinical psychologist, and virologist Ronald Glaser drew blood from 40 medical students at several points in the school year and again during exam week. Stress played havoc with their immune systems. The activity of their natural killer cells waned and their ability to manufacture interferon—a natural protein that inhibits viral infection—declined drastically during exams. So it was clearly no coincidence that the students reported suffering from more flu and colds.

Another article from that same *Reader's Digest* entitled, "WARNING! DAILY HASSLES ARE HAZARDOUS" continues on the subject:

University of Michigan sociologist Lois Verbrugge, who followed the daily lives of 589 men and women, found that daily
irritations triggered bad moods, which, in turn, were followed by
physical troubles. Studies among 210 Florida police officers
showed that it wasn't the dramatic but relatively rare stress of
apprehending criminals that caused distress. 'It was the accu-
mulation of everyday hassles like too much paperwork,' reports
Charles Spielberger, a psychologist at the University of South
Florida.

Psychologist Arthur Stone at the medical school of the State
University of New York at Stony Brook found that minor daily
stresses had increased three to five days before the onset of
upper respiratory illnesses among a group of Long Island hus-
bands. In an earlier study Stone had 50 couples rate their daily
experiences. The five most common hassles he found were
conflicts with one's spouse, children or business colleagues,
pressures at work and 'personal problems.' And he found that
minor hassles were better predictors of illness rates than were
major events from the past year.

Just what are hassles? Notice the above paragraph stated *common
hassles*, and *minor hassles*. The dictionary states, very simply, Hassle:
to irritate. So, hassles are daily occurrences that irritate you. And when
there are enough of them, they add up to stress. Why the irritation that
causes the stress? Again, identify the feelings involved with your situation which seem to trigger your stress.

It is easy to blame a lot of things on a nameless or faceless entity,
using the name of *stress* and accusing it of being the culprit—then justify and excuse ourselves for our problems because we are the "victim"
of this awful monster, stress. In reality, what triggers or causes our
stress/stressors are our unresolved feelings, our inability to identify
those feelings, and our reaction to those feelings. When we perceive that
something is becoming stressful to us, we need to stop immediately and

locate the feelings or the thoughts—the emotions—that are associated with that stress. After we identify those feelings (emotions), the next step is to process them through the Script. At this point, if you have identified your feelings accurately and replaced them in the Script with appropriate opposite feelings, the stress you were experiencing can be unlocked, diffused and dissipated.

An example of a stress I experienced: One of the things that used to really irritate me was having to stand in any kind of line. This was especially true in the grocery store when I only had three or four items to pay for. I don't know what it was that bothered me so much about that, but I would really *boil* inside. So, you could say that this situation caused me stress. I finally decided to go through the Script just asking my Spirit to "please locate the origin of my feelings of irritation and anger when I have to stand in line" . . . replacing the irritation and anger at the appropriate place with: "I choose Be-ing forgiving, I feel forgiving, I am forgiving. I choose Be-ing peaceful and calm while standing here. I feel peaceful and calm while standing here. I am peaceful and calm as I stand here. It's all right. It really doesn't matter. I feel happy to be here." Guess what? After doing this a couple of times, stating the feeling a little differently the second time than I did the first time, standing in lines no longer bothered me, nor does it bother me today. It has been such a relief—a small victory, nevertheless, a victory!

This is a simple example of how to work through something that stresses you. But, regardless of whether it's simple or complex—a little or big stress—it works the same way.

There are many situations in our lives that we just have to learn to make the best of, and we can accomplish this easily. Probably one of the major stressors in a metropolitan area is freeway traffic, especially at rush hour. When we find ourselves in a long line of traffic with no way out, we have a *choice* as to how we react in this stressful position. We can either sit there fuming and fussing, or we can be calm and unruffled, knowing that *this too, shall pass.* Here again, the *choice* as to how we react in this unpleasant situation, is usually ours. Are we going to choose inner peace or inner conflict?

UNCERTAINTY is said to be public stressor Number 1. This is understandable. Uncertainty automatically presses the FEAR button—fears of any and all kinds, and the mind can go wild with these fears! If you happen to suffer from the stress of uncertainty, zero in on the specific fears they create in you and process them with the Script, replacing the fears with "faith in myself and the future," and anything else you feel would be appropriate. You may be surprised at your accomplishment. Better yet, go for the feeling of "fear of uncertainty" and process that with the Script, replacing the negative with, "faith in the future," or something similar. Most often there is no need to be bothered by this stressor.

As already stated, before you can do anything about the stress, it is necessary, first, to be aware of what you are feeling . . . what is going on inside you. Or, as Dr. Joan Borysenko says, "Be mindful." When your *mindfulness* identifies the feeling that takes you out of a peaceful, calm state, then you are prepared to process with the Script. This allows your subconscious to uncover the memory of perfection and transform the negative vibrations into positive vibrations. Process the negative feelings so they change to positive feelings—which brings the feeling and the thinking together; integrating the Left brain and the Right brain; unifying the *Conscious* with the *Subconscious*; bringing the two sides of the self together—thus allowing you to be *Single-Minded*. Let me emphasize that when you bring the *Conscious* (Left brain) and the *Subconscious* (Right brain) part of your Be-ing together, peace ensues from the bottom of your feet to the top of your head. And, when you are at peace with yourself and the world, the internal artillery stops firing.

When you recognize your feelings of discomfort, uneasiness, irritation or whatever the stressful feeling may be, you are identifying your negative feelings and *owning* them (admitting they are actually there). At this point, you are no longer in *denial* and half the challenge is over.

Upon locating the *stressor(s)*, you are on your way to eliminating them. You may also choose to go deeper to locate and identify several additional feelings that surround the stressful situation, so as to more solidly approach a resolution of them. Note: If the stress continues it is only because the stressor feeling has not been accurately or adequately identified. Keep searching until you claim victory. FREEDOM is just around the corner! And PEACE is the ultimate victory!

Chapter 15

Eliminating Stressors

How important and desirable is it to eliminate the *stressors* in our life?

Our body responds to stress with an alarm reaction. This alarm reaction in our brain signals our adrenal glands to produce a stream of stress hormones which are chemical messengers that instantaneously increase our supply of energy, sustain blood pressure and assist other hormones in functioning more efficiently.

Our immune system, our autonomic nervous system and our brain are directly impacted by these hormones, helping our body to adapt to the stress. The body's magnificent intelligence always serves us during stressful crises. If the stress continues for a prolonged period of time, however, serious damage may be caused as the production of stress hormones can and does get out of control. When these stress hormones are out of control, our body's biochemical balance becomes upset and functions entirely out of harmony. This then impairs our immune system and leaves us open and vulnerable to invasion of dangerous infections and cancer cells. According to some scientists, stress hormones also hasten and compound the aging process, Cortisol being one of them.

To answer the original question, "How important and desirable is it to eliminate the stressors in our lives?", it is evident from the foregoing information that we would be doing our bodies a favor if we were taught how to minimize or eliminate as many stressors as possible on a daily basis.

Phobias

There is a condition that extends beyond the usual and normal stresses in life that is closely related to the stressors discussed in Chapter 14. This condition often manifests in a person when unidentified and unresolved feelings—deep stressors—are present in the body. This condition is known as a "Phobia." A phobia is an obsessive, irrational fear or anxiety which represents the ultimate panic attack. For example: Phobias or panic attacks often begin to occur after there has been a separation from a loved one or a major change in a person's life.

Phobias are a result of unresolved feelings/emotions or beliefs which may have been ticking inside you like a time-bomb for years. The "seed" of the phobia could have been there since the very first incorrectly perceived, unconscious belief you naturally established after having a bad experience. For instance, being locked in a closet could cause claustrophobia; falling from something high as a child could create a fear of heights. Each phobia has it's own personality, but all phobias are involuntary, irrational, and inappropriate to the situation.

There are over 40 million people in the United States who suffer from a phobia. When a phobia is in control, it's an indication that we are not in present time—that is, subconsciously (unknowingly) we are either living in the past or in the future. But a phobic person is mostly haunted by what has happened in the past and living with a horrendous fear of what can happen in the future. And . . . the other characteristic of a phobia is that it flourishes via illusion. The illusion is worry—what if—and our unconscious imagining takes it from there and runs wild. In other words, our phobic reality is a figment of our imagination and we are living in the past; we have moved in and are residing with our old fears. Something happened in our mind that facilitated the phobic behavior-reaction.

Whatever the feeling/belief may be that has created the phobia, it is usually rooted in some kind of fear. This fear has been stored, for who knows how long, in the subconscious mind which is connected to the nervous system. When this fear is triggered by a sight, a smell, a touch or a sound it arouses feelings of anxiety, fright and panic—almost like someone has a gun to one's head. The nervous system jumps into action, responding to the trigger by supplying all the unpleasant reactions that have been created by the fear stored in the subconscious and an unschooled imagination.

Major trauma in a person's life can also establish a fear that causes a phobia. If the trauma, at the time of its occurrence, is more than the person can cope with emotionally, often the mind provides a block that keeps the person from remembering the incident. Case in point is Sherry, a client who, at fourteen years of age, was left alone in a motel room by her parents for a short time. Two men broke in, turned the radio up very loud and proceeded to rape her. This trauma not only caused Sherry to panic thereafter every time she heard the stirring melody of *America the Beautiful,* (the piece that was playing on the radio as she was being violated) but the trauma (not resolved until about 20 years later), also caused her the phobia of being unable to drive on the freeway because she felt so "out of control." Sherry's mind had blocked the incident from her remembrance. Because her phobia caused her so much pain and was becoming continually worse, she was willing to see if the Script could bring her any relief. So, Sherry used the Script to instruct her subconscious to locate the origin of her feelings that caused her to panic every time she heard *America the Beautiful*. She also instructed her subconscious to locate the origin of her feelings that caused her to be so out of control on the freeway. By doing this, the block was removed and a remembrance of the incident returned. Several feelings associated with these phobias were successfully addressed with the

Script and a healing was affected. Needless to say, Sherry was extremely relieved and grateful when she found that she no longer was bothered by these old phobias.

Phobic victims are usually bound or locked up inside with two fears. First, they may have the fear of "driving on the freeway," then they have the second fear, "the fear of the primary fear," the fear that they will lose control, die or do something that is dangerous or embarrassing.

Even though buried feelings/beliefs may not have created a full-blown phobia yet, a person needs to be aware and recognize when one of their five senses triggers the start of a phobic reaction. At that very moment the feeling reaction (exactly what is being felt) needs to be faced, not resisted or denied. Resisting or denying a feeling creates a block in the energy flow which makes it worse. State exactly what is being felt and start processing those feelings that are coming to the surface with the Script.

An example of how to facilitate relief from a phobia attack as it is happening at the moment would be: Take a deep breath in through your nose, letting it out through your mouth slowly. Do it a second time and hold your breath after you inhale for 3 seconds, then let it out slowly allowing your body to totally relax. Then say, "Spirit, please locate the origin of the feelings that cause me to feel like I'm losing my mind!" (Or whatever.) Continue on through the rest of the Script, coming to the replacement line; . . . to transform. I choose Be-ing perfectly sane, I feel perfectly sane, I am perfectly sane, calm, serene and tranquil." These are merely suggestions of phrases to use for the positive replacements. You may have something you feel is more appropriate or better suits you. Use it. Here again, my suggestions are merely to assist you in processing with the Script.

Processing feelings at the onset of an attack can help relieve the phobia before it is fully developed. If a person is not able to process their feelings soon enough to have immediate positive results, they may want to recall their feelings at a later, calmer time and process each one of them with the Script then. Every person affected by a phobia will have a different experience when doing this, and there is no way to predict how many times it will be necessary to use the Script in the process of eliminating a phobia. The important thing is to continue with the processing and address any and every feeling surrounding the phobia.

Oftentimes, the person who experiences a phobia is in a chronic state of neurosis. The neurosis is due to the fact that they are being constantly irritated and agitated by their own thinking patterns. (Talk about the Conscious—thinking, and the Subconscious—feeling, being at war!) Fearful of when the next phobic attack will occur, their neurosis is compounded by this added state of fear. (Perhaps, if you haven't already, you now catch the vision and importance of "tuning" in to your feelings and thoughts immediately, if not sooner.)

What are some of the fears connected with phobias? The most common ones are:

> Fear of abandonment
> Fear of being alone
> Fear of being suffocated
> Fear of bridges
> Fear of cancer
> Fear of cats
> Fear of cemeteries
> Fear of closed areas
> Fear of confrontation
> Fear of crime
> Fear of criticism
> Fear of crossing streets
> Fear of crowds
> Fear of the dark
> Fear of dogs
> Fear of driving

Fear of driving on the freeway
Fear of dying
Fear of engulfment
Fear of falling
Fear of fires
Fear of flying/airplanes
Fear of going crazy
Fear of heights
Fear of illness
Fear of insects
Fear of loud voices
Fear of mice
Fear of meeting strangers
Fear of people in authority
Fear of public places
Fear of rape
Fear of rejection
Fear of riding in buses or trains
Fear of social interaction
Fear of speaking in public
Fear of tunnels
Fear of water

People who experience these phobic fears usually feel trapped. This trapped feeling creates terror; they feel out of control or, they feel they have no control of what is going on in their life. They feel there is no escape from this situation—there is no way out.

The phobic person makes a concerted effort to avoid the place, situation or thing which triggers the phobia. A phobic also fears that what they are afraid of will wake them up in their sleep—and then no sleep can come because of the panic, anxiety or terror of the situation, whatever it may be. Their plight becomes a "Catch 22" situation, like a squirrel in a round cage, running endlessly and getting nowhere.

A phobic attack can appear very quickly, and generally a person can not identify how or where it started. The thought pattern then becomes a behavior pattern—a habit, and the *squirrel* is off and running again, with the *rut* getting deeper and deeper.

Symptoms of a phobia are normal bodily reactions. They are just happening at the wrong time. These symptoms may include palpitation of the heart or shortness of breath, dizziness and light-headedness. A person may be very nervous and fidgety. Or, they may have a difficult time swallowing or breathing and start to sweat. Often they experience rubbery legs, feel faint and tremble. They may experience a strange tingling and their chest may hurt. A phobic often feels impending death or like they're going to go crazy! As one phobic stated it, "I feel like I'm sitting in the middle of a room that is raging with fire, but there are no windows or doors."

If any of these symptoms occur three times a week, this is the first sign of a phobia. Phobias usually happen in people from ages 25 to 45 years. If the phobia is not corrected, it increases in severity and eventually controls a person's life. Women are more prone to phobias than men and men will usually turn to alcohol in an attempt to minimize or avoid their phobia.

When a phobia starts to develop, there are several other things a person can do to distract the phobia and keep it from progressing while they are going through the Script:

- Focus on the present
- Wiggle the toes
- Tap on the table or lap with a pencil or fingers
- Massage the back of the neck
- Chew on the tongue
- Tense the hand and relax it
- Listen to music
- Carry a handkerchief sprayed with favorite perfume & smell it

• Draw an imaginary circle on the floor that represents present time and step into the circle

Any of the foregoing will facilitate a person's ability to maintain their focus and stay in present time. A positive affirmative statement that also helps keep a person in present time is, "I love myself just the way I am." Perhaps the most beneficial thing you can do, however, is go through the Script while standing in the imaginary circle, addressing your feelings of the moment. Doing the Script at this time is effective and one of the best applications of all the suggestions in this chapter to relieve or halt an attack.

Bear in mind that although the suggestions above have the ability to move one successfully through a tense moment, addressing the feelings one experiences at the time of the phobia is critical to eliminating the phobia.

Another factor valuable for your information is that hypoglycemia and phobias may be linked, according to Philip Bate, Ph.D., psychologist and former director of the Maitland Psychological Clinic in Maitland, Florida. Dr. Alan Goldstein, Ph.D., director of the Temple University Medical School Agoraphobia and Anxiety Center in Philadelphia made a similar observation. He says that the typical diet of their patients includes lots of sweets, as high as ten cups of coffee a day, and very few slow-release high-protein foods. Obviously, adequate, nutritious foods are very important to your health, chemical balance and well-being. So, you may want to evaluate your eating habits along with recognizing your feelings.

"Owning" the phobia and accepting it is a fundamental requisite on your road to overcoming the phobia. *The Complete Guide to Your Emotions & Your Health* tells us that two former phobics, when asked what their single most important advice would be for other phobics, recommended turning to family and friends for support rather than hiding the problem from them. They encourage phobics not to be embarrassed about telling others. It's important to believe that there is hope and that you are not alone. If the person experiencing a phobia has someone with them, they feel protected. Whereas, if the person is alone they feel isolated. The anxiety and apprehension they undergo from worrying that they will encounter their worst possible imagining, becomes their reality. These feelings can cause a person to become mentally, emotionally and physically crippled. Hormones and glands become imbalanced., and the longer the phobia continues the worse it becomes until 18% of the people who experience phobias or panic attacks commit suicide. So, help yourself by addressing your feelings as they occur.

Stress Can Cause Suicide

One Sunday afternoon in the early 90's, I received a telephone call from a 30 year old friend of mine in a neighboring state. We'll call her Jean. I wasn't prepared for Jean's declaration to me over the phone. She told me she was about to commit suicide! I had never heard anyone so despondent. The hopelessness in my friend's voice was heavy and oppressive. I persuaded her to talk to me about the reasons she didn't want to live any longer. As Jean talked I listened for cue words and phrases that indicated to me what she was really feeling, and wrote them down quickly. I knew it was possible Jean could be dissuaded from her intent, due to the fact that she called me.

When the person contemplating suicide tells another person they are about to kill themselves, they are really reaching out for help—for someone to stop them.

Whether a person succeeds in committing suicide or not, their intent to do so is usually a very strong indication they are trying to get a message through to someone. The old tapes that have been playing over and over again in their head have become worn out, but they don't know how to change them. So they just give up because they feel there is *no way out* of their situation. Their mind often drives them and gives them inappropriate messages until they are successful at ending their life.

The real message a suicidal person is actually communicating is, "I really don't want to die, I just don't want to live this way anymore. I can't stand the pain, and I can see no other way out." Their problems seem insurmountable, due to their unconscious conditioned inability to handle frustration and the stresses of life. The memory of perfection in their cells is definitely distorted. Very often a suicidal person is experiencing acute depression or extreme fear. Suicide, to them, seems the only way to overcome the pain. They feel that suicide is a permanent solution to their problems. Yes, it's a permanent solution, but to a temporary problem.

As Jean and I talked, a clearer picture of the intense internal conflict she was battling began to emerge. Her internal unresolved stressors had piled too high for her to handle. I asked if she would be willing to go through the Script. She agreed. I had Jean repeat it after me, to herself: "Spirit, please locate the origin of my feelings that cause me to believe everything is hopeless." We finished the Script and replaced "everything is hopeless" with, "I choose having faith in the future. I feel faith in the future. I am secure with the future. I choose Be-ing excited to be alive. I feel excited to be alive. I am excited to be alive. I feel the future can be bright and happy. I choose Be-ing optimistic and hopeful. I feel optimistic and hopeful. I am optimistic and hopeful."

After we zeroed in on additional key feelings and went through the Script a few more times, addressing some of her other fears, I heard a change in the timbre of her voice. The desperation she exhibited earlier had been reduced to semi-calm. I was finally able to reason with her and we talked further. Jean became amicable and subsequently agreed to forget about ending her life that day, promising to *stick it out*.

I told her that I would call her each night of the ensuing week to see how she was faring, which seemed to please her. I also encouraged

Jean to keep the Script available for her immediate use each time she felt any negative feelings or thoughts coming her way.

The suggestion was made to Jean that she quit running away and face the truth and inevitability of her suffering the natural consequences of something she had done which required that justice be met. We examined the worst case scenario of what could happen to her in this event, and discussed it for awhile. During our time on the phone I felt that Jean had experienced about an 180 degree shift, for which I was very, very relieved and grateful.

As a side-light, about two weeks after our conversation, Jean was offered the ultimate job in her profession. She could hardly believe her good fortune. Although Jean still continues to have her challenges, the quality of her life has improved to the degree she allows it.

As you can see, the neuroses that are possible to develop from stressors going unattended are wide and varied. How sad it is for a person if these stressors are not acknowledged and resolved. Yet, how simple it is to start addressing them now! Natural Laws ARE simple. It's human beings who make Natural Laws complicated. REMEMBER THE KISS PRINCIPLE: KEEP IT SIMPLE SWEETHEART!

No matter what degree of stress you are experiencing at this very moment, remember . . . the stress is caused by unresolved buried feelings. The feelings and thoughts are at war. The feeling and thinking need to get together—to be integrated so they become one. No matter what your challenges are or how many you have, they can all be addressed with the Script and healing can begin.

You are your own steward. You are your own director and you get to orchestrate the outcome of your life. Why not begin—right now! All it takes is a willingness to own the problem and a commitment to get started.

LET'S DO IT!

Chapter 16

Enjoy The "Now"

A regrettable tendency many of us experience on our journey through life is the inability to allow ourselves to be happy or satisfied in the "now." For example, when we're in grade school, we can hardly wait until we're in junior high school. Then we're in junior high and can't wait until we're in high school. In our early teens, we can hardly wait to be 16 so we can drive a car. Then we're waiting to graduate from high school, to leave home, then to get married, etc. We seldom, if ever, are able to be satisfied and content enjoying the *here and now*.

We don't seem to know how to stop along the way and *smell the roses*. And in some cultures we can't enjoy, or we think we're not supposed to enjoy life until we are *perfect* (whatever our perception of perfect is). Here is a question worth pondering: Why is it that so many of us think we can't enjoy life to it's fullest until we have arrived at our destination?

As our years start adding up and we become more aware of qualities in our life we'd like to improve, we might tell ourselves that we'll be happy when we've conquered this or that bad habit. Or, we'll be happy if we live through the next crises. We'll for sure be happy when we lose 30 pounds. And, oh yes, we really must have that new car, then we truly will be happy! We haven't been able to learn the art of enjoying where we are now! Too many of us have been conditioned to live with *fear* and *anxiety* as our constant companions, always in dread of the future, worried that we will repeat the past.

Remember when you were learning to ride a bicycle? Were you able to stay up the first time you tried? Did that deter or defeat you? You accepted the possibility that it might take more than one try. Each time you fell you were determined to do it over and over again until you finally figured out what the combination was that would keep you up and balanced. While you were going through this process didn't you enjoy the *now* of it, knowing you would eventually be triumphant? Remember the exhilaration of finally succeeding? It was the journey that was exciting!

If we can realize and recognize that the growth process is something to be savored and relished along the way—that enjoying the challenges of the now and seeing the positive aspects they bring to our life as we experience them—our existence can be so much more rewarding. Our Be-ing is developing and it is necessary to have these kinds of experiences in order to accomplish our growth.

It would be wise for us to remember as we lead and guide the lives of our children (or anyone else, for that matter), that we can't expect them to accept our knowledge, understand what we understand, or be where we are now in our knowledge and understanding. They simply don't have our points of reference. We can guide them to correct principles, but we need to allow them their own experiences and allow them to grow at their own speed. We can share our knowledge and experiences with them, but it is not wise to insist that they see things from our reference point. Nor do we want to control their thinking or their lives. We want to break the cycle of programming and control. Our purpose in their lives is to guide, enlighten and direct rather than to control. When we are *sharing* our knowledge or understanding with someone, we accomplish more by endeavoring to reach them from where their understanding is, not from where ours is. They will be more open and better able to comprehend and absorb new principles when we do this. In other words, allow them their own rate of growth.

A good guide to go by is: "Don't want something (understanding or conditions) for someone else, more than THEY want it for themselves!" If we sincerely desire to assist in lifting and building others:

The Greatest Example We Can Give Anyone, Is Our Life Working For Us!

Cynthia, a beautiful 22 year old client is a very bright, capable person. Her biggest problem is her mother who always wants to control what takes place in Cynthia's life. Cynthia never seems to be able to satisfy her mother. According to her mother, there is always something that needs to be changed or corrected in Cynthia's life. No matter who she is dating, Cynthia's mother always poses the big question as to whether he's good enough for her. It seems her mother has a definite picture of the type of young man she wants her daughter to marry, and unless the person Cynthia is dating measures up to that picture, he's not good enough. (Familiar story?) Well, right now Cynthia is suffering from anorexia, big time! Often the cause of this malady is, "not being able to satisfy parents, particularly mother." Her mother wants something more for Cynthia than Cynthia wants for herself, and Cynthia is becoming an emotional *basket case*.

The sad part about mother is that she lives in constant fear that her beautiful daughter is not going to make the *right* choices.

If we, as parents, only realized the deep emotional scars that are embedded in the soul of a child from parents trying to run their life for them, (particularly after the child is old enough to make his own decisions) we would surely back off and allow them their own experiences without interfering, unless invited by them to advise them. Even then it's important that we judiciously point out possible alternatives, helping them to recognize the potential natural consequences of their choices.

Reason with them and encourage them. Then allow them to make their own choices and support them in their decisions, regardless of whether or not we think they are wise. They will learn from their mistakes. But when they make a mistake, here again, if we just counsel them as to what might have happened if their choice had been different—rather than saying, "I told you so," or causing them to feel stupid, they will feel we are supporting them and allowing them their own experiences without judging them. The lines of communication between us are then open and they will be much more willing to talk with us about their problems the next time they have them.

As in learning to ride the bicycle, if we always steadied the bike for them, they would never learn to master it on their own or become independent of us. We would be robbing them of their growth experience.

Something else to consider as we are learning to enjoy the *now*, is this: How many of us seem to think that in order for life to work for us, that first—we have to HAVE something before we can DO something before we can BE something? For example, do we think that we have to HAVE money so we can DO the fun things in life that we want to do, so we can BE happy?

In reality it's just the other way around. We are better off BE-ing first, so that we can DO, so that we can HAVE. HAVING is a natural by-product of BE-ing.

Just what does BE-ing refer to? BE forgiving. BE non-judgmental. BE accepting. BE loving. BE grateful. BE caring. BE understanding. BE happy. BE willing to admit you don't know everything. BE the best you can BE everyday. BE efficient, DO the best job, HAVE the best pay. Little by little you can Be-come the kind of person that is most desirable for you to BE, then you will automatically DO the best you can DO. Let me say that one more time: When you are BE-ing the kind of person that is most desirable for you to BE, then you will automatically DO the best you can DO—then you will HAVE the peace and whatever else is most desirable in life for you to HAVE.

Here again, it's called the Law of Cause and Effect. HAVING, no matter what it is, is the natural by-product of what we are BE-ing and what we are DO-ing. We reap what we sow.

Lest you are overwhelmed feeling that you need to BE all of the above before you can DO or HAVE, just remember that it's a process getting there, and your BE-ing is developing in the *NOW* as you are accepting the challenges of each day. Eventually you can BE what you want to BE—your True-Self—and return to your perfect blueprint and the memory of your perfection.

As you can see, instead of HAVING...DOING...BEING, life works in better harmony when you are BEING...DOING...HAVING. After all, you are NOT a human HAVE-ing nor a Human DO-ing. You are a human BE-ing.

"So how do I get to this point," you may ask, "willing to BE, first?" Processing negative feelings through the Script is the perfect place to start. As you process your feelings you are BE-ing. It will be of great benefit for you to work through the hostilities and frustrations you may have so you can finally arrive at the place of 'live and let live' . . . of BE-ing, enjoying the peace of the NOW.

We are not Human Have-ings NOR Human Do-ings, but we are Human Be-ings. So instead of Having . . . Doing . . . Be-ing . . .

Life works best by Be-ing . . . Doing . . . Having . . .

Chapter 17

Feelings

The Feelings list in this chapter is designed to assist you in replacing negative feelings with positive feelings while Scripting. The "root" of the word is generally provided, as you may be using the words in the past, present, future tense, or as an action word.

Examples:

With Mercy as the root word—I *choose* <u>Be-ing</u> merciful. I *feel* merciful. I *am* merciful. Or, I choose <u>having</u> mercy for my sister. I feel mercy for my sister. I am merciful towards my sister.

With Love as the root word—I choose Be-ing loved. I feel loved. I am loved. Or, I choose loving my brother, John. I feel love for my brother, John. I am loving my brother, John. Or, I choose being loving. I feel loving. I am loving.

With Trust as the root word—I choose having trust. I feel trusting. I am trusting. I choose Be-ing trusting. I feel trust in this situation. I am trusting this situation.

The main point to keep in mind is that we are striving to BE the human Be-ing we intrinsically are. Nevertheless, it is necessary that we *choose* the characteristic we desire before we can *Be* (I AM) that characteristic.

In affirming something it is difficult for our psyche to jump to the I AM before it consciously *chooses* that characteristic. Then, the *feeling* is the bridge between the *choosing* and the I *AM*. Thus, the suggestion, I choose, I feel, I AM.

Please refer to my book, *Healing Feelings . . . From Your Heart* for a more in-depth discussion.

A

Abandoned . . . . .Cherished, Precious, Upheld, Cared For

Abused . . . . .Cherished, Sustained, Supported, Forgiving

Accused . . . . .Blameless, Innocent, Absolved, Vindicated

Afraid . . . . .Confident, Courageous, Peaceful, Reassured

Aggravated . . . . .Unprovoked, Senseless, Peaceful, Forgiving

Agitated . . . . .Forgive, Calm, Peaceful, Happy

Agony . . . . .Ecstasy, Peaceful, Love, Joyful

Aimless . . . . .Directed, Purposeful, Decisive, Resolute

Alarmed . . . . .Calm, Peaceful, Relaxed, Secure

Alienated . . . . .Forgive, Accepted, Loved, Cherished

Alone . . . . .Bonded, Upheld, Cherished, Connected

Aloof . . . . .Warm, Caring, Kind, Interested in Others

Ancient . . . . .Young, Vivacious, Exuberant, Happy

Angry . . . . .Forgive, Love, Peaceful, Calm, Merciful

Anguish . . . . .Relieved, Peaceful, Content, Happy

Animosity . . . . .Forgive, Love, Harmonious, Peaceful

Annoyed . . . . .Forgive, Accept, Undisturbed, Calm

Antagonistic . . . . .Agreeable, Harmonious, Cooperative

Anxiety . . . . .Trust, Reassured, Calm, Peaceful

Anxious . . . . .Confident, Peaceful, Trusting, Reassured

Apathy-Apathetic . . . . .Energetic, Interested, Concerned, Caring

Apprehensive . . . . . . .Confident, Calm, Trusting, Reassured

Argumentative . . . . . . .Agreeable, Harmonious, Peaceful

Arrogant . . . . .Humble, Loving, Teachable, Modest

Ashamed . . . . .Forgive Self, Repentant, Pleased, Merciful

Attacked . . . . .Defended, Protected, Supported, Upheld

Austere . . . . .Easy Going, Genial, Flexible, Friendly

Avoiding . . . . .Participating, Meet the Challenge, Comfortable

Awful . . . . .Wonderful, Good, Peaceful, Fulfilled

Awkward . . . . .Graceful, At Ease, Confident, Flowing

B

Backward . . . . .Forward, Progressive, Dynamic, Confident

Bad . . . . .Good, Worthwhile, Valuable, Pleasant

Bad Attitude . . . . .Good Attitude/Natured, Positive, Forgive

Bad Luck (It's My) . . . .Fortunate, Blessed, Life Works For Me

Baffled . . . . .Enlightened, Wise, Judicious, Comprehend

Banished . . . . .Welcomed, Accepted, Acknowledged, Honored

Bashful . . . . .Outgoing, Assertive, Confident, Forward

Beaten Down . . . . .Lifted Up, Elevated, Invigorated, Invincible

Befuddled . . . . .Collected, Confident, Composed, Congruent

Belligerent . . . . .Cooperative, Helpful, Cheerful, Good-Natured

Belittled . . . . .Built Up, Elevated, Praised, Valued

Bemoaning . . . . .Happy, Celebrating, Rejoicing in Life

Betrayed . . . . .Forgive, Merciful, Love, Peace

Bereft . . . . .Rich, Blessed, Provided For, Privileged

Bewildered . . . . .Enlightened, Understand, Comprehend

Bitter . . . . .Forgive, Love, Joyful, Peaceful, Sweet

Blah . . . . .Bright, Light, Enthused, Joyful, Anticipate

Blaming . . . . .Forgive, Non-Blaming, Merciful, Allowing

Bleak . . . . .Bright, Encouraged, Excited, Hopeful

Blew it . . . . .Forgive Self, It's Okay, Persistent, Move On

Blinders on (Have) . . . .See Things Clearly, Open to Truth, Teachable

Blocked . . . . .Unrestricted, Open, Flowing, Productive

Boastful . . . . .Modest, Sincere, Humble, Grateful

Boiling (Inside) . . . . . . .Forgive, Love, Calm, Peace, Merciful

Boisterous . . . . .Quiet, Tranquil, Peaceful, Placid, Serene

Bondage . . . . .Free, Liberated, Unconstrained, Independent

Bored . . . . .Excited, Interested, Enthused, Involved

Bothered . . . . .Forgive, At Ease, Comfortable, Accepting

Boxed In . . . . .Plenty of Room, Spacious, Released, Liberated

Bragging . . . . .Humble, Modest, Reserved, Unassuming

Brooding . . . . .Adaptable, Accepting, Happy, Cheerful

Brutal/ish . . . . .Merciful, Kind, Gentle, Sensitive, Loving

Bugged . . . . .Forgiving, Allowing, Loving, Peaceful

Burdened . . . . .Relieved, Light, Carefree, Liberated

Burned Up . . . . .Forgive, Cool, Calm, Peaceful, Tranquil

Burn(ed) Out . . . . .Invigorated, Enthused, Energized, Revitalized

C

Captive (Like a) . . . . .Liberated, Free, Independent, Restored

Careless . . . . .Careful, Accurate, Attentive, Thoughtful

Chaotic . . . . .Organized, Methodical, Purposeful, Resolute

Charlatan . . . . .Authentic, Genuine, Honest, Trustworthy

Chastened . . . . .Encouraged, Uplifted, Benefited. Rewarded

Cheap . . . . .Valuable, Cherished, Worthwhile, Unequaled

Cheated . . . . .Forgive, Unshaken, Treated Fairly, Restored

Childish . . . . .Mature, Sensitive, Wise, Understanding

Choking (Like I'm) . . .Breathing Freely, Unrestricted, Liberated

Chronic . . . . .Curable, Temporary, Short-Lived, Carefree

Chronic Anxiety . . . . . .Reassured, Peaceful, Serene, Tranquil

Churning Inside . . . . . .Calm, Composed, Comfortable, Secure

Clingy . . . . .Letting Go, Releasing, Relaxed, Yielding

Closed Off . . . . .Open, Accessible, Responsive, Unbiased

Closed-Minded . . . . . . .Open-Minded, Teachable, Embracing Truth

Clumsy . . . . .Forgive, Coordinated, Graceful, Comely

Cocky . . . . .Humble, Genial, Pleasant, Caring, Sincere

Competitive . . . . .Non-Competitive, Cooperative, Alliance

Complaining (Like) . . .Approving, Appreciative, Grateful, Enjoying

Complexes (Have) . . . .Understanding, Insightful, Directed

Comply (Need to) . . . .Independent, Self-Determining, Unique

Compromised . . . . . . .Secure, Honest, Steadfast, Strong

Compulsive . . . . .It's Unnecessary, Relaxed, Rational

Conceited . . . . .Humble, Teachable, Modest, Caring

Condemning . . . . .Forgive, Merciful, Accept, Allow

Confined . . . . .Free, Flowing, Released, Liberated

Conflict . . . . .Peacemaker, Peaceful, Forgive, Excuse

Confounded . . . . .Enlightened, Perceptive, Wise, Judicious

Confused . . . . .Clear-Headed, Enlightened, Understand

Conniver (Like a) . . . .Honest, Virtuous, Honorable, Sincere

Constricted . . . . .Expanded, Carefree, Released, Liberated

Contempt . . . . .Forgive, Merciful, Love, Accept, Allow

Contemptible . . . . . . .Decent, Honest, Kind, Truthful, Virtuous

Contentious . . . . .Agreeable, Pleasant, Courteous, Cheerful

Contradictory ....Accepting, Agreeable, Peaceful, Contrite

Contrary ....Yielding, Harmonious, Pleasant, Agreeable

Control (Want to) .....Letting Go, Releasing, Allowing, Flow With

Controlled ....Unrestricted, Let Go, Free, Liberated

Cope (Can't) ....Manage Successfully, Steadfast, Strong, Reliant

Covetous ....Generous, Unselfish, Grateful, Satisfied

Cowardly ....Heroic, Fearless, Valiant, Brave, Stalwart

Cranky ....Forgive, Good-Humored, Pleasant, Kind, Happy

Crazy ....Balanced, Together, Sane, Calm, Collected

Criminal (Like a) .....Unique, Authentic, Trusted, Admired, Valued

Critical ....Forgive, Accept, Love, Merciful, Allow

Criticized ....Accepted, Forgiven, Loved, Cared For

Cross (I Feel) ....Pleasant, Happy, Genial, Forgiving, Joyous

Cruel ....Kind, Gentle, Loving, Compassionate

Crummy ....Wonderful, Happy, Joyous, Fulfilled

Crushed ....Restored, Reconciled, Valued, Uplifted

Crying (Like) ....Rejoicing, Laughing, Exulting, Cheering

Cunning ....Genuine, Honest, Straightforward, Just

Cursed ....Forgiven, Blessed, Edified, Praised

Cynical ....Trusting, Accepting, Believing, Optimistic

D

Death Wish ....Love Life! Excited, Enthused, Joyous, Happy

Debased ....Purified, Restored, Cleansed, Redeemed

Deceitful ....Honest, Integrity, Honorable, True, Congruent

Deceived ....Informed, Discerning, Forgiving, Perceptive

Defamed ....Honored, Revered, Elevated, Uplifted, Valued

Defeated ....Victorious, Renewed, Sustained, Invincible

Defensive ....Assertive, Appropriately Aggressive, Forgive

Defiant ....Obedient, Peaceable, Yielding, Dutiful

Deficient ....Sufficient, Adequate, Capable, Competent

Defiled ....Restored, Purified, Cleansed, Renewed

Degenerate ....Good, Honest, Just, Kind, Virtuous, Pure

Degraded ....Honored, Promoted, Praiseworthy, Dignified

Dejected ....Happy, Cheerful, Tenacious, Erect, Uplifted

Delayed ....Moving Forward, Uninterrupted, Accelerated

Demanding ....Flexible, Yielding, Agreeable, Pleasant

Demeaned . . . . .Elevated, Uplifted, Supported, Cherished

Demoralized . . . . .Elevated, Exonerated, Valued, Glorified, Invincible

Denial . . . . .Responsible, Accountable, Owning, Accepting

Dependency . . . . .Liberated, Independent, Carefree, Self-Ruled

Dependent . . . . .Independent, Self-Reliant, Strong, Skilled

Depraved . . . . .Emancipated, Edified, Elevated, Righteous

Depressed/ion . . . . . . .Joyful, Enthused About Life, Happy, Excited

Deprived . . . . .Privileged, Favored, Pampered, Fulfilled

Derided . . . . .Approved, Applauded, Praised, Encouraged

Desecrated . . . . .Renewed, Replenished, Healed, Reverenced

Deserted . . . . .Cherished, Upheld, Protected, Cared For

Desolate . . . . .Happy, Secure, Joyful, Cheerful, Fruitful

Despair . . . . .Courage, Reassured, Trust, Hope, Faith

Desperate . . . . .Confident, Trusting, Unshaken, Composed

Despise . . . . .Forgiving, Loving, Caring, Allowing

Despondent . . . . .Cheerful, Radiant, Glowing, Elevated

Destroyed . . . . .Restored, Saved, Protected, Transformed, Invincible

Destructive . . . . .Constructive, Building, Elevating, Benevolent

Detached . . . . .Connected, Joined, Part of the Whole, Accepted

Detrimental (to Others) Beneficial, Valuable, Contributive, Constructive

Devalued . . . . .Valued, Respected, Appreciated, Esteemed, Prized

Devastated . . . . .Forgive, Liberated, Uplifted, Renewed, Encouraged

Destitute . . . . .Affluent, Prosperous, Sustained, Comforted

Detest . . . . .Forgive, Adore, Love, Favor, Approve, Accept

Devilish . . . . .Angelic, Kind, Virtuous, Pure, Honest

Dictatorial . . . . .Teachable, Humble, Giving, Compassionate

Different . . . . .Unique, Authentic, Original, Accepted

Difficult . . . . .Pleasant, Gracious, Comfortable, Simple

Dirty . . . . .Clean, Honorable, Kind, Good, Decent

Disagreeable . . . . .Allowing, Accepting, Loving, Pleasant

Disappointing . . . . . . .Pleasing, Encouraged, Satisfied, Content

Disappointment/ed . . . .Accepted/ing, It's Perfect, Allow, At Peace

Disappear (Could) . . . .Face the Issue, Be Present in the Moment

Disapproval . . . . .Approval, Favor, Support, Accept, Allow

Disapproved Of . . . . . . .Approve of Self, Cherished, Loved, Valued

Discontent . . . . .Content, Happy, Blissful, Serene, Peaceful

Discordant . . . . .Harmonious, In Tune With, Connected

Discouraged . . . . .Encouraged, Resolute, Eager, Excited

Discourteous . . . . .Courteous, Kind, Caring, Loving

Discredited . . . . .Vindicated, Credited, Valued, Honored

Disdain . . . . .Forgive, Regard Highly, Love, Merciful

Disgraced . . . . .Forgiven, Redeemed, Exonerated, Honored

Disgust/ing . . . . .Forgiving, Attraction, Admiration, Accept

Disharmony . . . . .Harmonious, Attuned, Balanced, Aligned

Disheartened . . . . .Encouraged, Happy, Jovial, Courageous

Dishonored . . . . .Honored, Worthy, Admired, Upheld, Valued

Dishonest . . . . .Honest, Forthright, Fair, Just, Scrupulous

Dislike (of Self/Others) Forgive, Like, Care About, Interested In

Disobedient . . . . .Obedient, Reliable, Stable, Steadfast

Disorderly . . . . .Orderly, Organized, Neat, Tranquil

Disorganized . . . . .Organized, Orderly, Neat, Systematic

Disown . . . . .Claim, Own, Admit, Acknowledge

Disowned . . . . .Claimed, Retained, Preserved, Valued

Displeasing (Fear of) . .Confident, Pleasing, Satisfying, Capable

Disrespect . . . . .Respect, Revere, Honor, Admire, Value

Dissatisfied . . . . .Satisfied, Pleased, Contented, Grateful

Dissension . . . . .Cooperation, Agreement, Peaceful, Harmonious

Distorted . . . . .Made Whole, Complete, Harmonious, Aligned

Distraught . . . . .Comforted, Supported, Calm, Peaceful

Distressed . . . . .Calm, Cheerful, Peaceful, Relaxed, Carefree

Distrust . . . . .Forgive, Trust, Reliable, Loyal, Dependable

Disturbed . . . . .Undisturbed, Quiet, Calm, Soothed, Accept

Divided . . . . .Connected, Bonded, Unified, Reconciled

Dominated . . . . .Empowered, Equal to, Strong, Capable

Doomed . . . . .Fortunate, Restored, Protected, Secure, Safe

Doormat (Like a) . . . . .Powerful, Strong, Self-Sufficient, Reliant

Double-Minded . . . . . . .Single-Minded, Integrated, Whole-Minded

Doubt/ful . . . . .Reassured, Trust, Believe, Confidence In

Downcast . . . . .Uplifted, Elevated, Happy, Joyous, Excited

Downtrodden . . . . .Stable, Strong, Resilient, Stalwart, Uplifted

Drab . . . . .Bright, Colorful, Exciting, Dynamic

Drained . . . . .Invigorated, Energized, Vibrant, Vital

Dread . . . . .Excited, Enthused, Fearless, Anticipating

Dreadful . . . . .Pleasant, Healthy, Happy, Joyful, Cheerful

Dreary . . . . .Bright, Happy, Vibrant, Joyful, Cheerful

Driven . . . . .Relaxed, Calm, Peaceful, Flowing, Carefree

Droopy . . . . .Revived, Uplifted, Happy, Elevated, Grateful

Drowning (Like I'm) . .Breathing Freely, Plenty of Air, Rescued, Invincible

Drudgery . . . . .With Spirit, Enthused, Happy, Excited About

Dumb . . . . .Smart, Intelligent, Bright, Comprehending

E

Egotistical . . . . .Meek, Humble, Selfless, Teachable

Embarrassed . . . . .Confident, Passive, Comfortable, Grounded

Emotional Stress . . . . .Emotionally Stable, Calm, Confident, Steadfast

Empty . . . . .Filled with Love, Reassured, Supreme Joy

Enmity . . . . .Love, Respect, Good, Kindness, Benevolent

Enraged . . . . .Forgive, Calm, Peaceful, Relaxed, Love

Enslaved . . . . .Free, Liberated, Unrestrained, Independent

Entangled . . . . .Liberated, Disentangled, Released, Restored

Envious . . . . .Accept, Pleased for Others, Benevolent

Envy . . . . .Love, Content, Accept, Happy, Delighted

Escaping (Feel Like) . . .Unwavering, Steadfast, Stalwart, Comfortable

Estranged . . . . .Forgive, Compatible, Harmonious, Bonded

Evil-Minded . . . . .Enlightened, Spiritual Minded, Virtuous

Exasperated . . . . .Patience, Tolerant, Accept, Forgive, Love

Excesses/ive . . . . .Moderation, Reasonable, Sensible, Sufficient

Excluded . . . . .Included, Accepted, Honored, Cherished

Exhausted . . . . .Invigorated, Revitalized, Energized, Refreshed

Exploited . . . . .Forgive, Appreciated, Valued, Respected

Exposed . . . . .Safe, Secure, Protected, Fortified, Forgive

F

Face up (Can't) . . . . . . .Decisive, Brave, Courageous, Valiant

Falling . . . . .Standing, Strong, Firm, Upright, Steadfast

Failing (Like I'm) . . . . .Encouraged, Supported, Succeeding, Competent

Failure (Like a) . . . . . . .Successful, Competent, Capable, Accomplished

Fainthearted . . . . .Resilient, Resolute, Masterful, Strong, Firm

Faithless . . . . .Faithful, Loyal, Stable, Steadfast, Strong

Fatigued . . . . .Revitalized, Replenished, Invigorated

Fear/Ful . . . . .Reassured, Trust, Confident, Resolute, Brave

Feeble . . . . .Stable, Strong, Erect, Energetic, Invigorated

Fickle . . . . .Constant, Loyal, Dependable, Faithful, True

Fierce . . . . .Gentle, Tenderhearted, Merciful, Kind

Fighting (Like) . . . . . . .Forgive, Calm, Peaceful, Composed, Unruffled

Filthy . . . . .Clean, Pure, Decent, Love, Honorable

Fixation . . . . .Mentally Stable, Disinterested, Balanced, Neutral

Flawed . . . . .Magnificent, Flawless, Distinctive, Noble, Beautiful

Flighty . . . . .Stable, Centered, Calm, Collected, Grounded

Flippant . . . . .Respectful, Considerate, Thoughtful, Caring

Floundering . . . . .Resolute, Grounded, Determined, Directed

Flustered . . . . .Calm, Collected, Peaceful, Competent, At Ease

Foolish . . . . .Brilliant, Wise, Bright, Exceptional, Focused

Forced . . . . .Liberated, Free Will, Able to Choose, Optional

Forgetful . . . . .Alert, Remember, Mindful, Retain Information

Forgotten . . . . .Remembered, Included, Revered, Honored

Forlorn . . . . .Happy, Cheerful, Exuberant, Enthused

Forsaken . . . . .Remembered, Favored, Indispensable, Restored

Foul-Mouthed . . . . . . .Respectful, Reverent, Humble, Honorable

Fragmented . . . . .Focused, Centered, Collected, Peaceful

Frantic . . . . .Relaxed, Flowing w/ Life, Calm, Peaceful

Fretful . . . . .Confident, Peaceful, Calm, Trust, Stable

Friendless . . . . .Popular, Well-Liked, Sought After, Valued

Frightened . . . . .Courageous, Confident, Brave, Calm

Frigid . . . . .Warm, Loving, Passionate, Responsive

Frustrated . . . . .Peaceful, Calm, Composed, Confident, Poised

Fuming . . . . .Forgive, Cool, Calm, Peaceful, Understand

Furious (Fury) . . . . . . .Forgive, Calm, Quiet, Restrained, Peaceful

Futile . . . . .Purposeful, Fruitful, Effective, Productive

G

Giddy . . . . .Responsible, Constant, Stable, Serious

Giving Up (Like) . . . . .Courageous, Purposeful, Future Reassured

Gloomy . . . . .Happy, Lighthearted, Bright, Excited

Goofed . . . . .Efficient, Capable, Competent, Confident

Greedy . . . . .Unselfish, Fair, Generous, Sharing, Giving

Grief . . . . .Solace, Understand, Joyful, Happiness, Peace

Grievance . . . . .Merciful, Forgive, Accept, Reunited

Grieved . . . . .Comforted, Consoled, Calmed, Soothed

Grouchy . . . . .Contented, Good-Natured, Cheerful, Happy

Groveling . . . . .Noble, Directed, Secure, Upheld, Confident

Grudge . . . . .Forgive, Compassionate, Understand, Love

Guilty . . . . .Innocent, Forgiving of Self, Repentant, Peaceful

Gullible . . . . .Discerning, Cautious, Perceptive, Wise

Gutless . . . . .Courageous, Confident, Assured, Resolute

Grumbler . . . . .Gracious, Happy, Content, Cheerful, Grateful

H

Hanger-On . . . . .Independent, Self-Sufficient, Confident, Strong

Harassed . . . . .Treated Kindly, Edified, Elevated, Respected

Hardened . . . . .Gentle, Open, Caring, Kind, Considerate

Hard-Hearted . . . . .Open-Hearted, Loving, Meek, Teachable

Harsh . . . . .Gracious, Courteous, Polite, Mannerly

Hasty . . . . .Patient, Cautious, Discerning, Wise, Prudent

Hate/ful . . . . .Tolerant, Forgive, Gracious, Accept, Love

Hatred . . . . .Forgive, Accept, Love, Peaceful, Allow

Haughty . . . . .Humble, Meek, Modest, Teachable, Grateful

Haunted . . . . .Liberated, Carefree, Secure, Protected

Headstrong . . . . .Yielding, Teachable, Manageable, Humble

Heartbroken . . . . .Consoled, Comforted, Courageous, Cheerful

Heartless . . . . .Caring, Loving, Sensitive, Benevolent

Heavy-Hearted . . . . . . .Light-Hearted, Consoled, Peaceful, Joyful

Hectic . . . . .Carefree, Calm, Collected, Organized

Helpless . . . . .Powerful, Self-Reliant, Capable, Competent

Helplessness . . . . .Powerful, Supported, Fortified, Adequate

Hen-Pecked . . . . .Masterful, Independent, Free, Assertive, Resolute

Hesitant . . . . .Eager, Willing, Assertive, Decisive, Resolute

High-Minded . . . . .Humble, Teachable, Meek, Grateful

High-Strung . . . . .Calm, Peaceful, Serene, Mellow, Tranquil

Hindered . . . . .Encouraged, Sustained, Supported, Blessed

Holding Back . . . . .Sharing, Giving, Letting Go, Benevolent

Hollow . . . . .Solid, Filled with Peace, Love, Joyful

Homely . . . . .Attractive, Beautiful, Favored, Radiant

Homesick . . . . .Happy, Content, Joyful, Cheerful, Renewed

Hopeless . . . . .Trust, Reassured, Hopeful, Optimistic

Horrible . . . . .Cheerful, Radiant, Happy, Glowing, Joyous

Horrified . . . . .Forgive, Calmed, Pacified, Serene, Buoyed Up

Hostile/ity . . . . .Accept, Peaceful, Love, Merciful, Gentle

Huffy . . . . .Forgive, Cheerful, Patient, Content, Gracious

Humiliated . . . . .Honored, Favored, Loved, Esteemed, Uplifted

Hurried . . . . .Unhurried, Paced, Relaxed, Easy Going

Hurt (Offended) . . . . . .Forgive, Comforted, Revered, Honored

Hurtful . . . . .Sensitive to Others, Caring, Kind, Loving

Hypocritical . . . . .Sincere, Genuine, True, Honest, Honorable

Hysterical . . . . .Calm, Peaceful, Stable, Relaxed, Grounded

I

Idiot (Like an) . . . . . . .Intelligent, Bright, Brilliant, Smart

Idler . . . . .Industrious, Endeavoring, Valiant, Zealous

I Don't Care . . . . .I Do Care, Sensitive, Kind, Compassionate

Ignorant . . . . .Intelligent, Brilliant, Smart, Capable

Ignored (Being) . . . . . .Noticed, Recognized, Acknowledged, Valued

Imbalanced (Grossly) . .Totally Balanced, Harmonious, Competent

Immature . . . . .Mature, Adult, Understanding, Wise

Immobilized . . . . .Mobilized, Free to Move, Trusting, Confident

Immoral . . . . .Moral, Virtuous, Honorable, Wholesome

Impatient . . . . .Patient, Calm, Pleasant, Accepting, Serene

Impossible . . . . .Determined, Anything Is Possible w/Faith & Trust

Imposter . . . . .Genuine, Authentic, Honest, Trustworthy

Impoverished . . . . . . .Replenished, Solvent, Abundant, Prosperous

Imprisoned . . . . .Liberated, Free, Restored, Victorious, Invincible

Impulsive . . . . .Focused, Purposeful, Stable, Cautious

Inability . . . . .Ability, Capable, Competent, Confident

In a Bind . . . . .Relaxed, Relieved, Centered, Confident

Inadequate . . . . .Adequate, Capable, Competent, Qualified

Incapable . . . . .Capable, Confident Of Abilities, Efficient

Incensed . . . . .Forgive, Merciful, Peaceful, Love, Kind

Incompetent . . . . .Competent, Capable, Skilled, Qualified

Incomplete . . . . .Complete, Centered, Whole, Fulfilled

Inconsiderate . . . . .Considerate, Concerned, Loving, Kind

Inconsistent . . . . .Consistent, Stable, Dependable, Congruent

Incorrect Perception . . .Changing My Perception, Accepting Truth

Indecisive . . . . .Decisive, Resolute, Certain, Stable, Settled

Indignant . . . . .Tolerant, Accepting, Loving, Caring

Indifferent . . . . .Attentive, Mindful, Concerned, Enthused

Indolent . . . . .Ambitious, Responsive, Active, Zealous

Ineffective . . . . .Effective, Productive, Capable, Competent

Inefficient . . . . .Efficient, Capable, Competent, Productive

Inept . . . . .Qualified, Efficient, Competent, Productive

Inferior . . . . .Extraordinary, Equal to, Valued, Capable

Inflexible . . . . .Flexible, Pliable, Adaptable, Yielding

Infuriated . . . . .Forgive, Accept, Love, Peaceful

Inhospitable . . . . .Hospitable, Gracious, Warm, Inviting

Injustice . . . . .Justice, Fairness, Fidelity, Equitable

Inner Pressure . . . . . . .Calm, Peaceful, Serene, Relaxed, Trust

Insane . . . . .Sane, Stable, Balanced, Competent

Insecure . . . . .Secure, Confident, Fearless, Certain

Insignificant . . . . .Significant, Important, Essential, Valued

Insincere . . . . .Sincere, Honest, Truthful, Congruent

Isolated . . . . .Connected, United, Linked, Accepted

Instability . . . . .Stability, Strength, Steadfast, Reliable

Insufferable . . . . .Tolerable, Bearable, Pleasant, Agreeable

Insulted . . . . .Complemented, Respected, Honored, Forgive

Intense . . . . .Relaxed, Calm, Tranquil, Peaceful, Carefree

Intense Depression . . . .Enthused About Living, Happy to Be Alive, Joyful

Intimidated . . . . .Confident, Assured, Masterful, Peaceful, Calm

Intolerant . . . . .Tolerant, Accepting, Open-minded, Patient

Introvert . . . . .Interested in Others, Caring, Out-Going

Irked . . . . .Forgive, Accept, Calm, Happy, Peaceful

Irritable . . . . .Pleasant, Agreeable, Good-natured, Happy

Irritated . . . . .Forgive, Accept, Peaceful, Calm, Tranquil

Irresponsible . . . . .Responsible, Dependable, Reliable, Caring

Irreverent . . . . .Reverent, Respectful, Honoring, Considerate

J

Jealous . . . . .Love, Accept, Harmonious, Benevolent

Jeopardy . . . . .Safe, Secure, Stable, Certain, Protected

Jittery . . . . .Tranquil, Relaxed, Contented, Calm

Joyless . . . . .Joyful, Happy, Grateful, Enthused

Judgmental . . . . .Non-Judgmental, Accept, Allow, Wise

Jumpy . . . . .Calm, Relaxed, Mellow, Serene, Relaxed

K

Know-It-All . . . . .Humble, Teachable, Meek, Unassuming

L

Lack Of: Affection . . .Demonstrate Love Easily, Accept Love Easily

    Consideration . . . . .Considerate, Kind, Caring, Thoughtful, Sensitive

    Courage . . . . .Courageous, Valiant, Brave, Daring, Assertive

    Encouragement . . . .Encouraged, Reassured, Supported, Upheld

    Faith . . . . .Abundant Faith, Trust, Belief, Hope

    Love . . . . .Loved, Cherished, Validated, Cared For, Adored

    Opportunities . . . . .Moving Forward, Plenty of Opportunities

    Self-Confidence . . .Self-Confident, Self-Assured, Secure, Important

    Support . . . . .Supported, Buoyed Up, Upheld, Sustained

    Trust . . . . .Trust, Assurance, Conviction, Fervor

    Understanding . . . . .Perceptive, Aware, Discerning, Understanding

Lacking . . . . .Adequate, Good Enough, Gifted, Valuable

Lazy . . . . .Ambitious, Industrious, Motivated, Resolute

Leech . . . . .Self-Sufficient, Contributing, Capable

Left-out . . . . .Included, Honored, Supported, Cared About

Less Than . . . . .Equal to, Important, Talented, Esteemed

Let down . . . . .Edified, Elevated, Built Up, Supported

Limited . . . . .Unlimited, Powerful, Effective, Efficient

Listless . . . . .Heedful, Concerned, Thoughtful, Enthused

Livid . . . . .Forgive, Merciful, Love, Calm, Peaceful

Loathe . . . . .Love, Harmonious, Peaceful, Benevolent

Loathsome . . . . .Lovable, Beautiful, Pleasant, Agreeable

Lonely . . . . .Love/Accept Self, Secure, Connected

Longing . . . . .Content, Accepting, Peaceful, Fulfilled

Looser . . . . .Winner, Competent, Confident, Capable, Secure

Lost . . . . .Purposeful, Directed, Decisive, Focused

Low . . . . .High, Wonderful, Exhilarated, Uplifted

Low Self-Esteem . . . . .High Self-Esteem, Accept/Love Self, Divine

Luckless . . . . .Blessed, Fortunate, Successful, Happy

Lukewarm . . . . .Responsive, Enthused, Spirited, Zealous

Lunatic . . . . .Sane, Rational, Sensible, Peaceful, Calm

Lustful . . . . .Moral, Temperate, Virtuous, Disciplined

Lusting . . . . .Wholesome, Upright, Noble, Respectable

Lying (Like) . . . . .Truthful, Honest, Straightforward, Honorable

M

Mad . . . . .Forgive, Happy, Joyful, Content, Loving

Maimed . . . . .Healed, Renewed, Regenerated, Soothed

Malice . . . . .Kindness, Forgive, Benevolent, Wholesome

Malicious . . . . .Virtuous, Honest, Honorable, Kind, Noble

Maligned . . . . .Pardoned, Vindicated, Exonerated, Honored

Manipulated . . . . .Masterful, Strong, Steadfast, Tenacious

Manipulative . . . . .Letting Go of Control, Allow, Accept

Martyr (Like a) . . . . . . .Noble, Mighty, Unshaken, Masterful

Materialistic . . . . .Accepting Self, Worthy, Meek, Humble

Mean . . . . .Loving, Kind, Caring, Considerate, Virtuous

Meddler . . . . .Uninvolved, Uninterested, Trustworthy

Melancholy . . . . .Happy, Spirited, Delighted, Cheerful

Mental Poisons . . . . . . .Releasing Negativity, Forgiving the Past

Merciless . . . . .Merciful, Love, Caring, Kind, Compassionate

Miffed . . . . .Forgive, Love, Kind, Merciful, No Blame

Mischievous . . . . .Harmless, Safe, Responsible, Prudent

Miserable . . . . .Comfortable, Happy, Pleasant, Calm, Settled

Miserly . . . . .Generous, Giving, Contributing, Sharing

Misfortune . . . . .Fortunate, Blessed, Grateful, Forgive

Mistreated . . . . .Defended, Protected, Honored, Favored

Misunderstand . . . . . . .Understand, Grasp, Comprehend, Enlightened

Misunderstood . . . . . . .Understood, Pardoned, Appreciated, Valued

Misused . . . . .Forgive, Confident, Steadfast, Masterful,

Mixed Up . . . . .Decipher, Understand, Comprehend, Realize

Moody . . . . .Stable, Steadfast, Happy, Cheerful, Constant

Morbid . . . . .Normal, Sound, Good-Natured, Sane

Mortified . . . . .Pardoned, Restored, Uplifted, Valued

Mournful . . . . .Happy, Cheerful, Joyful, Regenerated

Muddled . . . . .Focused, Clear, Rational, Sensible

Murmuring . . . . .Forgive, Accept, Content, Peaceful

N

Naive . . . . .Wise, Knowledgeable, Understanding
Narrow-Minded . . . . . .Open-Minded, Observant, Receptive
Naughty . . . . .Obedient, Responsive, Virtuous, Agreeable
Need For Approval . . . .Approve of Myself, Accept Self, Confident
Negative . . . . .Positive, Happy, Peaceful, Cheerful
Neglected . . . . .Attended to, Cared for, Cherished, Supported
Negligent . . . . .Attentive, Thoughtful, Responsible, Caring
Nervous . . . . .Calm, Relaxed, Confident, Peaceful, Serene
Neurotic Attachments . .Self-Secure, Independent, Balanced, Rational
No Good . . . . .Very Good, Valuable, Priceless, Worthy
Non-Acceptance . . . . . .Accept, Acknowledge, Allow, Open & Loving
Not Enough (I'm) . . . . .I AM Enough, Exceptional, Worthy, Important
Nothing (Like I'm) . . . .Valued, Cherished, Highly Regarded, Loved
Novice (Like a) . . . . . . .Expert, Authority, Proficient, Skillful
No Way Out . . . . .There is a Way Out, There is an Answer, I Choose
. . . . .Finding the Answer
Numb . . . . .Sensitive, Awake, Aware, Caring, Loving
"Nuts" (Driving Me) . . .Normal, Balanced, Positive, Happy, Flowing

O

Obnoxious . . . . .Pleasant, Agreeable, Delightful, Affable
Obsessed . . . . .Emancipated, Uninhibited, Uninterested, Relaxed
Obsessive . . . . .Rational, Indifferent, Unconcerned, Carefree
Obscure . . . . .Noticed, Significant, Distinguished, Honored
Obstinate . . . . .Flexible, Movable, Yielding, Manageable
Obstructed . . . . .Unobstructed, Open, Flowing, Relaxed
Offended . . . . .Forgive, Peaceful, Calm, Pardoned, Allow
On Edge . . . . .Peaceful, Calm, Relaxed, Mellow, Tranquil
Opinionated . . . . .Accepting, Open-Minded, Flexible, Movable
Opposing . . . . .Helping, Agreeing, Defending, Cooperative
Oppressed . . . . .Liberated, Released, Carefree, Happy
Outcast . . . . .Included, Accepted, Restored, Honored
Out Of Control . . . . . .In Control, Centered, Calm, Grounded
Out Of Sorts . . . . .Peaceful, Calm, Serene, Content, Happy
Outraged . . . . .Forgive, Calm, Peaceful, Collected
Outsider . . . . .Included, Cherished, Valued, Connected

Over-Analyzing ......Accepting, Allowing, Releasing, Letting Go
Over-Bearing ....Humble, Quiet, Gentle, Gracious
Over-Concerned ......Calm, Kind, Benevolent, Allowing
Over-Empathetic ......Allow Others Their Experiences, It's Okay
Overloaded ....Carefree, Relieved, Relaxed, Using Wisdom
Overlooked ....Recognized, Acknowledged, Honored, Respected
Overpowering ....Resistible, Controllable, Bearable, Enduring
Overwhelmed ....Calm, Carefree, Flowing w/Ease, Relieved
Overwhelmed Burden . .Burdens Lifted, Light, Relieved, Carefree
Overworked ....Wise, Knowing When to Quit, Resting
Over-Sensitive ....Forgiving, Accepting, Confident, Loving

P

Pained ....Comfortable, Eased, Soothed, Tranquil
Panic-Stricken ....Fearless, Calm, Peaceful, Trusting
Paranoid ....Normal, Calm, Centered, Together
Peculiar ....Normal, Usual, Ordinary, Conventional
Peeved ....Forgive, Merciful, Peaceful, Amused
Perfectionist (I'm a) ...Lenient, Relaxed, Easy-going, Moderate
Perplexed ....Enlightened, Understand, Clear Perception
Persecute (Self) ....Forgive, Accept, Love, & Validate Self
Persecuted ....Forgive, Cherished, Appreciated, Invincible
Perturbed ....Forgive, Allow, Connected, Relaxed
Perverted ....Balanced, Chaste, Pure, Modest, Directed
Pessimistic ....Optimistic, Hopeful, Happy, Jovial
Petty ....Forgive, Love, Accept, Benevolent
Phobia ....Grounded, Reassured, Trust, Fearless, Focused
Phony ....Authentic, Genuine, Sincere, Honest, Real
Pitiful ....Happy, Cheerful, Joyful, Delightful
Poor ....Rich, Wealthy, Prosperous, Grateful
Possessive ....Release, Let Go, Emancipate, Sharing
Poverty-Stricken ......Affluent, Prosperous, Wealthy, Abundant
Powerless ....Powerful, Strong, Resolute, Masterful, Invincible
Prejudice ....Tolerant, Accept, Allow, Forgive, Love
Prejudiced ....Unbiased, Objective, Open-Minded, Receptive
Pressured ....Relieved, Relaxed, Pacified, Soothed
Pretence ....Genuine, Sincere, Honest, Truthful

Pride . . . . .Humble, Modest, Teachable, Contrite
Prisoner (Like A) . . . . .Liberated, Pardoned, Vindicated, Free, Invincible
Protect Self (Have To) .Cautious, Trusting, Caring, Value Self
Procrastinator . . . . .Punctual, Motivated, Determined, Resolute
Proud . . . . .Humble, Grateful, Honored, Pleased
Punished . . . . .Forgive, Strong, Steadfast, Dauntless, Invincible
Punishing (self/others) . .Forgiving, Loving, Accepting, Merciful
Pushed . . . . .Encouraged, Supported, Competent

Q

Quarrelsome . . . . .Harmonious, Peacemaker, Good-Natured
Quick-Tempered . . . . . .Forgive, Slow to React, Patient, Serene
Quitting (Like) . . . . . . .Steadfast, Resolute, Strong, Dauntless

R

Rage . . . . .Understand, Peaceful, Forgive, Love, Calm
Rag, On (Someone) . . .Praise, Laud, Commend, Honor, Value
Rattled . . . . .Composed, Confident, Sure, Peaceful
Raving . . . . .Rational, Calm, Centered, Peaceful
Ravenous . . . . .Satisfied, Comfortable, Happy, Content
Rebellious . . . . .Submissive, Cooperative, Obedient, Content
Refusal . . . . .Cooperative, Compromising, Teachable
Regret . . . . .Forgive Self, Accept, Move Forward
Rejected . . . . .Accepted, Loved, Cherished, Favored
Reluctant . . . . .Eager, Willing, Inclined, Cooperative
Remorse . . . . .Forgive, Peaceful, Content, Love
Repel Others . . . . .Attract Others, Magnetic, Invite, Love
Repressed (Anything) . .Uninhibited, Bringing to the Surface, Face
Reprobate (Like a) . . . .Virtuous, Moral, Honest, God-Fearing
Reproved . . . . .Approved Of, Favored, Accepted, Recognized
Repulsive . . . . .Acceptable, Agreeable, Pleasant, Delightful
Resentful . . . . .Forgive, Charitable, Accept, Love, Understand
Resentment . . . . .Forgive, Tolerant, Compliant, Peaceful
Resistant . . . . .Agreeable, Flexible, Giving, Open, Caring
Restless . . . . .Quiet, Sedate, Relaxed, Calm, Content
Restrained . . . . .Forgive, Liberated, Free, Demonstrative
Restricted . . . . .Open, Free, Independent, Relaxed, Let Go
Retaliating (Like) . . . . .Forgive, Excusing, Merciful, Peaceful

Reticent . . . . .Eager, Enthused, Looking Forward To

Revenge . . . . .Forgive, Merciful, Pardon, Love, Remorse

Revolting . . . . .Appealing, Honorable, Creditable, Upright

Ridiculed . . . . .Praised, Approved of, Applauded, Commended

Ridiculous . . . . .Sensible, Confident, Dignified, Rational

Right (Have to Be) . . . .It's Unnecessary, Allow Others, Safe, Okay

Rigid . . . . .Flexible, Pliable, Flowing, Open, Loving

Rotten . . . . .Wonderful, Fantastic, Exhilarated, Vital

Rude . . . . .Gracious, Kind, Considerate, Courteous

Ruined . . . . .Restored, Mended, Prosperous, Preserved

Running Away (Like) . .Confronting, Responsible, Accountable

Rushed . . . . .Calm, Collected, Centered, Organized

Rut (In a) . . . . .Moving Forward, Learning, Growing

Ruthless . . . . .Forgive, Merciful, Compassionate, Gentle

S

Sabotage . . . . .Upheld, Supported, Reassured, Sustained, Steady

Sad . . . . .Happy, Jovial, Cheerful, Tenacious

Sarcastic . . . . .Flattering, Complimentary, Loving, Sensitive

Savage . . . . .Tamed, Gentle, Loving, Forgiving, Kind

Scapegoat (Like a) . . . .Vindicated, Liberated, Restored, Empowered

Scattered . . . . .Gathered, Focused, Collected, Concentrated

Scoffing . . . . .Praising, Approving, Applauding, Commending

Scorned . . . . .Acknowledged, Welcomed, Accepted

Scornful . . . . .Respectful, Admirable, Gracious, Caring

Scum . . . . .Worthwhile, Valued, Credible, Cherished

Seething . . . . .Forgiving, Accepting, Calm, Peaceful

Self-Centered . . . . . . .Selfless, Caring, Loving, Sensitive

Self-Condemnation . . . .Self-Love, Self-Praise, Self-Acceptance

Self-Contempt . . . . . . .Forgive Self, Accept Self, Facing Issues

Self-Conscious . . . . . . .Confident, Relaxed, At Ease, Assertive

Self-Doubt . . . . .Self-Trust, Self-Confident, Self-Assured

Self-Rejection . . . . . . .Self-Acceptance, Self-Love, Self-Worth

Self-Violence . . . . . . .Self-Love, Self-Acceptance, Forgiving Self

Self-Willed . . . . .Disciplined, Manageable, Obedient, Cooperative

Selfish . . . . .Unselfish, Selfless, Caring, Considerate

Separate/d . . . . .Unified, Connected, Joined, Bonded

Shallow . . . . .Having Substance, Meaningful, Depth

Shameful . . . . .Admirable, Credible, Decent, Worthy

Shameless . . . . .Modest, Reserved, Dignified, Sensitive

Shiftless . . . . .Efficient, Directed, Motivated, Focused

Shocked . . . . .Unshaken, Comforted, Humored, Renewed

Shoved Aside . . . . .Needed, Included, Appreciated, Cherished

Shunned . . . . .Included, Regarded Highly, Appreciated

Shy . . . . .Gregarious, Friendly, Appropriately Assertive

Sickly . . . . .Healthy, Vibrant, Vital, Robust, Exuberant

Silly . . . . .Reasonable, Rational, Logical, Fun, Sensitive

Sinful . . . . .Repentant, Virtuous, Honest, Chaste, Caring

Sinking . . . . .Buoyed Up, Elevated, Uplifted, Invigorated

Slandered . . . . .Approved Of, Favored, Credited, Appreciated

Slave (Like a) . . . . .Appreciated, Valued, Liberated, Renewed

Slighted . . . . .Recognized, Appreciated, Valued, Respected

Sloppy . . . . .Neat, Tidy, Organized, Particular, Clean

Slothful . . . . .Ambitious, Industrious, Motivated

Slow . . . . .Fast, Quick, Accurate, Surpass, Supersede

Sluggard (Like a) . . . . .Diligent, Steadfast, Resolute, Improving

Smothered . . . . .Breathe Easily, Free Flowing, Released

Smug . . . . .Modest, Retiring, Reserved, Humble

Sneaky . . . . .Reliable, Integrity, Honest, Responsible

Sore . . . . .Comfortable, Merciful, Peaceful, Calm

Sorrowful . . . . .Joyful, Happy, Full of Life, Cheerful

Speechless . . . . .Verbose, Expressive, Communicative

Spiteful . . . . .Forgive, Love, Pleasant, At Peace, Calm

Spoiled . . . . .Disciplined, Cooperative, Teachable

Stagnant . . . . .Progressive, Active, Moving Forward

Standstill (At a) . . . . . .Moving Forward, Motivated, Progressing

Stationary . . . . .Mobile, Changing, Moving, Progressing

Stifled . . . . .Encouraged, Making Progress, Supported

Stingy . . . . .Giving, Generous, Unselfish, Sharing

Stressed . . . . .Relaxed, Calm, Flowing w/Life, Peaceful

Strife . . . . .Peaceful, Contentment, Harmony, Love

Struggling . . . . .Flowing, Directed, Peaceful, Order & Ease

Stubborn . . . . .Flexible, Amenable, Good Natured, Agreeable

Stuck (Like I'm) . . . . . .Aware, Flowing, Moving Forward

Stuffing Feelings . . . . .Accept & Own Feelings, Resolving Them

Stupid . . . . .Brilliant, Wise, Understand, Astute

Suffering . . . . .Comforted, Healed, Renewed, Rescued

Suffocating . . . . .Breathing Freely, Spaciousness, Secure

Suicidal . . . . .Love Life, Enthused, Precious, Cherished

Sulky . . . . .Humorous, Sociable, Happy, Harmonious

Superficial . . . . .Unique, Authentic, Trustworthy, Real

Superior . . . . .Equal To, Humble, Teachable, Nurturing

Suppressed . . . . .Liberated, Restored, Nourished, Sustained

Survival (Fighting for) .Invincible, Supported, Cared & Provided for

Suspicious . . . . .Trust, Accept, Forgive, Allow

T

Tactless . . . . .Tactful, Considerate, Kind, Tender, Sensitive

Taker . . . . .Giver, Giving, Considerate, Kind, Sharing

Talk Too Much . . . . . . .Balanced, Concise, Disciplined, Quiet

Temperamental . . . . . . .Even-Tempered, Cool-Headed, Mellow

Tempted . . . . .Steadfast, Restrained, Courageous, Resolute

Tense . . . . .Relaxed, Yielding, Flowing, Flexible

Tension . . . . .Fearless, Relaxed, Peaceful, Effortless

Terrible . . . . .Wonderful, Great, Relieved, Tranquil

Terror/Terrified . . . . . . .Calm, Relaxed, Reassured, Protected, Invincible

Thin-Skinned . . . . .Thick-Skinned Unaffected, Confident

Thoughtless . . . . .Thoughtful, Considerate, Sensitive, Aware

Threatened . . . . .Safe, Protected, Sustained, Secure, Invincible

Thwarted . . . . .Encouraged, Supported, Accomplish Purpose

Ticked-Off . . . . .Forgive, Peaceful, Love, Letting Go, Allow

Timid . . . . .Out Going, Assertive, Eager, Forthright

Tired . . . . .Energetic, Vigorous, Vital, Alert, Peppy

Tormented . . . . .Untroubled, Tranquil, Serene, Peaceful

Traitor . . . . .Loyal, True, Honest, Virtuous, Steadfast

Trapped . . . . .Liberated, Relieved, Let Go, Carefree, Invincible

Trembling . . . . .Steady, Rooted, Stable, Strong, Secure

Tribulation . . . . .Steadfast, Blessed, Fortunate, Triumphant

Troubled . . . . .Content, Accept, At Ease, Settled, Calm

Turmoil (In) . . . . .Organized, Orderly, Focused, Peaceful, Invincible

Turned Off . . . . .Accept, Forgive, Love, Turned On

Two-Faced . . . . .Sincere, Loyal, Faithful, Principled, Honest

Tyrant (Like a) . . . . .Love, Kind, Helpful, Caring, Compassionate

U

Ugly . . . . .Beautiful, Comely, Graceful, Unequaled

Unable . . . . .Able, Capable, Gifted, Competent, Endowed

Unable To:

Express Self . . . . .Secure & Confident In Expressing My Self

Unacceptable . . . . .Acceptable, Approved Of, Acclaimed, Loved

Unappreciated . . . . .Appreciated, Loved, Valued, Revered

Unaware . . . . .Aware, Cognizant, Perceptive, Informed

Unbearable . . . . .Bearable, Tolerable, Endurable, Victorious

Unbeliever . . . . .Believer, Trusting, Reassured, Converted

Uncertain . . . . .Certain, Decisive, Resolute, Committed

Uncharitable . . . . .Charitable, Loving, Kind, Giving, Sharing

Uncomfortable . . . . . . .Comfortable, At Ease Undisturbed

Uncommitted . . . . .Trust Self, Constant, Confident, Committed

Uncompromising . . . . .Compromising, Cooperative, Giving

Unconcerned . . . . .Concerned, Caring, Supportive, Sensitive

Unconscious . . . . .Conscious, Aware, Mindful, Astute

Uncontrollable . . . . . . .Controllable, Cooperative, Manageable, Calm

Undecided . . . . .Decisive, Resolute, Settled, Committed

Understand (Don't) . . . .Do Understand, Comprehend, Grasp, Embrace

Undesirable . . . . .Desirable, Favored, Welcomed, Acceptable

Undeserving . . . . .Deserving, Worthy, Praiseworthy, Priceless

Undisciplined . . . . .Disciplined, Reliable, Steady, Constant

Uneasy . . . . .At Ease, Placid, Soothed, Relaxed, Comfortable

Unfair . . . . .Forgiving, Fair, Judicious, Merciful

Unfeeling . . . . .Feeling, Caring, Concerned, Loving

Unfit . . . . .Fit, Capable, Worthy, Skilled, Competent

Unforgivable . . . . .Forgivable, Merciful, Loving Exonerated

Unforgiveness . . . . .Forgiveness, Pardon, Excuse, Accept

Unfriendly . . . . .Friendly, Outgoing, Personable, Caring

Unfulfilled . . . . .Fulfilled, Pleased, Qualified, Content, Serene

Ungrateful . . . . .Grateful, Thankful, Appreciative, Humble

Unhappy . . . . .Happy, Joyous, Pleased, Accepting, Radiant

Unjust . . . . .Fair, Just, Equitable, Reasonable, Balanced

Unimportant . . . . .Important, Worthwhile, Valuable, Validated

Unkind . . . . .Kind, Caring, Considerate, Thoughtful

Unlovable . . . . .Lovable, Cherished, Honored, Favored

Unloving . . . . .Loving, Caring, Respectful, Accepting

Unlucky . . . . .Lucky, Fortunate, Successful, Trusting

Unmerciful . . . . .Merciful, Forgiving, Compassionate

Unmindful . . . . .Mindful, Aware, Cognizant, Conscious of

Unnoticed . . . . .Noticed, Recognized, Saluted, Valued

Unorganized . . . . .Organized, Systematic, Directed, Prepared

Unpleasant . . . . .Pleasant, Pleasing, Gracious, Agreeable

Unpopular . . . . .Popular, Well-liked, Approved of, Loved

Unprepared . . . . .Prepared, Well-organized, Skilled, Trained

Unproductive . . . . .Productive, Effective, Useful, Successful

Unprotected . . . . .Protected, Guarded, Secure, Strengthened

Unqualified . . . . .Qualified, Competent, Capable, Equal to

Unreasonable . . . . .Reasonable, Rational, Sensible, Prudent

Unreceptive . . . . .Receptive, Accepting, Enthused, Tolerant

Unrelenting . . . . .Relenting, Yielding, Merciful, Flexible

Unreliable . . . . .Reliable, Dependable, Responsible, Tenacious

Unrepentant . . . . .Repentant, Contrite, Reverent, Caring

Unresolved (Anything) . .Forgive, Understand, Love, Caring, Sensitive

Unsatisfied Needs . . . . .Important, Valuing My Self , Claiming My Needs

Unsettled . . . . .Settled, Organized, Stable, Steady, Secure

Unstable . . . . .Very Stable, Steady, Constant, Steadfast

Unsuccessful . . . . .Successful, Productive, Worthwhile, Capable

Unsupported . . . . .Supported, Encouraged, Defended

Unsure . . . . .Sure, Resolute, Confident, Certain, Steadfast

Unthankful . . . . .Thankful, Grateful, Appreciative, Praising

Untidy . . . . .Tidy, Neat, Orderly, Clean, Careful

Untrusting . . . . .Trusting, Comfortable With, Confident In

Untrustworthy . . . . .Trustworthy, Have Integrity, Honest, Valiant

Untruthful . . . . .Truthful, Honest, With Integrity, Congruent

Unwanted . . . . .Wanted, Welcomed, Invited, Cared For

Unwelcome . . . . .Welcome, Included, Desirable, Thankful For

Unwilling (To Change) . .Willing, Eager, Anticipating, Enthused, Grateful

Unwise . . . . .Wise, Prudent, Knowledgeable, Understanding

Unworthy . . . . .Worthy, Loved, Honored, Exceptional

Unyielding . . . . .Yielding, Flexible, Teachable, Accepting

Upset . . . . .Calm, Collected, Tranquil, Serene, Accepting

Uptight . . . . .Centered, Relaxed, Tranquil, Serene

Used . . . . .Forgive, Elevated, Appreciated, Honored

Useless . . . . .Useful, Worthwhile, Effective, Valiant

V

Vague . . . . .Succinct, Definite, Clear, Precise, Focused

Vain . . . . .Humble, Contrite, Teachable, Modest

Vengeful . . . . .Forgiving, Relenting, Loving, Tolerant

Vicious . . . . .Noble, Pure, Virtuous, Caring, Kind

Victim (Like a) . . . . . . .Masterful, In Control, Invincible, Steadfast

Vindictive . . . . .Unconditional Forgiving, Remorse, Loving

Violated . . . . .Healing, Benevolent, Forgiving, Pardoning

Violence (Self) . . . . . . .Forgiving Self, Self-love, Self-acceptance

Violent . . . . .Calm, Appeased, Tranquil, Peaceful

Void . . . . .Fulfilled, Peaceful, Joyful, Happy, Rooted

Vulgar . . . . .Decent, Moral, Respectful, Couth, Refined

Vulnerable . . . . .Protected, Guarded, Strong, Infallible

W

Wallowing . . . . .Elevated, Directed, Uplifted, Secure, Valued

Wasted . . . . .Invigorated, Energized, Nourished, Refreshed

Wavering . . . . .Stalwart, Steadfast, Resolute, Stable, Rooted

Weak . . . . .Strong, Resilient, Resolute, Stalwart, Masterful

Weak-Minded . . . . . . .Strong-Minded, Rational, Wise, Persevering

Weary . . . . .Vibrant, Energetic, Strong, Radiant

Weepy . . . . .Happy, Jovial, Balanced, Serene, Tranquil

Why Me . . . . .Why Not Me? I Can Handle It, I Have Faith

Wicked . . . . .Moral, Virtuous, Worthwhile, Honest

Willful . . . . .Obedient, Cooperative, Flexible, Teachable

Wishy-Washy . . . . . . .Focused, Purposeful, Strong, Steadfast

Withdrawn . . . . .Assertive, Active, Involved, Aggressive

Withholding . . . . .Honest, Truthful, Giving, Generous

Worried . . . . .Trusting, Reassured, Secure, Have Faith

Worry . . . . .Trust, Reassured, Tenacious, Steadfast, Calm

Worthless . . . . .Worthwhile, Valuable, Important, Competent
Wounded . . . . .Forgive, Pardoned, Healed, Vindicated
Wrong (Always) . . . . . .I Choose Being Correct, I Feel Correct, I Am

Y

Yearning . . . . .Satisfied, Content, Happy, Fulfilled
Yucky . . . . .Clear-headed, Happy, Peaceful, Serene

Feelings & Beliefs That Affect Success

This section will help you 'Script' for Negative Feelings that can affect your success, and replace them with Positive Feelings. With each number from 1-31, go all the way through the 'Script' to " . . . recorded in my DNA, to transform!" Replace the Negative with the Positive.

"Spirit, please locate the origin of the feelings that . . .

1) "...cause me to believe I am UNWORTHY & UNDESERVING OF HAVING FINANCIAL FREEDOM."   Replace with:
"I choose Be-ing worthy and deserving of having financial freedom.
"I feel worthy and deserving of financial freedom.
"I AM worthy and deserving of financial freedom."

2) "...created the belief that I MUST BE POOR IN ORDER TO BE HUMBLE/CLOSE TO GOD." Replace with:
"I choose Be-ing humbly grateful and close to God as I experience financial success.
"I feel humble, grateful, and close to God as my financial success expands.
"I AM humbly grateful and close to God as I experience financial success."

3) "...cause me to FEAR FINANCIAL SUCCESS/THAT I WON'T DO THE CORRECT THINGS WITH FINANCIAL SUCCESS." Replace with:
"I choose Be-ing financially successful. I welcome financial success with open arms.

"I feel financially successful. I handle financial success commendably
and wisely.

"I AM financially successful. I AM a wise steward of my success."

4) "...cause me to FEAR THE RESPONSIBILITY & ACCOUNTA-
BILITY THAT COMES WITH FINANCIAL SUCCESS." Replace
with:

"I choose Be-ing capable of the responsibility success brings.

"I feel capable of the responsibility financial success brings.

"I AM capable of the personal responsibility financial success brings.

"I choose trusting myself and accepting the accountability that comes
with financial success.

"I feel trust in myself and gratefully accept the accountability that success brings.

"I AM trusting in myself and my ability to be accountable with my
financial success."

5) "...created the belief in me that I'M SUPPOSED TO BE POOR/
MUST SUFFER FINANCIALLY/STRUGGLE FOR MY EXIS-
TENCE ALL MY LIFE." Replace with:

"I choose Be-ing financially abundant.

"I feel financially abundant.

"I AM financially abundant. Abundance is everywhere for me to enjoy.

"I let go of my 'lack mentality'. I give myself permission to be free of
financial oppression. In fact I claim financial freedom! I claim
continued abundance in my life!

"I choose enjoying financial freedom.

"I feel liberated from financial suffering—from struggling for my existence.

"I AM liberated from financial suffering—from struggling for my existence."

6) "...created the belief that I'M SUPPOSED TO FEEL GUILTY FOR
DESIRING FINANCIAL PROSPERITY/FOR HAVING FINAN-
CIAL ABUNDANCE." Replace with:

"I choose Be-ing peaceful in my desire for financial prosperity.

"I feel peaceful about desiring financial prosperity, and give myself permission to enjoy it.

"I AM peaceful in my desire for financial prosperity, and know it is God's desire for me, also.

"I choose Be-ing a wise steward and am very grateful for financial abundance.

"I feel deep appreciation for my financial abundance and feel it is a gift.

"I AM truly grateful for my financial stability, and rejoice in having prosperity."

7) "...cause me ANXIETY OVER MONEY MATTERS."
Replace with:

"I choose Be-ing calm and trusting with money matters.

"I feel a calm, trusting assurance that all is well with me financially.

"I AM trusting, calm, solid, and secure where my money matters are concerned."

8) "...cause me TO FEAR THE FUTURE/MY FINANCIAL FUTURE." Replace with:

"I choose Be-ing trusting and confident in the future/my financial future.

"I feel confidence, faith, and trust in the future/my financial future.

"I AM confident and trusting in the future/my financial future."

9) "...cause me to FEAR THERE IS NEVER ENOUGH/THERE'S NOT GOING TO BE ENOUGH ABUNDANCE." Replace with:

"I choose knowing there is always enough, plenty and more. God's universe is abundant!

"I feel confident there is always enough, plenty and more for me.

"I AM confident and secure in the knowledge that there is always enough, plenty and more money."

10) "...created the belief that IT'S UNFAIR FOR ME TO HAVE MONEY BECAUSE MY PARENTS DIDN'T." Replace with:

"I choose knowing my parents are very pleased and happy for me to enjoy prosperity.

"I feel my parents are happy and pleased for my financial freedom.
"I AM blessed with prosperity, and this pleases my parents."

11) "...have kept me from GIVING MYSELF PERMISSION TO BE
     FINANCIALLY INDEPENDENT." Replace with:
"I choose giving myself permission to be financially independent.
"I feel it is permissible for me to be financially independent.
"I AM comfortable in granting myself permission to be financially
     independent.
"I AM financially independent."

12) "...created the belief that I DON'T DESERVE/AM UNWORTHY
     TO HAVE FINANCIAL PROSPERITY." Replace with:
"I choose Be-ing deserving and worthy of financial prosperity.
"I feel deserving and worthy of financial prosperity.
"I AM deserving and worthy of financial prosperity."

13) "...cause me TO EXPECT TO FAIL." Replace with:
"I choose succeeding. I expect to succeed.
"I feel successful!
"I AM succeeding. I AM successful."

14) "...cause me TO FEAR HAVING TO PROVE MYSELF."
     Replace with:
"I choose Be-ing competent, resolute, self-reliant and secure in my
     own abilities.
"I feel competent, resolute, self-reliant and secure in the abilities God
     gave me.
"I AM competent, resolute, self-reliant and secure in my abilities."

15) "...caused me to BELIEVE I WILL FAIL AT EVERYTHING I
     ATTEMPT". Replace with:
"I choose succeeding in my endeavors, with the help of God.
"I feel and know that I can succeed in my endeavors.
"I AM succeeding in my endeavors, with God's help."

16) "...created the belief that NO MATTER WHAT I DO IT WILL
     BE 'WRONG'."

"I choose Be-ing capable, confident and correct in what I do.

"I feel capable and confident in what I do. I continually improve.

"I AM capable and confident and experience more and more success in what I do each day."

17) "...created the belief that I'M NOT GOOD ENOUGH TO EARN LARGE SUMS OF MONEY." Replace with:

"I choose Be-ing good enough to earn large sums of money.

"I feel I am good enough to earn large sums of money.

"I AM good enough to earn large sums of money."

18) "...created the belief that I'M UNIMPORTANT . . . WHO AM I TO THINK I SHOULD BE WEALTHY?" Replace with:

"I choose Be-ing important. I give myself permission to realize my own importance.

"I feel it's perfectly all right for me to be wealthy and prosperous.

"I AM important! I AM deserving of prosperity!"

19) "Spirit, please locate the origin of MY FEELINGS OF INADE-QUACY." Replace with:

"I choose Be-ing adequate, capable, and equal to any challenge.

"I feel adequate, capable, and equal to any challenge.

"I AM adequate, capable, and equal to any challenge."

20) "Higher-Self, please locate the origin of MY FEELINGS OF INCOMPETENCY." Replace with:

"I choose Be-ing competent and qualified.

"I feel competent, qualified and capable.

"I AM competent, qualified, capable, and gifted."

21) "Super-Conscious, please locate the origin of MY FEELINGS OF RESENTMENT OR JEALOUSY TOWARDS OTHERS WHO ARE SUCCESSFUL." Replace with:

"I choose Be-ing happy for others who enjoy success in any area of their life.

"I feel happy and pleased for others when they achieve success in any-
thing.
"I AM happy and pleased for others and delight in their success.
"I choose Be-ing forgiving and benevolent towards all whom I have
resented.
"I feel forgiving and benevolent towards all whom I have resented.
"I AM forgiving and benevolent of all those I have resented."

> (**Please note**: Often, when there is a great deal of resentment, it is neces-
> sary to specify the person and the situation the resentment is being held
> toward before this powerful feeling can be resolved.)

22) "...cause me TO BE CRITICAL OF MYSELF." Replace with:
"I choose recognizing and dwelling on my strengths.
"I feel I have many strengths, and I dwell on them instead of weak-
nesses.
"I AM recognizing and dwelling on my strengths.
"I choose Be-ing accepting, loving and approving of myself & others.
"I feel acceptance, love, and approval of myself and others.
"I AM accepting, loving and approving of myself and others."

23) "...cause me TO FEAR THE FUTURE." Replace with:
"I choose staying in present time and having faith and trust in the
future.
"I feel total faith and trust in the future, with the help of God.
"I AM in present time. I have faith in the future, with God's help."

24) "...cause me TO HAVE A POVERTY/LACK CONSCIOUS-
NESS/MENTALITY." Replace with:
"I choose establishing an abundance mentality within my Be-ing.
"I feel worthy, and give myself permission, to enjoy the best life has to
offer. Therefore, I embrace a prosperity/abundance conscious-
ness/mentality.
"I claim abundance. I claim prosperity. I claim the best life has to
offer.
"I AM enjoying abundance in every area of my life."

25) "…created SELF-DOUBT, LOW SELF-WORTH/A POOR SELF-
CONCEPT in me." Replace with:
"I choose Be-ing a person of genuine worth. I trust in my own magnif-
icence.
"I feel confident in my abilities and talents. I feel the nobility of my
Soul.
"I AM a person of magnificent worth. I AM a person of distinction."

26) "Sub-conscious, please locate the origin of my feeling HOPELESS
and/or HELPLESS." Replace with:
"I choose Be-ing optimistic, enthusiastic, and hopeful. I choose Be-ing
strong, tenacious, and resilient.
"I feel optimistic, enthusiastic, and hopeful. I feel strong, tenacious,
and resilient. I feel adequate, capable, and competent. I feel
resourceful!
"I AM optimistic, enthusiastic, and hopeful. I AM strong, tenacious,
and resilient. I AM adequate, capable, and competent. I AM
resourceful!
"I choose Be-ing secure, guided and directed to my highest good.
"I feel secure, guided and directed to my highest good.
"I AM secure, guided and directed to my highest good."

27) "Spirit, pleace locate the origin of my feeling OF DEFEATISM;
LIKE GIVING UP." Replace with:
"I choose knowing that challenges can be met without pain.
"I feel confidence and faith that challenges can be met without pain. I
feel courageous, steadfast and resolute.
"I AM confident that challenges can be met without pain. I AM coura-
geous, steadfast and resolute."

28) "…created the belief that I DON'T MEASURE UP/I'M A
LOSER." Replace with:
"I choose measuring up. I choose Be-ing what it takes to be successful.
I choose Be-ing a winner!
"I feel that I measure up. I feel I have what it takes to be successful. I
feel like a winner!
"I AM measuring up! I AM Be-ing successful! I AM a winner!"

29) "...cause me to BE DISHEARTENED/DISCOURAGED...WHAT'S
THE USE?" Replace with:

"I choose Be-ing capable and courageous in meeting the challenges
that come my way.

"I feel capable and courageous in meeting the challenges of life. They
assist me in growing and living to my full potential. I feel encouraged.

"I AM courageous and capable of resolving challenges. As I do this, I
receive growth. There are always answers to challenges with the
help of God. I AM encouraged."

30) "...created the belief that NO MATTER WHAT I DO, IT WON'T
BE ENOUGH."

"I choose Be-ing secure in my ability to do the correct thing and know
that it is enough.

"I feel secure and confident in my ability to do enough and be enough
in whatever is required of me.

"I AM confident in my ability to do the correct thing and it's always
enough. I AM a person who contributes much to life!"

31) "...created the belief in me that I MUST TAKE THE BLAME
FOR OUR LACK OF MONEY, or, I'M NOT SMART ENOUGH
NOR GOOD ENOUGH TO EARN A LARGE INCOME."
Replace with:

"I choose Be-ing blameless for our lack of money, however willing to
take whatever responsibility is necessary to correct the condition.

"I feel blameless for our lack of money, however, am willing to take
responsibility for my part.

"I AM blameless for our lack of money. I AM willing to take the necessary responsibility for my part, however. Things are looking up."

"I choose Be-ing intelligent, smart, bright and good enough to earn a
large income.

"I feel totally capable, competent and confident to earn a large income.
I feel intelligent, smart, bright and good enough to earn a sizeable
income.

"I AM totally capable, competent and confident in my ability to earn a large income. I AM intelligent, smart, and good enough to earn a sizeable income."

Many of the foregoing feelings are decidedly similar. However, they are varied just enough that they will register a different vibration inside you. Each word, each syllable, therefore, each sound has its own power. So it is helpful to do each one with which you identify in any way.

You will also notice that I have varied the way they can be Scripted. This is to indicate that there is no particular way it's *supposed* to be done. You can make Scripting as long or as short as you would like. Sometimes I feel like I'm carrying on a one-sided conversation, reasoning with my Higher Self for several minutes. Whatever feels comfortable is what it's all about.

REMEMBER . . .
THE MASTER PROGRAM
IN THE SUBCONSCIOUS
MUST BE CHANGED
BEFORE
THE CIRCUMSTANCES WILL CHANGE!!

The purpose of the next section is to show you how to use the Script when undesirable feelings come up during normal, daily activities. When you talk or express yourself in everyday situations, phrases just automatically come out of your mouth without conscious thought, so listen carefully to the words you speak. What you say is the best indication of what you are really feeling, so use that very expression. It may not be the actual feeling that is going on inside you, but it best symbolizes you at the moment, and your Intelligence/Spirit knows exactly what you are referring to.

EXAMPLE: A driver cuts in front of you on the freeway. Your natural response might be. "Boy, that ticks me off!" (Or stronger words.) Whether you know it or not this reaction pumps up your blood pressure.

What you really want to accomplish, at this point, is changing the way you feel when someone does this to you so you won't have this same reaction over and over again. Wouldn't it be wonderful to go down the freeway and not be bothered by someone else's driving?

So, you quickly say, "Spirit, please locate the origin of my feelings that caused me to be so ticked off at that person who cut in front of me.

"Take each and every level, layer, area and aspect of my Be-ing to this origin. Analyze and resolve it perfectly with God's truth.

"Come through all generations of time and eternity, healing every incident and its appendages based on the origin. Do it according to God's will until I'm at the present—filled with light and truth, God's peace and love . . ." Continue with the Script. When you come to the second blank line, a good replacement would be: "I choose Be-ing merciful and forgiving. I feel merciful and forgiving. I AM merciful and forgiving. It's all right when someone does that because I am alert and a very good driver. I feel peaceful. Bless you." Then finish the Script.

How do I know this works? Because, I've had this very thing happen to me. It's really a great feeling to be driving and not have anyone bother me or push my buttons! You too can experience this feeling.

Another example might be one of those days when nothing seems to go as planned. (Here again, listen to what your internal dialogue is saying.) Do you catch yourself saying, "Nothing is going good for me today. I can't do anything right!" Or something similar to that? However you express yourself . . . just take those words and go through the Script. "Spirit, please locate the origin of my feeling like I can't do anything right today!"

Continue on through the remainder of the Script replacing the negative with something like, "I choose doing everything to the best of my ability today. I feel like doing everything to the best of my ability today.

I AM doing everything to the best of my ability today. I choose Be-ing capable and competent. I feel capable and competent. I AM capable and competent. Things go smoothly for me." Then complete the Script.

Do you ever find yourself making the statement, "It's a hard life!"?

This is a belief or feeling you have. Just take it through the Script by stating, "Spirit, please locate the origin of the feelings that created the belief in me that it's a hard life." Continue through to the positive replacement, stating, "I choose seeing/experiencing life as wonderful, beautiful, and exciting! I feel life is wonderful! I AM having a wonderful life! My life flows with order and ease as I meet my challenges with confidence and in a relaxed and positive manner."

The purpose of doing this is to reprogram the statement, "It's a hard life." The heavy vibration of hard life changes to a much lighter vibration. Wouldn't you rather have a light feeling than a heavy feeling?

Do you ever feel like saying, "I give up!" and mean it? Process the feeling of "I give up!" through the Script, and replace that feeling with something similar to, "I choose Be-ing resolute! I feel resolute! I AM resolute! I feel courageous! I feel happy! I feel tenacious! I love life and all that is in it!"

Examples of Daily Situations

The following examples show how you can utilize the power of the Script in everyday life. For each example insert the Negative Feelings and Positive Feelings listed below, into the proper place in the Script.

". . . , please locate the origin of the feelings that cause me to believe. . .

1) I'M TAKEN FOR GRANTED." (Negative Feelings)
   (Positive Feelings) "I choose Be-ing loved. I feel loved. I AM loved. I choose Be-ing appreciated and valued for my contribu-

tions. I feel appreciated and valued for my contributions. I AM appreciated and valued for who I am."

2) I'M GOOD FOR NOTHING."

    "I choose Be-ing a very valuable person. I feel I'm a very valuable person. I AM truly a valuable person. I value myself. I feel I am of great worth."

3) THINGS NEVER WORK OUT FOR ME!"

    I choose Be-ing a fortunate person! I feel fortunate! I AM a fortunate person. Things usually work out for me! I AM blessed.

4) I CAN'T REMEMBER NAMES OR FACES."

    "I choose remembering names and faces. I feel like remembering names and faces. I AM remembering names and faces. Names and faces usually come to me at the precise moment I have a need to recall." (This example will probably need to be reinforced several times.)

5) I DON'T BELONG; EXCLUDED; LEFT OUT; LIKE A STRANGER."

    "I choose belonging. I feel like I belong. I AM included now. I choose Be-ing friendly. I feel friendly. I AM friendly. People enjoy my company. I enjoy my company. I choose feeling comfortable wherever I am. I feel comfortable wherever I am. I AM comfortable wherever I am."

6) I'M SICK AT HEART."

    "I choose Be-ing at peace with this situation. I feel at peace with the situation. I AM at peace where this situation is concerned. All things work together for my good."

7) CAUSES ME TO WANT TO SCREAM."

    "I choose forgiving the situation/this person. I feel forgiving of the situation/person. I AM forgiving this situation/person. I chose Be-ing serene, peaceful and tranquil. I feel serene, peaceful, and tranquil. I AM serene, peaceful, and tranquil."

8) THERE'S NO WAY OUT!"
   "There is a way out! There's always a way out and I choose finding it! I feel resolute! I AM resolute. There is an answer to every challenge, and it's close at hand!"

9) EVERYONE HASSLES ME!"
   "I choose Be-ing forgiving. I feel forgiving. I AM forgiving. I forgive them. I feel everyone loves me, including myself. My life flows with order and ease. I feel at peace."

10) I AM RESPONSIBLE FOR MAKING EVERYONE HAPPY."
    "I choose allowing others to be responsible for their own happiness. I only feel responsible for my happiness. I AM expressing my love, concern and acceptance to others. I assist in any way I am able, nevertheless, I allow them their own experiences."

11) I'M A FAILURE."
    "I choose Be-ing a success. I feel successful. I AM successful. I feel competent, I feel confident, I feel capable. I achieve my goals in all my endeavors."

12) I'M WORTHLESS."
    "I choose Be-ing worthwhile! I feel worthwhile. I AM worthwhile. I choose Be-ing important. I feel important. I AM important. I choose Be-ing useful. I feel useful. I AM useful. I choose Be-ing valuable. I feel valuable. I AM valuable."

Perhaps these examples give you a better idea of how to facilitate the Script for daily use in many different ways. Have fun working with it. When you first process your feelings it is a little scary because it's a new concept. Be imaginative and creative. You really can't do anything wrong. Just be sure to use the dialogue of the Script as it is written. In order to have consistency and the desired affect, this is very important.

If at first you are unable to feel a significant difference when using the Script, keep persisting. The more you use it the more of a shift—the more of a change you will feel inside you. It is a very subtle change to begin with, but little by little you will start seeing people and situations differently, and you will start responding to them differently. You will also notice a change in your attitude. Then one day you will step back, mentally, and watch the scene you are involved in without the old, negative emotional responses.

Remember, there are only two main feelings. LOVE and FEAR. Have you noticed after reading these lists that our negative feelings stem from FEAR?

An acronym for FEAR is: False Evidence Appearing Real. Fear keeps us locked in immature and unsatisfying behavior. The stress that results from this behavior lies at the core or root of all dis-ease, whether that dis-ease be phobias, relationships, finances or physical ill-ness. Fear and its resultant vibrations literally sap and drain our life force. Fear diminishes the energy that is available for life-enhancing activities.

Adversity is Energized By Human Fear!!

If all feelings, indeed, do have vibrations, and negative feelings or vibrations cause us to thrust and repel ourselves away from our Source, thereby diminishing our peace—think of what we could accomplish and become by changing all negative feelings to positive feelings!

The Bottom Line Is . . . .
Rid Yourself Of Fear!!

Dr. Gerald G. Jampolsky truly knew what he was talking about when he titled his book, "Love is Letting Go of Fear." When we let go of FEAR, the only thing left for us to experience is LOVE. When we allow vibrations of LOVE to fill the immensity of our "space," we are then "enabling" ourselves to discover the great and glorious BE-ing God designed us to BE!!

Chapter 18

Probable Feelings Causing Ill-ness

A Personal Experience

"The 'will to live' is an undeniably powerful force for survival—probably THE most important factor in health and healing." (*Love, Medicine & Miracles*, Dr. Bernie Siegel) When someone has lost this *will* to *live*, many things can go wrong in their life. It's like a giving up. And when a person gives up, no matter what kind of treatment they obtain to correct their illness, a healing is very slow in taking place (if, indeed, it takes place at all). How can a person recover their *will to live*? One of the simplest ways is to use the Script.

"Spirit, please locate the origin of the feelings that have caused me to lose my 'will to live' . . . " (taking it through to the replacement), " . . . based on the negative origin recorded in my DNA, to transform. I choose life and living. I feel like living! I reclaim my 'will to live.' I choose Be-ing enthused about life. I feel enthused about life and the future. I am enthused about life and the future! I choose taking an active part in life and living! I feel like an active participant in life. I am an active participant in life and look forward to the future! I LOVE LIFE!" Then finish it on out.

One of the most profound experiences with a health condition that we have had in using the Script, came to our family in the Spring of

1988. My husband had suffered several unfortunate experiences which caused extreme financial stress. Nothing seemed to be working for him. Not only had he lost most of the assets he had taken years to build, but he lost his self-worth, self-respect, self-esteem, yes, and his *will to live*. He really didn't care whether he lived or died. In fact, he would rather have died than lived.

For several months I watched him become more and more despondent. He is normally 6' 2" tall, but he was literally starting to shrink, and he had no zest for anything in life.

For quite some time he had been complaining about how he was aching clear down into his bones. He just hurt all over and had a difficult time getting warm. It was all he could do to face each day. Then I started to notice a real peculiar odor about him. It wasn't his breath or body odor, in the usual sense. The only way I can describe it is to say that it was a metallic odor . . . unlike anything I had ever smelled before on a person. He also had terrible headaches. His face broke out with several huge horrible sores. He would wake up each morning and prepare for the day only to run out of strength and energy in about an hour. Then he would feel the need to go back to bed.

He was diagnosed as having leukemia. Of course, that was the last thing we needed! We had no insurance nor money with which to begin treatment.

One evening after my husband had retired early, I decided to study the syllabus from a conference I had attended the previous year at a major university. The conference was a "Behavioral Medicine and Health Psychology" Conference. There were six guest clinicians who are leading M.D.'s and Ph.D.'s involved in PSYCHONEUROIMMUNOLOGY, which is a new branch of medical science. Two of these participants were Joan Borysenko, Ph D., and Steven E. Locke, M.D., of Harvard Medical School.

Psychoneuroimmunology is concerned specifically with the impact of mental attitudes on the body's resistance to disease, especially exploring the links among and between the mind, the brain and the immune system. The researchers involved in this field have established solid evidence that emotions, mental attitudes and a person's ability to cope all strongly affect and determine the function of the immune system.

The guest doctors at this conference had a remarkable understanding of how feelings, emotions and attitudes affect a person's health. It was obvious from participating in this conference that these professionals were on the *cutting edge* of this information. The syllabus I was studying was a compilation of articles these doctors had written for professional publications. This particular night I was hoping to locate additional clues as to the emotional causes of leukemia to validate or invalidate information I already had from previous research. When I discovered that "deep depression" was one of the emotional causes of leukemia, I KNEW that was my husband's problem. There was no doubt in my mind!

It was about midnight and I was preparing to go to bed when my husband came into the den where I was studying. He knew that I had been searching for some answers, so he asked me what I had found. When I told him that *deep depression* was one of the feelings that causes leukemia, he quickly sat down on the couch and said, "Let's take care of it." Now, mind you, this man is one of the world's greatest doubters and skeptics where things like the Script are concerned. He had silently observed, however, some of the very beneficial effects our son and I had experienced from using the Script over the previous few years. At this point, with his health going down hill so fast, he was ready and willing to do ANYTHING in order to feel better!

I sat down with my husband and assisted him in wording the Script, substituting *deep depression* with, "Forgiveness of myself for an incorrect perception. I feel excited to be alive! I am excited to be alive! I choose loving life. I feel love for life. I am loving life! I choose living. I feel like living. I am living life to the fullest. I choose being happy, joyous, and tenacious! I feel happy, joyous and tenacious! I am happy, joyous and tenacious." (Or words to that affect.) I also took him through the Script for having a death wish, because it was obvious to me that if he had a deadly disease it would indicate he had a death wish. (However, a person does not necessarily have to have a deadly disease in order to have a death wish.) We then went to bed.

When my husband awoke the next morning he couldn't believe the difference in the way he felt! I know it's difficult for one to believe, and we might not have believed it ourselves if we hadn't experienced it, but he felt like a different person, and there was no denying that! His bones no longer ached, he had energy for the first time in months and the metallic odor was gone. All day he just relished in how good he felt, and the next day was the same.

The third day after this experience, however, my husband woke up and was hurting in the area of the kidneys. I didn't pay much attention to his complaint and perhaps I should have because he is *not* a complainer. I was just so happy to have him feeling better that I thought the pain in that area would surely go away soon.

Well, it didn't. All day he walked around bent over and by night he was completely doubled over from the pain. We finally looked up the feelings that cause kidney problems and went through the Script for those feelings. He went to bed and when he awoke the next morning, the pain was gone. And to this day, 14 years later, the pain has never reoccurred. Could it be that simple? Our experiences have been that the answer to this question is an absolute and resounding "YES"! It's just we human beings who make it so complicated.

For the next ten days my husband experienced one health problem after another. It was like he was re-tracing emotional pains of the past. The vibrations of the negative feelings he had been holding onto for s-o-o-o-o long were finally manifesting themselves. His physical pain was now letting him know that he needed to get *in touch* with the inappropriate feelings he had buried . . . feelings that were on their way to manifesting dis-ease. This experience gave him the opportunity to release some of the old feelings he didn't even realize he had, let alone that he had hung on to all through the years. Needless to say, he was very, very grateful for this *tool*, and as his health continued to improve, along with other aspects of his life, he became one of the greatest supporters of the Script.

When I read *Love, Medicine and Miracles*, by Dr. Bernie Siegel, I reflected back on my husband's and my experiences that Spring of 1988. I was drawn like a magnet to the part of his book that talked about leukemia:

> Depression as defined by psychologists generally involves quitting or giving up. Feeling that present conditions and future possibilities are intolerable, the depressed person 'goes on strike' from life, doing less and less, and losing interest in people, work, hobbies, and so on. [This was a perfect description of what had taken place with my husband.]
>
> Such depression is strongly linked with cancer. Dr. Bernard Fox of Boston, for example, found that depressed men are twice as likely to get cancer as non-depressed men. A study of identical twins, one of whom in each pair had leukemia, showed that the one with the disease had become severely depressed or suffered an emotional loss before-hand, while the healthy twin had not.

In *The Will to Live*, Arnold Hutschnecker tells us that depression is a partial surrender to death, and that cancer seems to be despair experienced at the cellular level. He tells us that the mind does not act only through our conscious choices. Many of its effects are realized directly in the body's tissues, without any awareness on our part. He points out some of our common expressions: "She's a pain in the neck/ass." "Get off my back." "This problem is eating me alive." "You're breaking my heart."

The body responds to the mind's conditioned messages whether they are conscious or unconscious. Generally, these may be either *live* or *die* messages. Dr. Hutschnecker is convinced we not only have survival mechanisms, such as the fight-or-flight response, but we also have a "die" mechanism that actively stops our defenses, slowing the body's functions and bringing us toward death when we feel our life is not worth living.

May I tell you that the first time I read a list of probable emotional causes of physical illness, I became indignant! To think that someone would have the audacity to insinuate that I feel such and such, thereby causing the particular health problems I had been plagued with during my life. This was almost more than I could tolerate and accept. I literally threw down the list and walked off in a huff! "It's totally impossible," I thought for over a week, "that feelings could cause a person's health problems." (What I didn't understand at this point was that these feelings were either hidden or unconsciously buried.) Well, it (this new idea) wouldn't leave me alone, nor would the idea go away. So, I decided I had better look at it squarely. When I finally did, I had to admit there was definitely a lot more truth to the theory than I could have possibly imagined.

The following list may indicate one or several possible feelings for a dis-ease or ill-ness. It doesn't mean that you have to be bothered by all those feelings. You may only feel one out of five, or you may feel two or three. Keep in mind that these feelings are usually on a sub-conscious level. Whatever your feelings are, or whatever you recognize as being a part of you, take those feelings through the Script. Remember, these feelings have probably been buried for a long, long time, completely covering over the memory of perfection in your cells, so you may have become totally numb to them. To realize results requires *owning* whatever feelings you can identify, and processing them through the Script.

Thankfully, you may have experienced health problems that have been treated successfully. But, as Barbara Ann Brennan so strongly suggests and states in her book, *Hands of Light*, . . . "if the 'inner' healing is not also done and the faulty belief system not challenged, illness will again precipitate into the physical body, even after present symptoms have been removed."

In other words, symptoms of an illness may be removed, but in order to achieve a complete resolution of that illness, an "inner" healing and changing of belief systems must take place before the dis-ease is eradicated.

To accomplish this, look at the illness list; locate the feelings that could be the probable cause for you. Then go through the Script stating those probable feelings, and replace them with appropriate opposite feelings.

The following are two examples of how to process the feelings indicated for the first illness on the list.

Examples

1. ". . . locate the origin of feelings that cause my incorrect use of judgment or my incorrect use of wisdom." A possible replacement would be, "I choose opening my mind and heart to truth. I feel to open my mind and heart to truth. I am opening my mind and heart to truth. I choose accepting truth. I feel like accepting truth. I am accepting truth. I choose making correct decisions. I feel to make correct decisions. I am making correct decisions. I accept truth with all my heart." Then finish the Script.

2. ". . . locate the origin of my feelings that cause me to identify with my possessions and have little sense of self." Replace with something like, "I choose finding my own identity. I feel like finding my own identity. I am finding my own identity. I feel a great sense of self. I feel love and respect for myself. I am loving and honoring myself just the way I am." Then finish the Script.

Probable Feelings Causing Ill-ness

Abdominal Area:

Incorrect use of judgment (wisdom)

Identifies with possessions and has little sense of self

Feeling possessive of someone

Worrying about others/needs introspection to change self

Feels responsible for giving understanding, help and encouragement

Feeling undue tension, fear & anxiety which constricts the energy
flow

Disharmony and bondage in relationships

Bound up in present fears and not trusting

Abscess:

Seething; unresolved hurt feelings

Wanting revenge

Festering feelings

Stagnation

Holding on to an old concept

Accidents:

High levels of stress

Tense and worried

Feeling a need to punish self

Feelings of resistance towards authority

Feeling defenseless

Unable to take a stand—wishy-washy

Feeling of being in the wrong place

No feeling of purpose (Aimless)

Aches:

Feeling of being all alone

Feeling separated from source of love

Feeling that *nobody loves me*

Aching to be held and loved

Feeling efforts have been thwarted

Feelings of sadness

Acne:

Feelings of guilt

Feelings of self-rejection/dislike of self

Disowning what is happening in life—"Denial"

Unwilling to face up to issues

Addictions:

Distorted memory in the DNA

Unable to think rationally

Unable to perceive clearly & correctly

Disapproval of self/running from self

Feelings of self-rejection

Feelings of despair

Feeling a void in the Soul

Wanting to avoid feeling

Addison's Disease:

Lacks understanding of self/no sense of self

Anger at the self

Inability to understand own emotions

Feels no mercy for self

Adenoids:

Acute disharmony in the home

Feels restricted in life/in breathing

Child feels unaccepted or hostility from someone

Feels unwelcome, in the way

Adrenal Problems:

Feels defeated

Feels like a victim

No belief in self

"Don't care what happens to me" attitude

Lack of courage

Feelings of anxiety

Misusing the will

Subconscious belief that life must have burdens

Being disloyal to self

Unresolved jealousies & fears

Feels that one must struggle for success, power or position

Aging Problems:

Inability to accept NOW

Fear of being one's self

Long standing unresolved negative feelings

Agoraphobia:

Not using/unable to use the power of discernment

AIDS:

Feeling defenseless & hopeless

Feels nobody cares

Belief of "not good enough"

Denial of the self

Extreme deep-rooted anger

Negative thoughts against yourself

Lack of inner peace

Alcoholism:

Inability to cope/futility/"What's the use?" attitude

Feelings of worthlessness/self-rejection

Feelings of living a lie/guilt/inadequacy

Locked in by unresolved negative emotions

Locked in by believing the negative words of others

Protecting against feelings one is afraid to feel

Worried/bothered by lack of communication with others

Allergies:

Suppressed weeping

Imitation substitute for colds

Feelings that don't seem to have an answer to change

Fear of sharing feelings with people

Feeling stifled

Denying own power

Feeling aggravated by someone or something

Alzheimer's Disease:

Tired of coping

Can't face life anymore

Feels unable to be in control of own life

Feelings of inferiority & insecurity

Suppressed anger

Wants to live in own little world

Feelings of hopelessness & helplessness

Amnesia:
Unable to be assertive/to stand up for self
Wanting to escape life's problems/running from life
Fear of the future

Anemia:
Angry at self for inability to control things
Feeling life is not going the way I want
Feelings of "I'm not enough"
Not loving yourself
Manipulative but resentful if being manipulated
Devoted/possessive of someone else
Feels there is no joy
Lack of order in life

Anemia: (Pernicious)
Feelings of total helplessness
Have given up
Deep, unresolved grief

Ankles:
Fears falling or failing
Inflexibility
Instability in present situation

Swollen:
Feeling overworked, but can't quit
Feels there is no relief from pressures in life

Anorectal Bleeding:
Anger
Frustration

Anorexia:
Feels totally unable to please parent (usually mother)
Feels unable to live up to expectations of others
Feelings of self-rejection/self-hatred
Lack of spiritual understanding/of knowing yourself
Don't know how to love self or be self
Your soul wants to leave (self-destruction)

Aneurysm:
Dealing daily with more responsibility than the body can handle

Not facing the need to change day to day situation

Feels the need to be everything to everyone all the time

Anus:

Survival is threatened by outer conditions

Feeling powerless in some area

Anxiety:

Feels unable to "call the shots" in life

Feels boxed in

Feels helpless to affect a change

Apathetic:

"Spark of life" has been turned off

Doesn't want to feel

Appendicitis:

Undue fears about life

Unable to deal with fear: energy flow is constricted

Wanting something but feel you can't obtain it

Appetite:

Loss of: Incorrect perceptions causing distrust & a form of depression

Excessive: Feeding the need for love, acceptance & protection

Arms:

Left: Not bringing enough spirituality to yourself

Right: Not doing enough physically for yourself

Arteries - Hardening:

Fears being disappointed

Hard-hearted

Being dictatorial

Feeling obstructed or delayed in life

Unresolved feelings obscuring the flow of life

Perfectionism

Arteriosclerosis:

Long-standing inability to express feelings and emotions

Unable to see the good

Layers of unresolved feelings built up inside

Refusing to be open-minded

Worried about not being perfect

Arthritis:
Severely criticizing self or others
Holding onto feelings of hostility
Holding onto own opinions & beliefs
Long term tension or anger in life
Feelings of anxiety and/or
Depression endured over long periods of time
Belief that it's wrong to get angry which creates:
Repressed anger that *eats you up*
Need to be *right*
Rigid in thinking & feelings
Uncompromising attitude
Inflexibility

Arthritis - Rheumatoid:
Body is receiving conflicting messages, like:
Laughing on the outside, but crying on the inside
Feels totally helpless in ability to change life's burdens

Asthma:
Reliving childhood fears
Need for dependence
Chronic anxiety & fear
Unconscious dependency wishes
Feeling dominated by a parent
Wanting to protest, but unable
Being over-sensitive
Suppressed sorrow or crying
Feelings of being stifled
Not satisfied with yourself

Autoimmune System:
Laughing on the outside, but crying on the inside
Feels totally helpless
Have given up
Deep seeded/seated grief

Back Problems:
Feeling no support
Can't cope with emotional difficulties

Feeling burdened emotionally

Feelings of frustration

Wanting someone to "get off my back"

Back - Upper:

Feels unsupported or burdened emotionally

Withholding your love from others

Feeling agitated or anxious

Feelings of frustration

Back - Middle:

Feeling guilty

Lacking self-support

Lacking in self-confidence

Back - Lower:

Feels unsupported financially

Experiencing fear where money is concerned

Wanting to back out of something

In a relationship that hurts

Running away from a situation

Bad Breath:

Worrying instead of priority planning

Reacting to plans that have gone awry

Bedwetting:

Feelings of fear toward parent (usually father)

Unconscious anger

Don't know how to get what you want

Need for attention

Bladder Problems:

Repression of sexual feelings

Inharmonious male & female emotional relationships

Sexual identity going unexpressed

Unable to release things or ideas no longer needed

Feels over concerned with survival issues (money, job, health)

Lack of order or obsessed with order

Yearning

Bleeding Gums:

Inability to feel joy over decisions

Blisters:
Feeling unprotected emotionally
Resisting the flow of life
Staying in a habit that irritates you

Bloating:
Feeling stuck in your life situation
Unable to change what you don't like/have to live with it
Unable to express your true feelings (you swallow them)

Boils:
Letting out stirred up feelings
Something stagnant finally coming to a head

Blood Disorders:
Root cause: Lack of pure self-love & love for others
Feeling powerless in some area of life
Feelings of deep anger
Feelings of long-standing ill will
Intense depression

Blood Problems:
Not feeling joy in life
Stagnant thinking
Unable to flow with life
Feelings of fear

Bones: (Broken)
Feelings of separation
Feelings of resentment going unresolved
Rebelling
The feeling nature is very obstinate or fixed

Bone Problems:
Resisting authority
Internally punishing self

Bowels:
Fear of displeasing a loved one
Fear of releasing the old that is no longer useful
Fearful of not having ample means
Unable to control outer situation; tries to control a substitute

Unwillingness to relinquish control
Inability to eliminate possessive attitudes

Bowel - Irritable Syndrome:

Not being open about what you really feel
Holding back
Loss of enthusiasm & drive

Brain:

Extreme nervousness
High anxiety
Feeling unable to control life
Not open to what you really feel.
Holding back/keeping things to yourself
Not relaxed enough to give of your knowledge

Breasts:

Conflict of worthiness
Denying individual worth
Feels conflict in nurturing ability
Not nurturing yourself

Bronchitis:

Extreme disharmony in the home
(A baby always feels the disharmony is their fault)
Wanting to be able to change things, but can't
Wanting to be in charge, but can't

Bruises:

Feels a need to punish self
Not resolving feelings toward a certain situation

Bulimia:

Mistaken self-image
Inability to accept self
Feelings of no control over one's self
Unsatisfied needs never met
Feelings of self-contempt
Feels unable to measure up to others expectations
Need for spiritual growth

Bunions:

Constant & chronic fear

Being stubborn and inflexible in your direction

Bursitis:

Feelings of anxiety

Feelings of anger which have been repressed

Feel you have lost control

Feeling helpless to change a situation

Tension built up

Holding back hitting someone

Frustrated with the flow of life

Calluses:

Inability to flow with life

Not wanting to circulate & be open to new learning

Cancer: A FORM OF SELF-DESTRUCTION

Of blood-Leukemia: Intense depression, anger or ill will

Lack of pure love for self & others

Of cervix: Repressed anger

Of female organs:

Repressed anger (Usually at male authority figures)

Feeling an emptiness in life

Unresolved resentments

Feelings of hostility being suppressed

Rejecting the self

Feelings of despair

Feelings of loneliness being repressed

Poor relationship with parents

Inability to cope with a traumatic loss

Feelings of hopelessness/helplessness being repressed

Mental depression

Holding on to deep anger, resentment, hate, revenge or jealousy

Not open to "light' or divine help

Subconscious death wish—no desire to live

Cancer - Skin: A form of destruction due to-

Feeling inadequate or unworthy

Cancer - Small of Back: Continual inside strife, but appearing happy

Carrying life's burdens

Unresolved emotional burdens

Cancer - Stomach: Feelings of condemnation & hatred
Feelings of malice
Feelings of wanting to get even
Unforgiveness

Candida:

Begins with doubting your Self
Resentment multiplying inside
Inability to claim ones own power
Unresolved negative feelings molding in the body
Continually blaming others on a sub-conscious level

Canker Sores:

Unresolved negativity
Overwork coupled with emotional stress
Emotional upset
Anxious over details

Carpel Tunnel:

Feeling that life isn't fair
Inability to claim ones own power
Feeling justice is never served in your behalf

Cardiovascular Disorder:

Driven to compete, achieve and acquire material wealth
Feelings of agitation and impatience
Wanting matters to move more quickly
Low self-esteem

Chest:

Belief & emotional center
Unidentified unresolved fears
Not feeling approval
Inability to claim ones own power
Lack of self love
Feelings of being unprotected
Hurts where love is concerned

Childhood Disease:

Child responding to mother's feelings
Feelings of helplessness
Emotional needs not being met

Feeling shoved aside

Cholesterol:
Belief that "I'm not supposed to be happy"
Denying self joy

Chronic Diseases:
Distrusts the process of life
Unwilling to change for the better

Chronic Fatigue Syndrome:
Feeling totally alone
Feelings of desolation
Feelings of despair
Feeling hopeless/"It's no use"
Tired of trying to prove yourself
Low self-worth
Has lost the will to live

Circulation Problems:
Feeling overloaded
Not enjoying job, but can't quit or let go
Feelings of tension & discouragement
Feeling "I must prove myself, but how?"
Putting yourself down
Love of self and others drives circulation

Colds:
Unkind feelings toward someone
Confusion in the home
Confusion in life
Belief in seasonal sickness

Cold Sores: (Fever Blisters)
Inability to express anger
Feeling pressured or burdened by responsibilities
Unable to cope with pressures of life
Feeling resentful of the load you are carrying
Not wanting to accept specific news

Colic:
Not happy with surroundings
Feelings of irritation

Feelings of impatience

Colitis:

Overly concerned with order (lose freedom)

Worrying excessively

Feelings of oppression

Feelings of defeat

Feeling a need for more affection

Colitis - Ulcerative:

Often manifest in those with obsessive-compulsive behavior

Indecisiveness

Feelings of anxiety

Unable to express hostility or anger to whom you feel it

Feels a need to conform

Feels like a martyr

Colon:

Bottled up hate

Ascending: Not being generous to yourself (need to be)

Transverse: Not being open/truthful with self or others

Descending: Unable to be relaxed within yourself

Color Blind:

Unable to see things the way they are

Concussion:

Not wanting to know something you need to hear

Needing to accept new insights

Conjunctivitis:

Feelings of frustration at what you see in life

Feelings of anger towards life

Not seeing the perfection in people & life

Constipation:

Constantly fretting

Unwilling to release old feelings & beliefs

Resisting the flow of life

Blocking what you want to say

Feelings of anxiety

Unresolvable problems/determined to carry on

Corns:
Holding onto hurts of past experiences
Hardened feelings

Coughs:
Nervousness
Feelings of criticism
Feelings of annoyance
Feels present conditions & future possibilities are intolerable
Feel like you're choking on life

Cramps:
Fear of pain
Holding onto incorrect perceptions of femininity
Tension built up
Feelings of guilt about what you have or haven't done

Cysts:
Feeling sorry for self
Inability to resolve hurt feelings

Cystic Fibrosis:
The belief that "life works for everyone but me"

Cystitis:
Unresolved irritability
Habitual unhappy thought patterns
Burning feelings inside
Can't get what you want

Dandruff:
Feels a strong need to have things done a certain way
Impatient with the way others do things
Self-acceptance is being blocked

Deafness:
Not wanting to hear what is going on
Lack of self-love
Feeling of poor self-worth
Wanting to be isolated
Feels more comfortable in own little world

Dementia:

Feeling hopeless & helpless

Tired of having to struggle with life

Unresolved anger

Depression:

Feeling "I'll never be able to be enough or do enough"

Feeling "It's no use"

Feeling "Things are beyond my control"

Hopeless/helpless feeling

Feels like quitting or giving up on life

Anger turned inward

Insufficient exposure to sunlight (usually in Winter) can also cause depression

Diabetes:

Judging self or others severely

Disappointed in life

On-going feelings of sorrow

Emotional shock

Joy of life is gone

Feeling "It should have been different"

Obsessed with wanting to control

Ashamed of something you did in the past

Diarrhea:

Rejecting the visualization of something you don't want to accept

Wanting to be done with someone or something

Running away from a situation

Fear of something in the present

Obsessed with order

Giving up your goals when unable to have what you desire

Diverticulitis:

Having a difficult time being sociable

Won't express your true feelings

Dizziness:

Lack of solid self-direction

Ego wants to be the boss

Not taking personal time for self

"Going around in circles" due to being unorganized

Feeling overloaded

Feeling "I don't want to cope anymore"

Not wanting to accept things as they are

Dowagers Hump:

Unresolved anger

Built up resentment

Carrying others burdens

Dry Eye:

Unable to express grief

Feelings turned off

Incorrect perceptions from early years; keeping tears from flowing

Dysentery:

Fear of the present

Cannot face what is going on

Hate what you are seeing

Feeling unjustly dealt with

Need to have empathy, be generous, honest, relaxed & open

Dysmenorrheal:

Feelings of anger toward self

Inability to forgive self

Ears:

Hearing corresponds to the understanding

Intolerance

Impatience

Feels nobody is listening to you, OR-

You don't want to listen to others

Hearing problems:

Trying to force someone to hear things your way

What are the advantages of not hearing?

Wax: Does not want to hear about new things

Infection: Stagnating, impatience, not tolerating new information

Earache: Feelings of anger at what you are hearing

Can't tolerate new information

Don't want to hear what is going on

Children: Can't abide the turmoil in home

Eczema:

Over-sensitive

Feel you are being interfered with or prevented from doing something, thus feeling frustrated

Unresolved hurt feelings

Unresolved feelings of irritation

Edema:

Sympathy for self, keeping you from moving too fast

Body's way of putting on a cast

Feeling a need to be immobilized in some area of body

Holding onto something that is not necessary

Elbow:

Inability to accept new experiences

Inability to change focus

Resisting achievement or sense of confidence

Elimination Problems:

Deep subconscious resentments

Holding on to past experiences

Not letting go, which creates blockages

Tension built up

Emphysema:

Feeling unworthy to live

Fears taking in life to the fullest

Unable to be yourself

Endocrine System:

Drastic imbalances in life

Endometriosis:

Deep-seeded unresolved sadness going unanswered

Feelings of frustration

Feelings of insecurity

Lack of self-love

Wanting to blame problems on others

Lacking in understanding of self

Dwelling in old limiting concepts

Energy: (continual lack of)
  Unresolved deep-seeded sadness
  Tired of the day to day struggle
  Wishing you could "quit"

Epilepsy:
  Feeling a need to persecute self
  An inability to accept how you do things
  Wanting to reject life
  Violence against the self

Eyes:
  Retina represents your feelings; Fovea represents your thinking.
    They need to work together for proper vision. When we are not
    single-minded they begin to separate.
  Not wanting to understand what you are seeing
  Not seeing the truth
  Fearing the future
  Not wanting to see life as it is
  Life is weak and out of focus
  Not seeing eye to eye with another
  Not forgiving
  Inability to see ones own self-worth
  Bags under: Holding on to old inaccurate concepts
  Blinking (uncontrolled)*:* Always running out of time, which causes:
  Not wanting to see what you haven't done
  Wasting time in between opportunities
  Cataracts: Not wanting to see the future
  Not seeing any future for yourself
  Failing to share your knowledge or skills
  Circles under: Bitterness
  Resentment/hurt
  Self-condemnation
  Feeling unfulfilled
  Deep-seeded grief
  Remorse/regret
  Glaucoma: Protracted hostility
  Itching: Feel you're not doing what is best for you

Not seeing what needs to be done
Feel you aren't doing a good job
Sty: Not seeing the best in another person
Unresolved anger towards someone
Hanging on to feelings of resentment
Watery: Unable to express an inner grief
Unable to say what you would like to

Eyelids:

Flaky skin: Feeling inadequate or unworthy
Unable to say what you feel
Protruding: Resenting change
Do not want to voice how you feel
Red: Not speaking truth of what you see
Feeling resentment because of this

Face:

Has to do with identity
Forehead: Reacting to recent conscious thoughts
Paralysis: Judging self harshly
Putting self down in favor of others
Feeling rejected
Feeling fear and anxiety
Having doubts about own competence
Can't *face* a situation, someone or something
Afraid of *losing face*
Problems with relationships

Fainting:

Fear of the present
Feeling unable to cope
An excuse to blank out
Not facing what you need to learn
Nothing to look forward to

Falling Over:

Not sure of self
Insecure within

Fallopian Tubes: (Blocked)

Nervous tension of long duration

High-strung temperament

Fat:

Feel a need for protection

Resistance to forgiving

Hidden anger

Fatigue:

Resisting life

Feeling bored

Not enjoying your place in life

Experiencing "burn out" in one's job or relationship

Feet:

Not liking the direction you are going

Fear of the future

Fear of stepping forward in life

Pigeon-toed: Inhibited in your direction

Pointed outward:

> *Left foot* - Fear of spiritual direction

> *Right foot* - Fear of physical/material direction

Toes curled under: Unbalanced direction

Feeling inferior

Walking on insides: Fear facing what needs to be done

Difficulty in planting feet squarely on ground

Walking on sides: Not feeling solid in your direction

Lack of understanding in many aspects of life

Female Problems:

Emotional block where own sexuality is concerned

Feeling inadequate in sexual role

Feelings of fear or guilt about sex

Refusing to "let go" of the past

Rejecting feminine nature

Emotional block where mate is concerned

Fever:

Feelings of anger unable to be expressed

Feelings of resistance

Emotionally "burning up" about something

Being affected by lack of order

Holding onto the past

Fibromyalgia: (See Chronic Fatigue Syndrome)

Fibroid Tumors & Cysts:

The ego has been injured

Unexpressed & unresolved hurts

Fingers: (Fussing over details of life)

Thumb: Affected by Worry, Depression, Hate, Anxiety,
Guilt & Self-protection

Index: Affected by Fear & Resentment

Middle: Affected by Anger, Bitterness & Sexuality

Ring: Affected by grief & Inability to flow with life

Little: Affected by Pretense, Deceit & Unforgiveness

Fingernails:

Biting: Wanting to destroy oneself

Resisting authority

Over-analyzing tiny details

(See Nail biting)

Flu:

Fear

Belief in the worst happening to you

Belief in mass negativity

(See Immune System)

Frigidity:

Unresolved fears, resentments or guilt having to do with sex and
sexual relationships

Fixations, complexes or neurotic attachments affecting emotional
nature

Fungus:

Inability to let go of the past

Allowing the past to rule the now

Hanging on to old concepts/can't change

Gallbladder:

Feelings of bitterness

Feelings of anger

Wanting to force things

Gallstones:
Feelings of bitterness
Feelings of condemnation
Being unyielding
Feelings of pride
Refusing to forgive

Gangrene:
Morbidity running wild
Unresolved poisonous feelings
Inability to love self with enthusiasm

Gastritis:
Feelings of uncertainty
Feelings of anxiety

Gingivitis:
Fears own incapability
Putting off doing things/responsibilities

Glandular Problems:
Living in the past
Long term inappropriate feelings
Unresolved feelings that have created gross imbalance

Goiter:
Feeling unfulfilled
Feelings of *being used*
Feel purposes have been thwarted

Gout:
Judging others harshly
Feelings of impatience
Feelings of anger held inside
Rejecting others or world around you
Wanting to dominate or control others

Growths:
False sense of pride
Unresolved anger and resentments
Inability to accept Divine help
Spiritual understanding & values out of balance

Nursing buried hurts

Gum Problems:

Not carrying out decisions once they are made

Bleeding: Pressuring yourself to quit procrastinating

Hair:

Crown Baldness: Feelings of unworthiness

Difficulty/inadequately accepting self

Dry: Unaware that you can achieve

Holding back

Don't know self

Feelings of inadequacy

Falling out: Unable to be flexible in changing your thinking

Not using your own power

Relying on others for your sense of security/safety

Graying--Back of head: Not accepting yourself

Front of head: Not believing in what you do and say, which--

Changes your perception of yourself

Overnight: Shock from letting go of your power

Receding: Feeling inadequate and/ or worthless

Hands:

Has to do with the ability to grasp or let go of ideas

Left: Receiving or being passive

Right: Giving, reaching out or acting aggressively

Fearing new ideas

Fearing lack of opportunities

Hands have the ability to give or grab; explore or push away, hold on
    or let go; caress or punch

Hands - Arthritis:

Rigid, perfectionist or controlling personality

Severe self-criticism and criticism of others

Inflexible feelings repressed & mirrored in the hands

Hands - Cramps: Conflict over ability & how to communicate it

Feels unable to communicate well verbally

Hands - Sweaty: Fears making mistakes

Fears appearing incompetent or foolish

Hay Fever:

Unresolved feelings of rage or fear
Unresolved feelings of grief or sadness
Repressed tears held back
Repressed aggression
Wanting to *get even*
Feelings of guilt
Not satisfied with self

Headaches:

Tension & stress

Inability to resolve emotional upsets
Hurt feelings going unexpressed
Feelings of inner pressure working on you
Feeling unable to control
Feelings of fear & anxiety getting the best of you
Unpleasant relationships
Inability to face an issue
Manifesting the need to laugh, sing, praise & express gratitude
Impatience with self that you haven't done enough

Frontal

Holding on to old limitations
Not seeing the good in anything
Feeling you're better than other people

Heart Problems:

Violating the laws of love; knowingly or unknowingly
Feelings of compassion or rejection being blocked
Feelings of resentment and/or hurt
Not feeling approval from others
Upsetting family problems
Has a difficult time forgiving (including self)
Wanting release from responsibility
In a relationship that hurts

Hemorrhoids:

On-going feelings of being burdened
Feeling pressured or anxious
Feeling fear or tension

Inability to let go

Hepatitis:

Not wanting to change

Feelings of anger

Feelings of fear

Feelings of hate

Hernia:

Angry with what's happening in your life

Feelings of being burdened

Punishing self

Herpes:

Feelings of guilt

Feelings of shame

Feelings of anxiety

Feelings of anger

Herpes-Simplex Virus:

Not allowing yourself to be the *love* that you are

Lack of inner peace

Feelings of guilt, shame, anxiety and/or anger

Wanting to speak words of bitterness

Wanting to complain royally

Hips:

Fears making major decisions

Has nothing to look forward to

Lack of emotional & physical self-support

Hip joint: Not wanting to accept present experiences

Non-acceptance of physical experiences

Hives:

Small hidden fears

Fears that are finally surfacing

Feeling mistreated

Inability to view things with the correct perspective

Anger—perceiving someone has inflexible behavior

Wanting to protest, but unable to

Hodgkin's Disease:

Inability to accept self

Frantic need to feel accepted

Feels a continual need to prove self

Huntington's Disease:

Feelings of resentment for inability to change others

Feelings of hopelessness & helplessness

Feelings of deep sorrow

Hyperactivity:

Always wanting needs to be met, but feels helpless to have it happen

Frustrated due to inability to feel peace

Hypertension: (High Blood Pressure)

Feels a strong need to be in control of everything

Allowing people or situations to bother you

Letting your emotions and reactions rule you

Not minding your own business/interfering with others

Hyperthyroidism:

Feelings of rage for being overlooked

Hyperventilation:

Distrusting the flow of life

Feelings of resistance to life and it's uncertainties

Hypoglycemia:

Feelings of overwhelmed burdens

Feeling a lack of joy in life

Feel unsuccessful so pressure yourself to be successful

Hypotension: (Low Blood pressure)

Being more devoted to outside things than to yourself

Not loving yourself

Loss of enthusiasm and drive

Hypothalamus: Governs pituitary & pineal gland which in turn governs endocrine system

Feelings of rage

Feelings of insecurity

Feelings of displeasure

Feelings of sadness

Feelings of anxiety

Feeling restricted in some area of your life

Immune System:
Any feelings that go against your inner peace
Giving up
Inability to care (feeling) for others
Feeling that "everything is out of my control"
Feeling "there's no use trying anymore"
Feeling "I'm not enough"

Impotence:
Conflicting ideas about sex
Fear, resentments or guilt having to do with sex and sexual
    relationships
Unresolved fears towards mother
Psychic obsessions or sexual frustration
Emotional nature affected by complexes, fixations or neurotic
    attachments

Incontinence:
Weary of controlling the emotions
Overflowing emotions
Guilty of not being loyal to yourself

Incurable Disease:
Long standing condemnation of self & others
Need to forgive all situations & people of the past

Indigestion:
Feeling everyone is against you
Feel you need to fight your way through life
Feelings of anxiety
Fear of losing job; losing security
Lack of understanding what, how, when, where or why in life

Infection:
Feelings of hostility
Feelings of anger being manifested
Feelings of suspicion or annoyance

Inflammation:
Feelings of rage
Feelings of anger or fear

Influenza:
Believing the worst will happen to you
Fearing the worst

Injuries:
Feelings of guilt & a need to be punished
Feeling angry toward self, so needs to suffer

Insanity:
Unable to let go of old ideas or things of the past
Wanting to escape
Strong desire to separate or withdraw from life
Inability to cope
Wanting to flee from family

Insomnia:
Tensions in life
Deep seeded guilt
Feelings of fear & anxiety
Reaction to potential threatening situations
Worrying about being able/good enough to do what is needed

Intestinal Diseases:
Inability to assimilate & absorb the new in life
Wanting to live in the past
Desire to stay in comfort zone

Itching:
Desires gone unfulfilled
Having a difficult time accepting where you are in life
Wanting more than you are getting out of life
Feelings inadequate or unworthy

Jaw Problems: (T M J Syndrome)
Feelings of rage
Subconsciously wanting revenge
Inability to express how one feels

Joints:
Feelings of resentment
Suppressing hurt feelings

Jaundice:

Not allowing self or others to just "be"

Experiencing difficulty in loving self

Jet Lag:

Living in the past/Not in present time

Kidney Problems:

Extension of bladder but more severe

Insensitive to situations where caring & concern should be exhibited

Trying to control life

Being disloyal to self

Being over judgmental

Feeling emotional confusion

Deep subconscious resentments toward people & experiences
of the past

Unfounded criticism of others

Repressed emotions

Don't have a good relationship with yourself

Leaving your self out to please someone else

Kidney Stones: Hardened anger

Poor relationship with self & others

Knee Problems:

Unable to be flexible

Not wanting to bend, usually to authority

Ego gets in the way

Pride gets in the way

Stubborn—wanting own way

Knee - Left: Need to be more receptive to events

Feelings of insecurity

Experiencing unresolved stress

Knee - Right: Need to be more assertive

Not wanting to give in to authority

Knuckles:

Lack of flexibility in feeling nature

Lack of Acceptance

Inability to change viewpoint

Laryngitis:
Fears voicing opinions

Feelings of resentment toward authority

Repressed emotions & fears

Gripped anger

Irritation at someone or some situation

Left-Right Split:
Left: Spiritual direction/Feminine side/Protecting/Receiving/Taking side

Right: Physical direction/Masculine side/Fighting/Giving/Releasing side

Leg Problems:
Fear of moving ahead with life

Fear of change

Has difficulty in being resolute about issues

Inability to understand

Leg Paralysis:
Avoiding situation you don't like

Avoiding something you are afraid of

Leukemia:
Feelings of deep depression

Feelings of anger or ill will

Significant loss of a parent or a career position

Feelings of total helplessness

Giving up or quitting

Unable to express emotions

Feeling present conditions & future possibilities are intolerable

Feelings of despair & futility

Leukorrhea:
Sexual guilt

Feeling powerless

Feeling anger toward mate

Ligaments:
All about control

Controlling others or letting others control you, or-

Not being able to control yourself

Lips:

Cracked corners: Feelings of frustration
Can't say more for fear of saying wrong thing
Parched: Feeling frustrated at inability to impart knowledge

Liver: (Anger Center)

Feelings of unresolved anger
Feelings of resentment & pettiness
Being judgmental
Critical thoughts
Not forgiving self & others
Feelings of injustice & revenge
Feelings of self-condemnation
Feelings of regret over the past
Feelings of sadness
Being possessive

Lock Jaw:

Feelings of rage
Wanting to control
Inability to express how one feels

Lou Gehrig's Disease:

Unwillingness to accept self-worth
Denial of success

Lumps:

Feeling inadequate or unworthy
Not trusting yourself
Frustration at not moving forward in life
Feeling blocked

Lungs:

Feelings of grief
Not feeling approval
Hurts where love is concerned
Feels life is monotonous
Not being able to do things your way

Lupus:

Feelings of deep-seeded (seated) grief

Feels like "giving up"

Laughing on the outside, but crying on the inside

Lymphatic Vessels:

Breaking the laws of love

Breaking the laws of peace & joy

Resentment, hatred or anger built up inside

Lymph System:

Lack of enthusiasm

Unable to feel acceptance

Negative thoughts against yourself

Male Problems:

Feeling inadequate in sexual role

Refusing to let go of the past

Feeling guilt for sleeping around

Holding onto unpleasant memories of previous relationships

Feeling unfulfilled in love

Mastoiditis: (Most often in children)

Not wanting to hear what is happening in surroundings

Fears that affect the understanding

Feeling left out

Memory: (Lack of)

Feel others aren't interested in what you know

Don't feel valued

Meningitis:

Not open to new insights

Feels to know it all

Menopause:

Fears this time of life & getting older

Fears being rejected

Feeling useless

Hot flashes: False belief that they can't be avoided

Anger at not having control of own body

Menstrual Problems:

Unresolved feelings of guilt

Fears role as a woman

Feels no joy in being a woman

Migraine Headaches:
Unable to flow easily with life
Want to take things at own pace
Dislikes being pushed
Inability to handle pressure or stress for long periods
Pushing to control; wants to control

Mind:
Over analyzation
Fear of the unknown

Miscarriage:
Fears timing is "wrong"
Fears what the future will bring
Fears the responsibility of baby

Mononucleosis:
Feeling unloved
Feeling unworthy
Feelings of anger from not being appreciated

Moles:
Feeling inadequate or unworthy (usually generational)
Growths from false beliefs about the self
Can be congenital

Motion Sickness:
Fears not having control

Mouth Problems:
Resistant to change
Fears moving out of comfort zone
Opinionated

Multiple Sclerosis:
Unwilling to be flexible
Unreceptive to new ideas
Hard on self; blames self
Incorrect use of will
Unforgiving of self or others
Lack of communication with others

Muscles:
Feelings of guilt
Not performing to your standard
Unable to 'own' something you have or have not done

Muscle Cramps:
Stubborn nature
A willful attitude
Resists moving forward in life

Muscular-Skeletal Diseases: (Muscular Dystrophy)
A form of self-created paralysis to keep from hitting someone or
   moving forward
Deep seeded anger that has not been resolved
Feels "I must experience pain"

Myasthenia Gravis:
Laughing on the outside, but crying on the inside
Feelings of helplessness in being able to change conditions
Deep-seeded grief
Feels like giving up
Fears a change in life

Nail-Biting:
Unfulfilled desires
Feeling spiteful towards parents
Feelings of frustration

Narcolepsy:
Wishing you were somewhere else
Don't want to cope anymore
Weary of responsibilities
Wishing responsibilities would go away

Nausea:
Rejecting the visualization of something you don't want to see
Wishing an undesirable situation had never happened
Fear of something about to happen

Neck Problems:
Moving under pressure
Want to let feelings out but don't dare

Inflexible state of mind

Not wanting to yield to opinions you think are wrong

Non-acceptance & rejection of others

Nephritis:

Feelings of disappointment

Feelings of failure

Feeling life is unfair

Nerves:

Influenced by thoughts & feelings

How the body communicates within

Parasympathetic:

Holding onto things or people of the past that need releasing

Need to be congruent in your communication with self

Nervous Breakdown:

Inability to communicate true feelings

Fear of the future

Not recognizing/accepting own power

Nervousness:

Inability to communicate feelings adequately

Fear of the future

Feelings of anxiety

Confused thinking

Neuritis.

Feeling of being irritated without your consent

Your power is negated because of being irritated

Neurosis:

Feeling of overload; pressures in life too hard to bear

Feeling there is no letting up; "can't quit"

Nodules:

Feelings of frustration & resentment

Feel you always have to prove yourself

Ego feels in jeopardy

Nose:

Bleeds: Feeling overlooked

Blocked: Not enjoying life

Broken: Rebelling against learning due to resentment

Bulbous: Continually going against your feelings
Compromising your principles
Runny: Crying on the inside; wanting help, or running away from
unwanted responsibility
Stuffy: Not accepting your worth; Desire for love; Impatience;
Unwilling to just be your Self
Numbness: Not expressing love; Not expressing consideration

Obesity:
Using food as a substitute for affection
Inability to admit to self or others what you really desire
Inability to express true feelings
Seeking love
Protecting the body
Trying to fulfill the self
Stuffed feelings

Osteomyelitis:
Feeling a lack of support
Feeling frustrated with life
Feeling angry at life

Osteoporosis:
Feeling totally unsupported in life

Ovaries:
Feelings of loneliness
Desire to feel love and respect
Feeling inadequate in sexual role

Over-Eating: (Compulsive)
Tension
Feeling a material-emotional lack
Craving closeness
Putting on emotional armor
A symbol of power & desire to throw one's weight around
Emotional energy based on anger & resentment

Overweight:
Feelings of insecurity
Feelings of self-rejection
Wanting to protect the body

Seeking love & fulfillment
Attempting to fulfill the self
Feelings are being stuffed inside
Unexpressed, mis-perceived & inappropriate feelings

Pain:

God trying to get your attention
Repressed anger & frustration
In a relationship that hurts
Feelings of guilt
Indicating that something is imbalanced

Palsy:

Feeling stagnant in life
Feel you can't move forward

Pancreas:

Feelings of judgment
Feelings of guilt
Low self-esteem
Suppressing laughter
Incorrect use of ego
Feels the joy of living is gone/not allowing joy
Ashamed of something you have done

Paralysis:

Feeling overwhelmed by responsibilities
Sub-consciously wanting to escape
Resisting life
Fear of the future

Paralyzed Arms:

Left arm: Difficulty in receiving from others
Right arm: Difficulty in giving to others
Resistance to an unexplained hardness of will
Tension of the mind

Parathyroid:

Unresolved anger

Parkinson's Disease:

Not understanding a fear you have, which-
Stops you from believing in what you do and say

Lack of inner communication

Wanting full control

Fears not being able to control

Pelvis:

Unable to remain grounded or focused in emotional activity

Relates to holding on to sexual feelings

Peptic Ulcer:

Feels a lack of self-worth

Feels responsible for pleasing everyone

Phlebitis:

Feelings of being trapped

Feeling there is no way out

Feels life's immediate problems can't be solved

Pimples:

Unresolved frustrations

Hidden anger surfacing

Dislike of self

Pineal Gland:

Corresponds with inner seeing & hearing

Refusing to receive understanding & enlightenment

Misusing faith

Pink-Eye:

Feelings of frustration

Feelings of anger at present situation

Wanting to obscure what is going on around you

Pituitary Gland:

Continually picturing ill health or sickness

Feelings of being a constant recipient of bad luck/misfortune

Not being able to see good in all things

Plantar Wart:

Frustrated about life & the future

Deep seeded anger

Pleurisy:

Feelings of antagonism

Feelings of hostility

Lack of enthusiasm for what you are doing

Pneumonia:
Weary of life
Deep emotional hurts that have not healed
Feelings of desperation

Post-Nasal Drip:
Crying on the inside
Feelings of inner grief
Feeling you are a victim

Premenstrual Syndrome: (PMS)
Relinquishing power to others
Rejecting the feminine aspect of self

Prostate Problems:
Ideas are in conflict about sex
Refusing to let go of the past
Fear of aging
Feels like throwing in the towel
Prostate Cancer: Repressed anger at being restricted

Psoriasis:
Emotional insecurity
Holding onto feelings/fears that go against you
Not speaking your truth with love
Unwilling to be accountable for own feelings
Unresolved, deep-seeded hurt feelings surfacing

Pyorrhea:
Angry at self for not being able to make decisions

Rash:
Being irritated by something or someone
Unable to flow with life

Respiratory Problems:
Not feeling approval
Lack of love
Fears living life to the fullest

Rheumatism:
Feelings of resentment & wanting revenge

"I'm a victim" syndrome

Long-standing bitterness

Has a problem loving self & others

Right-Left Split:

Right Side: Physical direction/ Masculine side/
Fighting/Giving/Releasing side

Left Side: Spiritual Direction/ Feminine side/
Protecting/Receiving/Taking side

Sacroiliac Problems:

Feel you're in the wrong place (job, city, relationship, etc.)

Sciatica:

Mental anxieties regarding creative abilities

Sexual abnormality or frustration

Over-concerned with money issues

Disregarding your own desires

Being double-minded

Salivary Gland: (Sublingual Gland)

Not following through with your insights

Senility:

Inability to stay in the present

Longing to return to security of by-gone years

Wanting to control those around you

Not willing to change your life

Don't want to be in the situation you're in

Unhappy with this time of life

Sex Organs:

Feelings of apathy

Feeling separated

Shins:

Not being true to ideals & values

Shingles:

Fear things won't work out the way you want

Over-sensitive

On-going tension concerning a situation

Hostile energy being manifest
(Herpes Zoster) Lack of inner peace
Recurring problem of unworthiness

Shoulders: (Our expressive part)
Bearing burdens that don't belong to you
Life is too great a burden to bear
Carrying stressful responsibilities
Lacking in courage
Hunched & Sloped: Feels life is a tough struggle
Round: Feelings of Hopeless/Helpless
Scoliosis: Inability to trust life
Right: Relates to financial
Left: Relates to family

Sickle Cell Anemia:
Feelings of inferiority

Sinus Trouble:
Trying to call the shots in someone else's life
Dominating possessive
Being irritated by a person close to you

Skin Disease:
Unresolved feelings of irritation
Unresolved feelings of criticism
Disturbed reactions over trivial things
Lack of security
Feelings of impatience
Feeling bored
Feeling unsettled

Skin Rashes:
Inner conflicts surfacing
Someone or something is irritating you
Feeling frustrated at not being able to accomplish something

Slipped Disc:
Feeling indecisive about life
Feeling no support in life

Snoring:
Refusal to eliminate old patterns
Not being devoted to self

Sore-Throat:
Feelings of anger going unexpressed
Other negative feelings going unexpressed

Spasms:
Thoughts & feelings of fear

Spastic Colon:
Intense feelings of insecurity
Unable to let go and flow with life

Spine: (Has to do with the ego)
Ego getting carried away in pride
Allowing your intellect to let you down
Afraid to live in your feelings
Feelings of shyness
Feelings of inferiority
Not supporting or standing up for yourself

Spinal Meningitis:
Unresolved feelings of rage
Inflammatory thoughts

Spleen:
Lack of self-love
Not being sincere with self and others due to lack of self-love
Not allowing self to feel others' love/feeling rejected
Emotional conflicts
Feelings of intense anger/antagonism
Feelings of agitation & melancholy

Sprains:
Feelings of resistance
Inability to change directions in life

Spur:
A build-up of resentment

Sterility:
Extreme nervous tension

Hard & cold in attitudes

Stiffness:
Inability to give

Inflexible in opinions & attitudes

Rigid feelings in whichever area it is in

Stomach Cancer:
Feelings of wanting to get even

Feelings of spite

Wanting revenge

Stomach Problems:
Our sense of security feels threatened

Fears new ideas

Lack of affection

Condemning the success of other people

Unhappy feelings

Stuttering:
Wanting to protest, but dares not

Feels inferior

Doesn't accept self

Unable to express self

Emotionally insecure

Having to always please authority figures

Stroke:
Rejecting life at a deep level

Extreme resistance

Impatience with self for not improving a situation

Impatient for not being able to perform like you want to

Self-violence

Feeling overloaded with the pressures of life

Feel like "giving up"

Sty:
Not seeing the best in another person

Unresolved feelings of anger toward someone

Hanging on to feelings of resentment

Suicidal:
Feeling totally unable to resolve life's problems
Feels there is no hope for tomorrow
Feeling "What's the use"
Feels "Everyone would be better off without me"

Swelling:
Holding onto negative feelings

Tailbone:
Unduly concerned with material needs & survival needs

Teeth:
Painful: Inability to be decisive
Upper: Not understanding the big picture
Lower: Impatience
Abscess: Procrastinating in carrying out plans

Tendons: (Knots in)
Mental poisons
Unwilling to accept full stature
Need to forgive self
Inflexibility in mind sets

Testicles:
Rejecting masculinity

Thalamus:
Impatience
Feeling criticized

Thighs:
Fat: Feelings of frustration about moving forward in life
Fear of the future

Throat:
Feelings of anger that have been restrained
Strong critical words have been spoken
Swallowed emotional hurts
Not having your own way
Feelings of confusion
Lack of discernment
Knowledge used unwisely

Thrush:
Feelings of anger for making incorrect choices

Thymus: Master Gland
Feeling persecuted

Feeling picked on

Feeling life is unfair

Feeling unprotected

Thyroid:
Conflict between the conscious & the subconscious

Lack of love for Self

Fears self-expression

Deep sense of frustration/anxiety

Lack of discernment

Tinnitus:
Refusing to hear ones inner voice

Not wanting to listen to higher laws

Intolerant

Toes:
Worrying about minor details of the future

Ingrown Toenail: Continually worrying

Guilt feelings about your right to move forward

Holding Self back

Tongue:
Not speaking truth

Inability to taste the beauty & joy of life

Tonsils:
Tense will

Repressed fear or anger

Irritation at someone or something

Not getting own way

Toxins:
Negative feelings and thoughts against yourself

Giving away your power

Tuberculosis:
Continual selfishness

Feeling possessive

Being cruel to others

Tumors: (False growths)

Suppressed emotional hurts

Holding onto feelings of hatred & anger

Feelings of remorse

Jealousy

Not trusting self or others

False sense of value & pride

Results from not forgiving & releasing (forgetting) resentment

Feeling of "No one cares"

Doesn't feel close to parents

Forgiveness & Love are the two greatest solvents

Ulcers:

Worrying over details

Conflict as to capability

Frustration at not having things go the way you want

Pressures are too much to bear

Feelings of anxiety, fear or tension

Seeking revenge

Feelings of conflict/helplessness/powerless

Underweight:

Worries/Fears

Distrusting life

Feeling extreme tension

Urinary Infections:

Putting blame on others for your problems

Allowing another to irritate you

Uterine Cancer:

Being 'ticked off' at the male gender

Repressed anger

Feeling like a martyr

Uterus:

Has to do with unresolved feelings towards mother

Negative feelings toward creative aspect of life

Vaginitis:
Feels sexual guilt

Feels a need to punish self

Feels a loss of someone or something loved

Varicose Veins:
Pronounced tension

Wanting to run away

Feelings of discouragement

Feelings of negativity & resistance

Feeling overburdened

Venereal Disease:
Feels a need to be punished

Feeling guilty about sexual activities

Viral Infections:
Bitterness & ugliness overshadowing the beautiful & good in life

Belief that "I get everything that comes along"

Vomiting:
Rejecting the visualization of what you don't want to accept

Feelings of disgust

Wanting to get rid of these emotions

Warts:
Refusing to see the beauty in life

Feelings of hate taking form

Built up feelings of inadequacy or unworthiness

Wrists:
Holding onto outmoded beliefs about life and self

Imbalanced in giving or receiving/doing 'overs' on one or the other

Yeast Infections:
Deep and unresolved resentments

Lack of self love

Inability to claim ones own power

Unable to love & support the self

Unable to accept the self

Not recognizing own needs

Chapter 19

Self-Fulfilling Prophecies, or The Words We Use, Use Us!

While being mindful of your feelings and thoughts, you would be wise to also be conscious and aware of the words you speak, as words have vibrational energy along with everything else. Words are spoken thoughts that are generated by your feelings. And the words you use, as well as the thoughts you think, definitely register in your cells—in your DNA.

In *Quantum Healing*, Dr. Chopra says, "You may not think you can talk to your DNA, but, in fact, you do continually." For instance, if a person is always saying, "I'm sick and tired of . . . ," they shouldn't be surprised if they are tired a lot or become sick.

Be careful of what you claim! If you are always calling the health condition your body is registering, YOURS . . . then you are faithfully claiming it! For instance, by saying "my cancer," "my varicose veins," "my diabetes," "my bad eyes," "my sore throat," "my allergies," etc. you actually command, or lay claim to the manifestation of that which you are calling yours. Instead, refer to the health condition you are experiencing as, "the cancer," "the problem with these eyes," "the varicose veins." Or, simply say, "This person is experiencing a sore throat."

I had a friend who was continually saying, "The words we use, use us." She drew my attention to the words I used that didn't truly express what I meant to say. After being reminded over and over again, she ultimately convinced me that I was not thinking about—or aware of—what I was saying. I was mindlessly using words out of mere habit. So, I decided to be more alert and vigilant in my speech and to say what I meant and mean what I said. This was a distinctly different experience for me. I actually began hearing how I talked for the first time in my life. My goal has been, since then, to be more succinct with the words I use in my communication.

Someone else I knew was always saying, "It nearly killed me," or "That just kills me." Then my response to her would be, "Please don't let it kill you." You've heard the expression, "I'm dying to see you." Another friend said this quite often. Again, I would say, "Please don't die," and I wasn't saying it to be funny, but I would say it in a humorous manner so as not to offend. At first, when I would comment or mirror back to them what they had said, these friends would look at me with a start, as if to ask, "Did I really say that?"

When bringing my friends' attention to the words they had just used, they quickly grasped and understood the message. They also knew there was no harm intended.

Many people stand in amazement when they realize how they talk, once they listen to what they say. Everyone willingly admits they didn't really mean what they said, ("It nearly killed me!") . . . it's just a figure of speech. Usually they will smile, correct themselves and finish what they were communicating—being a little more aware in their choice of words. Unfailingly, they will express appreciation for someone bringing their attention to their mindless words so they can be more aware of their own inner and outer communication.

At first, when we become mindful of the words we speak, it helps to have someone point out our slips of the tongue—our incongruencies.

Have you ever noticed how people use so many negative words to express positive feelings in communicating? For instance: When a person really wants something, they will habitually say, "I want it so BADLY, I can almost taste it!" This could cause you to wonder if the negative cancels out the positive of the statement. Instead of using the word *badly*, perhaps a more concise way to say it is, "I want it so MUCH."

Develop the habit of listening to what you say. And whenever you feel to say, "I am _____," be prudent, aware and mindful, because "I am" is extremely powerful. Be certain that that which you choose to manifest or come into your life, BE exactly what you desire when you say, "I am _____."

An example: If you could not comprehend what someone was discussing or talking about, instead of saying, "I'm so stupid!" (whether to yourself or aloud), say, instead, "It's not like me to miss details like that," or, "I'm usually smarter than that."

A relative of mine repeatedly said, "I don't understand, I don't understand." And you know what? Eventually he became very confused when someone would explain something to him, until it became more and more difficult for him to understand new information. He was rudely awakened when he realized what he had been programming himself to do. "I don't understand" had registered inside him so strongly that his mind responded to what he kept telling himself!

Can you see how this principle affects us all?

It would be advisable to keep in mind that EVERY WORD HAS A VIBRATORY ENERGY; therefore, it has power! And depending on the negativity or the positivity of the word(s), every word that leaves our mouth will have an effect for truth or for error, for good or for bad, for light or for darkness. Which side of the coin do we wish to represent on a daily basis?

In a real sense, when we use words to express ourselves that do not convey the message of our true intent, we are lying. We are being untruthful, false and deceitful (as lying is defined in the dictionary). Here again, our body's intelligence knows when truth is not honored and spoken. Conflict and imbalance occurs in the electrical system of our body when we use words to express ourselves that don't actually mean what we are saying and truly feeling. We literally short-circuit the electrical energy in our body, and the DNA becomes confused because it is receiving garbled messages.

How do we, as human Beings, face the challenge of expressing our true feelings verbally and non-verbally?

According to the book, *The Day America Told the Truth*, James Patterson and Peter Kim report that 91%, or, nine out of ten Americans lie regularly.

Where do we, as individuals, fall statistically? Are we one of the 91% or the 9%? Each person must answer this question for himself. But, how truthful are we going to be when we do answer?

A further breakdown of the authors' statistics indicate that:

> 86% of the people lie to their parents
> 75% of the people lie to their friends
> 73% of the people lie to their siblings
> 69% of the people lie to their lovers
> 61% of the people lie to their boss
> 59% of the people lie to their children

What a calamity! These statistics indicate a very serious deterioration of the moral fiber of America. What happened to integrity? Has it become a word without a meaning?

William Shakespeare counseled us most wisely when he said, "To thine own self be true." When we are true to ourselves then it is easy to be true to others.

One can see how important it is to become more vigilant where our true feelings, thoughts and words are concerned.

Speaking of words, the offensive and shocking words used in the movies and on the airwaves today could cause us much concern. Why? Let us recall that thoughts create thought fields which can be very powerful (for good or for ill). And . . . before we say a word, we have a thought, fleeting though it may be. When thoughts are expressed in words, the thought becomes even more powerful because the thought has also been released as an audible vibration, which then creates a compounded effect of the thought. When this energy has been released out there in the ethers of the air, does it have an affect on humankind? Absolutely! How important then, is the quality of our words?

Remember when people used to express themselves adequately without resorting to language that is sordid and foul (which is so prevalent in our Western society today)? Oh, that we could return to purer thoughts and purer words.

The following Biblical references remind us of how important it is to be mindful of each word we speak:

Proverbs 12:18
There is that speaketh like the piercings of a sword: but the tongue of the wise is health.

Proverbs 13:2
A man shall eat good by the fruit of his mouth: but the soul of the transgressors shall eat violence.

Proverbs 13:3
He that keepeth his mouth keepeth his life: but he that openeth wide his lips shall have destruction.

Proverbs 16:24
Pleasant words are as an honeycomb, sweet to the soul, and health to the bones.

Proverbs 18:7
A fool's mouth is his destruction and his lips are the snare of his soul.

Proverbs 18:21
Death and life are in the power of the tongue.

Proverbs 21:23

Whoso keepeth his mouth and his tongue keepeth his soul
from troubles.

Eph. 4:29

Let no corrupt communication proceed out of your mouth,
but that which is good to the use of edifying, that it may
minister grace unto the hearers.

James 3:6

And the tongue is a fire, a world of iniquity: so is the tongue
among our members, that it defileth the whole body, and
setteth on fire the course of nature;

James 3:8

But the tongue can no man tame; it is an unruly evil, full of
deadly poison.

James 3:10

Out of the same mouth proceedeth blessing and cursing. My
brethren, these things ought not so to be.

Author Unknown - "Profanity indicates poverty of intellect."

Thoughts precipitate words. Feelings precipitate thoughts.

If we understood . . . if we were fully and genuinely aware of the
far reaching consequences the words we use have on and in our lives, as
well as the lives of those we come in contact with, we would assuredly—beyond question—want to be influential in affecting a reversal of
this condition in our society today.

Chapter 20

A More Harmonious Be-ing

In Chapter Two we discussed a few Natural Laws and how they influence our lives. We learned that regardless of our awareness of natural laws, we suffer natural consequences if we break a law. In like manner, when we observe a natural law, we reap the benefits and enjoy the positive effects of that law in our lives. (The Law of *Cause* and *Effect*.)

In accordance with the laws of Nature (God's laws), certain feelings affect particular parts of our body or aspects of our life. When we suffer physical, mental or emotional pain of any kind, it's our body's way of getting our attention to let us know there is imbalance of some kind in our life . . . there is disharmony in the body's energies. We are out of *sync* with God's laws . . . the laws of Nature. God talks to us through our body. Anytime a natural law is disobeyed—like holding onto resentment or not forgiving, for instance—it is possible that we could experience kidney problems.

Franz Alexander, the father of psychosomatic medicine, recognized over forty years ago: "There is much evidence that, just as certain pathological microorganisms have a specific affinity for certain organs, so also certain emotional conflicts possess specificities and accordingly tend to afflict certain internal organs." (*Love, Medicine and Miracles*, Dr. Bernie Siegel)

Each emotion releases a different hormonal chemical into the body. For example, with the emotion of *fear for our life—fight or flight*—ACTH is released into the bloodstream to assist us in the challenge we are momentarily facing, and propels us into an action that helps preserve our life. Research further indicates that each feeling/emotion creates tears of a different chemical composition. This is why it feels so good to cry when we feel some of the feelings we do. So, contrary to what some people think, tears are important. Crying literally serves to relieve the stress that is caused by an over-abundance of chemicals created by a particular feeling. Never apologize for crying or shedding tears. We service our health as well as our emotions when we cry.

The chemical present in our tears during a particular emotion, is simultaneously present in other parts of our body. A prolonged negative feeling of any kind can cause a continual chemical emission that eventually brings about a chemical imbalance in our body. This can subsequently lead to illness. Nevertheless, feelings and emotions are absolutely necessary in our lives . . . they help us survive. It's the continual suppression of unresolved feelings/emotions that cause the problems we experience in our lives. And, the feelings that are buried—that haven't been resolved—continue to govern our thoughts and beliefs.

Is it just a coincidence you get a sore throat, have a liver problem, cancer, diabetes, or anything else you may happen to have? I think not. The laws that govern the proper functioning of your body parts have been broken. Whether it be the laws of good nutrition, the laws of physical maintenance, the laws of correct thinking, the laws of appropriate feelings, the law of "do unto others." Regardless of what the problem is, the problem is there because of broken laws which, in turn, have created imbalance and inharmonious vibrations within your body.

In his book, *Quantum Healing*, Dr. Chopra gives further clarification of this principle:

Many people still think that the nerves work electrically, like a telegraph system, because until fifteen years ago, that is what medical texts contended. However, in the 1970's a series of important discoveries began, centering on a new class of minute chemicals called neuro-transmitters. As their name implies, these chemicals transmit nerve impulses; they act in our bodies as 'communicator molecules,' whereby the neurons of the brain can talk to the rest of the body.

Neuro-transmitters are the runners that race to and from the brain telling every organ inside us of our emotions, desires, memories, intuitions, and dreams. None of these events are confined to the brain alone. Likewise, none of them are strictly mental, since they can be coded into chemical messages. Neuro-transmitters touch the life of every cell. Wherever a thought wants to go, these chemicals must go too, and without them, no thoughts can exist. To think is to practice brain chemistry, promoting a cascade of responses throughout the body.

Dr. Chopra continues:

. . . the mind and body are like parallel universes. Anything that happens in the mental universe must leave tracks in the physical one . . . your body is the physical picture, in 3-D, of what you are thinking. We don't see our bodies as projected thoughts because many physical changes that thinking causes are un-noticeable. They involve minute alterations of cell chemistry, body temperature, electrical charge, blood pressure, and so on, which do not register on our focus of attention. You can be assured, however, that the body is fluid enough to mirror any mental event. Nothing can move without moving the whole.

The latest discoveries in neuro-biology build an even stronger case for the parallel universes of mind and body. When researchers looked further, beyond the nervous system and the immune system, they began to discover the same neuro-peptides and receptors for them in other organs, such as the intestines, kidneys, stomach, and heart. There is every expectation of finding them elsewhere, too. This means that your kidneys can 'think,' in the sense that they can produce the identical neuro-peptides found in the brain. Their receptor sites are not simply sticky patches. They are questions waiting for answers, framed in the language of the chemical universe. It is very likely that if we had the whole dictionary and not just our few scraps, we would find that every cell speaks as fluently as we do.

Dr. Candace Pert, one of the most progressive and accomplished researchers in the field of brain chemistry and director of the brain biochemistry division at the National Institute of Mental Health, refers to the entire mind-body system as a network of information. Dr. Pert feels that we cannot separate the mind and the body, and prefers to use one term for both—BODYMIND.

Dr. Chopra states: "It has now been absolutely proved that the same neuro-chemicals influence the whole bodymind. Everything is interconnected at the level of the neuro-peptide; therefore, to separate these areas is simply bad science." He also tells us that the human brain changes its thoughts into thousands of chemicals every second. We may do well to ask ourselves if the chemicals we are creating are healthy or unhealthy chemicals.

Perhaps a more meaningful question at this point is, "Do I want to change the construction or design of my life?" If the answer is "yes", you will be encouraged and motivated to know that reconstruction with a new design is entirely possible! You CAN be in control of your life. By becoming more conscious and mindful of your feelings and thoughts, then, by using your new *tool*—the Script, all of this is possible. You CAN change the *undesirable* causes in your life. You CAN bring desired effects to your life. YOU are the one who determines the outcome of each day. YOU are the master of your destiny—your Soul.

Now that you have the Script as a vehicle with which to change your inharmonious vibrations into a more harmonious state of Be-ing—consider supporting this process by including in your daily living the following:

1. Eat nutritious foods. Eat an abundance of complex carbohydrates; fruits, vegetables and whole grains. Low fat and very low refined carbohydrates. Avoid overeating.
2. Drink plenty of water—eight or more glasses a day.
3. Consistently participate in some form of exercise at least four days a week, 20-30 minutes a day.
4. Take a good source of minerals. Minerals are the catalyst to the spirit. They provide the electrolytes (turn on the electrical energy).
5. Eliminate foreign or deleterious substances from your body that are known to be detrimental; i.e. alcohol, drugs, tobacco, etc.

And why are the foregoing guidelines important? Let's think of each cell in our body operating as though it were a miniature powerplant. The DNA is the intelligence—the receptor of light, or the supervisor of the powerplant (the cell).

Under normal circumstances, when the cell receives fuel or substances that are in harmony with mother nature, the receptor of light (DNA) embraces this positive energy, synthesizes it to full advantage and continues to produce it's own life supporting and life enhancing energies from the harmonious fuel it receives. The cell (powerplant) responds positively and continues to operate and function to it's full potential.

When foreign substances such as alcohol, drugs, tobacco or other deleterious substances are used by a person, mass confusion is created in the DNA, because these substances are not in harmony or compatible with the cell. Little by little, due to this incompatibility each time these negative energies are used by the body, they shut down the receptors of light in the DNA, which then allows darkness or confusion to enter. Eventually, after layers of inharmonious energy is impacted over the DNA, darkness takes hold and totally covers the memory of perfection in the cell. The electrical system of the cell (powerplant) will eventually function without order. Compound this by adding all the cells of the body together. The edifice that houses the cells then turns into chaos with disfunctioning cells throughout the body as a result.

For these same reasons you can comprehend why it is so important to feel positive feelings, to think positive thoughts, to use positive words and to eat correct foods. The powerplant must be stoked with appropriate energy in order for the cells to receive correct information and to receive light.

By incorporating the foregoing five suggestions into your life, and processing your feelings through the Script, you can bring your body into a more balanced and harmonious state of well Be-ing. You can also refurbish and accelerate the efficiency of your power plant.

If you are presently involved in an exercise program and are participating in a good nutritional regimen, you've undoubtedly seen the positive results that come from doing this. Now, dealing with your feelings will be an added benefit for you in bringing your body into an even more balanced state. Just keep in mind that all these things work together for your good—for a happier, healthier, and more harmonious Be-ing.

Wherever you are in your quest for peace, personal balance and harmony, remember, you are a five-dimensional Be-ing. As you participate in eliminating your negative feelings and resultant blocks, you are healing the Emotional and the Spiritual aspects of your life. However, at the same time you are accomplishing an Emotional and Spiritual healing, you are also facilitating the Physical, the Social and the Mental aspects of your life. The healing that automatically occurs in each area of your life just by concentrating on resolving your feelings, will naturally bring you closer and closer to wellness, wholeness, and balance.

Allow and give yourself every advantage on your road to becoming whole and complete. Use whatever is available to further assist you in your reconstruction and new design; food, supplements, exercise and beautiful music. Yes, music is extremely important. (But that's a whole other subject.) Suffice it to say, you'll want to listen to music that brings peace and tranquility to your soul in order to support your combined efforts. And you will also want to wear and surround yourself with harmonious colors. (Which is another wonderful subject!)

Chapter 21

Freeing The Soul

When we enter this sphere of existence, each one of us is innately blessed with our own *power*. Some people may think of *power* in a negative sense, but for our purposes here, power, as described in the dictionary in the positive sense of the word is: "Ability to act; capability. Potential capacity. Great or telling force or effect."

How we choose to use this *power*—this aptitude for genius and fulfillment we all have been given—determines our capacity to function in life; determines the effects in our lives; determines our sense of well-being or not so well-being. Our FEELINGS, THOUGHTS and EMOTIONS are what influence the application or use of this *power*.

When we utilize our power in observance of Universal Laws, we preserve our own *power*. And, when we break a Universal Law—where our own power is concerned—or when we allow others to usurp or sap our power from us, we lose that power. This leaves us handicapped, crippled and impotent. In other words, we become helpless in effectively directing the outcome of our own day to day living.

Let me give an example to illustrate what I mean: In a seminar setting where deep personal issues were examined very closely, a married couple, desirous of working out some of their issues, were participating. At one point the husband wanted his wife to participate in a role playing situation that would help her find what her belief was in one area of her life. She was being very resistant to becoming involved in this little exercise, but could understand that it would undoubtedly be very beneficial to her.

He cajoled, persuaded and insisted that she do this. She was particularly resistant at first, but finally made her decision. Turning to her husband, this is what she said, "I'm going to do this, but I want you to understand that it's NOT because you want me to. It's because I CHOOSE to. I can see the benefits I would receive, and so I'm doing it because I DESIRE the benefits . . . and for no other reason!" She kept her power by making the decision to do it for her own growth experience, even though it was going to be uncomfortable going through it. This was her choice. And because it was her choice, she kept her power.

How do we break the laws that cause our loss of power on a day to day basis? The laws are broken when we allow another person to interfere, control or manipulate us or our life against our will. Likewise, if we try to interfere, control or manipulate another person's life or circumstances against their will—and they allow it—we rob them of their power, which renders them powerless to be who and what they came here to be.

As a parent, have you ever imposed *your will* over your child's *will*? This is one of the most devastating things we can do to a child (or anyone, for that matter). When a child has to give up his/her *will* to a parent, a part of their soul is violated. It's true that children need to learn to be obedient, but if you are involved in a situation with a child that turns into a power struggle—where you feel you've GOT to have control—be assured that no one will win, even if you break the child's *will*. (This can also happen between husband and wife, teacher and student, employer and employee, etc.) If you break a person's *will*, you rob them of the most valuable gift they possess. When this happens, it's as if their integrity, their soul has been ripped from them. And it's impossible to measure the devastation it causes or the lifetime scars it creates in an individual.

I believe that when a person is raped physically or raped emotionally, this is exactly what happens—their *will* is literally ripped from them. And this is one of the reasons most rape victims have such a difficult time healing. How do they get back their *will*, after it has so forcibly been taken from them? Usually, this is a difficult process.

Then there are the races, the groups of people who have had this done to them on a larger scale. All we have to do is look at history and recount the millions of people who have been captured, tortured, forced at gun point and made to submit to another's *will*, to recollect man's inhumanity to man. Could this treatment be part of the cause of so much hatred and so much prejudice? How many people are crying from their graves for justice to be served in their behalf? When can a healing be realized? If you are the descendent of any of these kinds of victims, put yourself in their place to feel what they may have felt. Then go through the Script for those feelings. The results may surprise you. In a way, you can affect a healing for them.

Once someone's *will* is gone, they are like a boat without a rudder. Not that they can't function, but they just don't have the direction they had while their "will" was still intact.

For you who feel someone has robbed you of your *will*, claim it back! Just go through the Script, stating at the beginning, "Spirit, please locate the origin of the feelings that were created in me when I unknowingly allowed my will to be taken." Continue through the remaining Script and replace the negative with the positive, "I choose claiming back my *will*. I forgive the person who robbed me of my *will*. I forgive myself for it happening. I now claim back my *will* and am grateful for its return. I choose functioning with my will intact from this day forward. I feel myself functioning with my *will* intact. I AM allowing my *will* to thrive once again in my Soul." Then complete the Script.

Have you ever known parents who thought they were supposed to run their child's life even after the child had left home and been on his own for several years? I knew a young man, David, who was a very obedient and dutiful son—always desirous of pleasing his parents. The parents' love and acceptance of David was a conditional love, however (meaning—they would love and accept him—IF he did what they dictated), so naturally, he was trained that he must always follow their instructions in order to maintain their love and acceptance. David was very cooperative in doing exactly what his parents wanted him to do concerning his schooling and preparation for a future career—as well as every other aspect of his life. He seemed to be anxious and on edge much of the time, but he was still very pleasant to be around.

One of David's characteristics that intrigued me was his stuttering. He didn't stutter all the time—only occasionally. The stuttering was especially noticeable when he talked to his parents on the telephone or got excited. I couldn't help but wonder if David's stuttering was triggered by an anxiety to please his parents. (I have since learned that one of the emotional causes of stuttering is "wanting to protest, but dares not.")

There finally came a point in David's life when he asserted his independence and took over his own life—he completely defied his parents on a major issue. David's parents practically disowned him and rarely communicated with him for about a year. To begin with, he was at a loss, because for the first time in his life he was making his own decisions without any input from his parents.

It was fascinating to watch David try to find his own identity. With the help of a friend who totally allowed him to be himself and imposed no conditions on their friendship—extending unconditional acceptance—David began to realize his unique capabilities and strengths. As he gained confidence in his ability to make correct choices, David claimed back his power by not allowing anyone to run his life! He eventually outgrew the stuttering and has continued admirably to direct and manage his own affairs. I might add, David's parents eventually recognized his ability to wisely govern his life and they now allow him his individuality.

Another way we break laws and surrender our power is by allowing someone or something to make us angry, irritated, bitter, resentful, or any other negative feeling. The feelings we *hang onto* and don't resolve will create, to some degree, a loss of our power. And where does this power go?

Some of us give our power away by simply feeling responsible to keep peace *at all costs*, and this usually costs us our *power*. We end up swallowing or burying our feelings just to keep peace, when our goal and challenge is to communicate what we are feeling in a mature, non-threatening and non-accusing manner.

Accomplishing this may require us to confront and monitor ourselves. By so doing, we could eventually become experts in the *language of feelings*, which is the most difficult and misunderstood language there is on the face of the earth! Nevertheless, communicate we must!

Many people, when expressing themselves in a confrontive situation, come from feelings of hostility, anger, bitterness, pride, hurt, resentment or worthlessness. They don't necessarily understand their own motivation for what they say, why they say it, and how they say it. In an attempt to express what they are feeling, they usually say the first thing that pops into their mind. When this happens, the true picture of what's going on inside a person is seldom communicated adequately or correctly.

The person who is listening to another's attempt to communicate has their own perception of the situation being discussed, so their attitude may be, "Someone has to win and someone has to lose in this exchange (the need to be *right*), and, by darn, it's not going to be me who loses," or, "I'm not giving in."

We are so busy trying to put over our point of view to the other person in hopes they will understand what we are talking about—so they can feel what we're feeling—that a true awareness, understanding, comprehension, or exchange is rarely accomplished.

If we, as human Be-ings, have a sincere desire to eliminate this kind of an impasse, we will always practice coming from a position of *no blame* and *no judgment*. We will extend our unconditional love and understanding at all times toward others. We will listen with interest—in calm and peace—and be willing to put ourselves in the other person's shoes. We will do our *best* to see through the other person's eyes.

One of the greatest benefits we will enjoy when we come from the posture of love and understanding—rather than blame and judgment—is the gift of maintaining our own power. At the same time, this then allows others to do likewise.

When we become involved in an issue (argument, disagreement, emotional tirade) and are putting our entire energy into *winning*, that issue rules us and takes our power. So, while we are participating in that issue, we are in literal bondage. And, if we feel a person has gotten the best of us . . . that we are defeated, and yet we continue to hang onto any negative feelings concerning that issue, our power is still neutralized.

If we don't want our power neutralized, we will *let go* of the entire issue and all the feelings surrounding it. At this point, we would do well to ask ourselves, "In the final analysis, what difference does it make, anyway?"

If we feel that we have won the issue, but the other person is upset about the whole exchange, their power is neutralized. And when a negative situation is not resolved by both or all participants involved—when there are still festering feelings—the energy created by that situation is misplaced (misplaced because it does not belong) . . . it stops progress.

Nevertheless, that energy resides in, and is a definite part of, the thought field of each person involved, creating a literal barrier between the two (or more) people—as documented with Kurlian photography in the book, *The Body Electric*, by Thelma Moss, Ph.D.

The negative energy created by this kind of situation connects and links these people together. It's as if they are having a tug of war with a rope, but neither one of them can let go. This negative energy is continually with them like a thick cord, connecting them—with a big barrier in between. This energy literally holds these two (or more) people back and keeps them from progressing.

Misplaced energy is also like a negative vapor that is endlessly present with the people involved, contributing to personal negativity and confusion which restricts and blocks their good and their moving forward in life. The individual power of the two people in this negative energy exchange is subsequently sapped and drained.

If you have had several of these exchanges with other people throughout your life that remain unresolved, your power is incessantly being drained from you. This gives you a clearer understanding of why it is so important to resolve any issues or negative feelings you now have or have had with anyone. (We DO want to operate with our own, full power, don't we?)

How can a person accomplish this? Process unresolved issues you have with anyone that stands out in your mind, using the Script. Feelings of resentment, hostility, animosity, anger, bitterness or pride are often the culprits that stifle, suffocate, smother, choke, restrain and limit you. When these feelings have not been resolved, they are deeply buried (seeded) and entrenched inside you—having some kind of impact on you, whether you recognize it or not. If they haven't already caused some recognizable problems in your life, eventually they will. Don't stop with just the feelings mentioned (resentment, hostility, animosity, anger, bitterness or pride). Discover any others you might have.

Even though we think we want to operate at our full power and potential, often we allow resentment, bitterness or our natural prideful nature to interfere with this desire. If we feel we have been unjustly treated or maligned, but have felt helpless to do anything about it—have been unable to resolve the situation—do we allow bitterness to creep into our Be-ing? The longer the situation goes unresolved, the more the resentment and bitterness festers and grows, thereby becoming a bigger, deeper, and more powerful energy. Eventually this energy can become all-consuming and even obsessive—motivating our every thought and action. (How unfortunate.)

Rather than going to the person(s) who has supposedly been the cause—as you see it—of creating your resentment or bitterness and resolving it, do you just keep hanging on to it?

Some people in this scenario may feel it would show a sign of weakness to approach the party with whom they were in conflict and ask for a resolution of the situation. At this point, *pride* is added to resentment and bitterness. And, *pride* can be SO great in some people that they would rather DIE than to seek forgiveness of, or give forgiveness to the offending or offended person. What does this accomplish? Just a lot of negativity that is extremely counter-productive and impedes our growth.

Pride, in this regard, denotes an unwarranted sense of one's own superiority (as defined in the dictionary). But pride often creates a wall between parents and children; children and parents; brothers and sisters; aunts and uncles; nieces and nephews; cousins; friends; employer and employee; co-workers, etc. In other words, walls are created in all human relationships. And yet, many people CHOOSE to function this way. Sometimes pride keeps loved ones apart for decades and creates animosity for generations. For what purpose? To be *RIGHT*? To satisfy the EGO—Edging God Out? How unfortunate, because all we are doing is sabotaging ourselves. Think of the wasted years; the joy and happiness that has been missed; the lack of inner peace; the unfulfilled dreams.

Negative feelings of any description, either felt by you or directed toward you or toward anyone else (knowingly or unknowingly), need to be resolved immediately. "Total unconditional forgiveness" and "unconditional love" are two of the most powerful solvents as positive feelings you can use to replace the old negative feelings in the Script.

Heighten your awareness in all phases of your life. As you become more conscious of what you are feeling, what you are thinking, what you are saying and what you are doing, you will experience how heightened awareness facilitates results. And as you begin seeing and feeling results you will have a greater appreciation for how extremely important your feelings, your thoughts, your words and your actions are to your well Be-ing. Your feelings and thoughts can bring you peace and joy or misery and unhappiness. And the beautiful part is . . . the *choice* is yours. All that is necessary is for you to become more consciously aware.

There are many references in the Bible that underlie the importance of our being mindful of our thoughts. My favorite is: 2 Corinthians 10:5: "Casting down imaginations . . . and bringing into captivity every thought to the obedience of Christ."

Avoid the wild imaginings your thoughts can create in you (as illustrated in the story about your boss requesting your presence in his office), and bring each thought you have into alignment with what Christ taught.

You will find that as you become more and more aware, observant, and alert to your challenges as they occur, and see them for the opportunities and gifts they are—opportunities for growth—you will want to give thanks for them, otherwise your growth will be empty and void. GIVE THANKS IN ALL THINGS because JOY is preceded by GRATITUDE. And, as it says in the scriptures, "Man is, that he might have joy." Have you experienced a fullness of joy yet?

When you allow balance, harmony and order to enter your life by transforming negative vibrations into positive vibrations, joy will accompany your harmony in unlimited abundance. This joy, harmony and balance is at your fingertips. Make a commitment to yourself to:

☐ 1. Become aware/mindful/conscious of your feelings, thoughts, emotions, words and actions.

☐ 2. Let go of blame and judgment.

☐ 3. Let go of force and control.

☐ 4. Sincerely forgive the past (everyone and everything, including yourself) and let go of it.

☐ 5. Resolve all resentment, bitterness and pride.

☐ 6. Love without putting conditions on that love (again, including yourself).

☐ 7. Recognize that everyone is perfect the way they are.

☐ 8. Accept responsibility and accountability for self.

☐ 9. Quit resisting.

☐ 10. Quit denying.

☐ 11. Give thanks in ALL things . . . be grateful for the challenges and the pain! (It gets your attention to let you know you're out of balance.)

☐ 12. Be excited about getting to know the REAL you.

☐ 13. Utilize the "Script" on a consistent daily basis.

☐ 14. Pray to God to have Him assist you in your efforts.

By taking these steps toward a more fulfilling and satisfying life, you are putting yourself in the position to gain control . . . where you become the *master* of your life's circumstances and destiny rather than remaining a *victim*.

After incorporating these principles into your daily life, it will become evident to you that you DO have the ability to communicate the language of feelings . . . to be congruent in what you feel, think, say and do. You DO have the ability to change your vibrations . . . to uncover the memory of perfection in your DNA so that you function from the perfect blueprint of your Be-ing. You DO have the ability to become the *master* of your Soul. You CAN keep your own power. You CAN become closer and eventually return to your *Source*.

The *quantum* strides possible for you to make in your life will be determined by your diligence in seeking self-awareness. In order to open that *quantum* door and make the desirable changes you are anticipating, CONSISTENCY is the "key." Don't be timid about using that "key" and opening that door . . . thus, allowing those strides to be made.

If you ever had a desire to contribute to society . . . to make a difference, THIS is your opportunity.

By becoming acutely aware of your own feelings and changing the undesirable ones to desirable ones, you will be contributing to the establishment of a more humane and a more genuinely caring society.

It would please me to learn of your experiences in utilizing the Script in your life. Keep in mind that as you use it, you are on a journey—you are in a process—an on-going process. My hope is that its application in your life will assist you in accomplishing your goals and your desires. May the quality of your life improve beyond your fondest dreams.

May your ability to communicate the language of feelings become one of your greatest assets. May your efforts uncover your **True** and **Glorious Self**. May your endeavors be rewarded with peace, love, joy, success and genuine fulfillment!

Prayer
by
St. Francis of Assisi

Lord, make me an instrument of Thy peace.
Where there is hatred, let me sow love.
Where there is injury, pardon.
Where there is doubt, faith.
Where there is despair, hope.
Where there is darkness, light.
Where there is sadness, joy.
Oh, Divine Master, grant that I may not so much seek,
To be consoled, as to console.
To be understood, as to understand.
To be loved, as to love.
For it is in giving, that we receive.
It is in pardoning, that we are pardoned.
It is in dying [the false self], that we are born
To Eternal Life

Copyright Acknowledgments

For permission to use copyrighted material the author gratefully acknowledges the following:

Babbel, Frederick W.
"Bring Forth Your Light."
Bookcraft, Salt Lake City, Utah, 1987
Bloodworth, Venice
"Key to Yourself."
DeVorss & Company, Marina del Rey, California 90294, 1980
Borysenko, Joan B., Ph.D.
"Minding The Body, Mending the Mind." © 1987 by
Joan Borysenko.
Reprinted with permission of Addison-Wesley Publishing Co., Reading,
Massachusetts, 01867
Bradshaw,John
"Reprinted with the permission of the publishers
HEALTH COMMUNICATIONS, INC.,
DEERFIELD BEACH, FLORIDA
from HEALING THE SHAME THAT BINDS YOU, by JOHN BRADSHAW,
copyright date 1988"
Brennan, Barbara Ann
"Hands of Light."
Bantam Books, New York, New York, 10103, 1988
Carey, Ken
"Terra Christa." Uni-Sun Publications, Kansas City, Missouri
Chopra, Deepak, M.D., F.A.C.P.
"Quantum Healing: Exploring the Frontiers of Mind/Body."
© 1989 by Deepak Chopra, M.D.
Used by permission of Bantam Books, a division of Bantam
Doubleday, Dell Publishing Group, Inc., New York, New York, 10103,
"COMPLETE GUIDE TO YOUR EMOTIONS AND YOUR HEALTH (THE)"
    © 1986 by Rodale Press, Inc. Permission granted by Rodale Press, Inc;
    Emmaus, PA 18098. Price $24.95. To order, call 1-800-441-7761
Dougherty, Sarah Belle
Sunrise Theosophic Perspectives: "Mysteries of Prenatal Consciousness."
February/March, 1990
© National Geographic Society
"The Incredible Machine" 1986, 1989, Washington, D.C. 20036

Lybbert, Carolyn
> The "Script." Suquamish, Washington 98392, 1984

Pearce, Joseph Chilton
> "Magical Child." © 1977 by Joseph Chilton Pearce. Used by permission of the publisher, Dutton, an imprint of New American Library, a division of Penguin USA, Inc., New York, New York 10014-3657,

Peterson, Norma
> "Mind Over Disease: II. Warning! Daily Hassles Are Hazardous." Readers's Digest Association, Inc.,
> Reprint, April 1987 issue, Pleasantville, New York

Ritchie, George G. and Elizabeth Sherrill
> "Return from Tomorrow."
> Fleming H. Revell, 184 Central Ave., Old Tappan, New Jersey 07675, 1981

Robinson, Donald
> "Mind Over Disease: I. Your Attitude Can Make You Well." Readers's Digest Association, Inc.
> Reprint, April 1987 issue Pleasantville, New York

Sanford, John A.
> "The Kingdom Within."
> ©1979 HarperCollins Publishers, San Francisco, CA 9411

Siegel, Bernie S., M.D.
> "Love, Medicine & Miracles." Copyright notice 1986
> HarperCollins Publishers, New York, New York 10022-5299

Stowell, Jerome W., Dr., M.D.
> "Testimony of a Scientist." Kellirae Arts, Provo, Utah 84602, 1973

Wickett, Michael
> "IT'S ALL WITHIN YOUR REACH."
> ©1987 Nightingale-Conant Corporation, Chicago, Illinois

Winter, J. A., M.D.
> "The Origins Of Illness and Anxiety."
> Matrix House Ltd., New York, New York 10003, 1966

Suggested Reading

Ader, Robert
    "Psychoneuroimmunology"
    Academic Press, New York, New York, 1981
Allen, Charles L.,
    "God's Psychiatry"
    Jove Publications, Inc., New York, New York 10016, 1978
Arterburn, Stephen
    "Hand-Me-Down Genes & Second-Hand Emotions"
    Fireside (Simon & Schuster), New York, New York 10020, 1994
Asimov, Isaac
    "The Human Brain, Its Capacities and Functions"
    Boston: Houghton Mifflin, ©1963
    "Understanding Physics: Light, Magnetism and Electricity"
    A Mentor Book, New American Library, Inc.,NewYork, NewYork, 10019, 1966
Babbel, Frederick W.
    "Bring Forth Your Light"
    Bookcraft, Salt Lake City, Utah, 1989
Barnett, Lincoln
    "The Universe and Dr. Einstein"
    William Sloane Associates 1957, New York
Benson, Herbert
    "The Mind-Body Effect"
    Simon & Schuster, New York, New York, 1980
Bloodworth, Venice
    "Key to Yourself"
    DeVorss & Company, Marina del Rey, California 90294, 1980
Borysenko, Joan B.
    "Minding The Body, Mending The Mind"
    Addison-Wesley Publishing Co. Reading Massachusetts 01867, 1987
Braden, Greg
    "Walking Between The Worlds"
    Radio Bookstore Press, 1997
Bradshaw, John
    "Healing The Shame That Binds You"
    Health Communications, Inc., Deerfield Beach. Florida, 1988
Brennan, Barbara Ann
    "Hands of Light"
    Bantam Books, New York, New York 10103, 1988
Brinkley, Dannion

"At Peace in the Light"
Harper Collins Publishers, Inc., New York, New York 10022, 1995
Buscaglia, Leo
"Living, Loving & Learning"
Ballantine Books, a division of Random House, Inc., New York, 1982
Carey, Ken
"Terra Christa"
Uni*sun Publications, Kansas City, Missouri
Carroll, Lee & Jan Tober
"The Indigo Children"
Hay House, Inc., Carlsbad, California 92018, 1999
Chopra, Deepak, M.D., F.A.C.P.
"Quantum Healing: Exploring The Frontiers Of Mind/Body Medicine"
Bantam Books, New York, New York 10103, 1990
Chopra, Deepak, M.D., F.A.C.P.
"Perfect Health"
Harmony Books, a division of Crown Publishers, Inc. N.Y., N. Y., 10012, 1990
Clark, Glenn
"The Man Who Tapped the Secrets of the Universe"
The University of Science and Philosophy, Swannanoa, Waynesboro, Virginia
First Edition, 1946. 14th Edition, 1981
Cohen, Alan
"The Dragon Doesn't Live Here Anymore"
Alan Cohen Publications & Workshops, Somerset, New Jersey 08875, 1981
Cousins, Norman
"Anatomy of an Illness as Perceived by the Patient"
Norton, New York, 1987: Bantam, New York, 1981
Covey, Stephen R.
"The Divine Center." Bookcraft, Salt Lake City Utah, 1982
Covey, Stephen R.
"Seven Habits of Highly Successful People"
Simon & Schuster, Rockefeller Ctr, 1230 Ave of Americas, N.Y., N.Y. 10020
Custer, Dan
"The Miracle of Mind Power"
©1960 by Prentice Hall Press, New York, New York, 19923
Diamond, John, M.D.
"B K, Behavioral Kinesiology"
Harper & Row, Publishers, New York, New York 10022, 1979
Dougherty, Sarah Belle
Sunrise Theosophic Perspectives: "Mysteries of Prenatal Consciousness"
February/March, 1990

Dyer, Wayne W.
   "Pulling Your Own Strings"
   Avon Books, New York, New York 10019, 1979
Dyer, Wayne W.
   "The Secrets to Manifesting Your Destiny"
   Nightingale-Conant Corp., Niles, Illinois 60714
Dyer, Wayne W.
   "The Sky's the Limit"
   Pocket Books, New York, New York 10020, 1980
Eadie, Betty J.
   "Embraced by the Light", and "The Ripple Effect"
   c/o Onjinjinkta, Seattle WA 98125, 1999
Eyre, Linda & Richard
   "Teaching Your Children Sensitivity"
   A Fireside Book (Simon & Schuster) N.Y., N.Y. 10020, 1995
Frankl, Viktor E.
   "Man's Search for Meaning"
   Pocket Books, New York, New York 10020 1959, 1963, 1980
Glasser, Howard and Jennifer Easley
   "Transforming the Difficult Child"
   Center for Difficult Child Publications
Goleman, Daniel
   "Emotional Intelligence"
   Bantam Books, N.Y., N.Y. 10036, 1995
Helmstetter, Shad, Ph.D.
   "What to Say When You Talk to Yourself"
   Pocket Books, New York, New York, 1987
Helmstetter, Shad, Ph.D.
   "The Self-Talk Solution"
   William Morrow & Co., Inc., New York, New York, 1987
Jampolsky, Gerald G., M.D.
   "Listen To Me ..."
   Celestial Arts, Berkeley, CA 94707, 1996
Jampolsky, Gerald G., M.D.
   "Love Is Letting Go Of Fear"
   ©1970, Bantam Books, New York, New York 10103
Johnson, Denny
   "What The Eye Reveals . . . "
   ©1984 Rayid. Model Publications, Goleta, California 93117
Joslyn, Joy Tsuya & Don
   "The First Note"
   Art Farm Productions, Coloma, CA 95613, 1995

Keyes, Ken Jr.
"Prescriptions for Happiness"
Living Love Publications, St. Mary, Kentucky 40063

Kimball, Spencer W.
"The Miracle of Forgiveness"
Bookcraft, Inc., Salt Lake City, Utah, 1969, 17th Printing, 1974

LaHaye, Tim and Bob Phillips
"Anger is a Choice"
S. John Bacon Pty. LTD. Victoria 3149, Australia © 1982 by Zondervan
Corporation

Latham, Dr. Glenn I.
"Christlike Parenting"
Gold Leaf Press, 415 Neal Armstrong Rd., Salt Lake City, Utah 84116, 2000

Lundberg, Gary B. & Joy Saunders
"I Don't Have to Make Everything All Better"
Viking Penguin Press, Hudson, New York, 10014, 1995

Miller, Saul
"Food for Thought"
Prentice-Hall, Inc. Englewood Cliffs, New Jersey 07632, 1979

Mills, Roy
"The Soul's Remembrance"
Onjinjinkta Publishing, Seattle, WA 98125, 1999

Moss, Thelma, Ph.D.
"The Body Electric"
J.P. Tarcher, Inc. Los Angeles, California 90069, 1979

MacIvor, Virginia and Sandra LaForest
"Vibrations"
Samuel Weiser, Inc., York Beach, MN 03910

Murphy, Dr. Joseph
"The Power of Your Subconscious Mind"
Prentice Hall, Inc., Englewood Cliffs, New Jersey, 1963, 1980

©National Geographic Society
"The Incredible Machine"
Washington, D.C. 20036, 1986, 1989

Noontil, Annette
"The Body is the Barometer of the Soul"
Victoria 3131 Australia, 1994

Padus, Emrika and the editors of Prevention Magazine
"The Complete Guide to Your Emotions & Your Health"
Rodale Press, Emmaus, PA 18098, 1986

Pearce, Joseph Chilton
"Magical Child"

Penguin USA, Inc., New York, New York 10014-3657,1977

Peterson, Norma
   "Mind Over Disease: II. Warning! Daily Hassles Are Hazardous,"
   Readers Digest Association, Inc. Reprint, April 1987 issue, Pleasantville, N.Y.

Ritchie, George G., and Elizabeth Sherrill
   "Return from Tomorrow."
   Fleming H. Revell, 184 Central Ave., Old Tappan, N.J. 07675, 1981

Robinson, Donald
   "Mind Over Disease: I. Your Attitude Can Make You Well"
   Readers Digest Association, Inc. Reprint, April 1987 issue, Pleasantville, N.Y.

Sanford, John A.
   "The Kingdom Within"
   ©1979 HarperCollins Publishers, San Francisco, CA 94111

Schneider, Meir
   "Self-Healing—My Life and Vision"
   Routledge & Kegan Paul Inc., New York, New York 10001, 1987

Siegel, Bernie S.,
   "Love, Medicine & Miracles"
   HarperCollins Publishers, New York, New York 10022-5299

(Skinner), Valerieann Giovanni (Cover artist. See www.Valerieann.com)
   "The World of Mirrors"
   Inner Light Creations, Georgetown, ID 83239, 2002

Smith, Harry Douglas
   "Instantaneous Healing"
   Parker Publishing Co., Inc., West Nyack, NY, 1965

Swindoll, Charles R.
   "Dropping Your Guard: The Value of Open Relationships"
   Guideposts edition, Carmel, New York 10512, 1983

Tuttle, Carol
   "Return To Wholeness"
   Elton-Wolf Publishing, Inc. Seattle, WA, 2002

Russell, A.J. - (Two Listeners)
   "God Calling", Jove Book, N.Y., N.Y. 10016, 1978

Robbins, Anthony
   "Awaken the Giant Within"
   A Fireside Book (Simon & Schuster), N.Y., N.Y. 10020, 1992

Wickett, Michael
   "It's All Within Your Reach"
   Nightingale-Conant Corporation, Chicago, Illinois, 1987

Winter, J. A., M.D.,
   "The Origins Of Illness and Anxiety"

Previous Script

Spirit/Super-Conscious, please locate the origin of my feeling(s), thought(s) of _____.

Take each and every level, layer, area, and aspect of my Be-ing to this origin. Analyze and resolve it perfectly with God's truth.

Come through all generations of time and eternity, healing every incident and its appendages based on the origin. Do it according to God's will until I'm at the present—filled with light and truth, God's peace and love, forgiveness of myself for my incorrect perceptions, forgiveness of every person, place, circumstance, and event which contributed to this feeling(s)/thought(s).

With total forgiveness and unconditional love, I allow every physical, mental, emotional, and spiritual problem, and inappropriate behavior based on the negative origin recorded in my DNA, to transform.

       *I Choose Be-ing _____.
       I Feel _____.
       I AM _____.

It is done. It is healed. It is accomplished now!

Thank you, Spirit, for coming to my aid and helping me attain the full measure of my creation. Thank you, thank you, thank you! I love you and praise God from whom all blessings flow.**

*Basically, use the same appropriate positive feeling on each of the three blanks to replace the negative feeling.
**You can do the Script in the name of Jesus Christ if you choose.

About The Author

    Karol K. Truman is a practicing therapist and Spiritual healer. She is dedicated to assisting people achieve emotional and spiritual well-being through resolving and healing their "core issues." In her book, *Feelings Buried Alive Never Die . . .* (now in 3 languages with over 300,000 copies sold), she addresses the importance of resolving "buried" feelings, and introduces the concept of "Scripting."

    Mrs. Truman is an accomplished pianist and music instructor, having taught piano—until she started writing books—since she was a young teen-ager.

    Over fifty years ago, the author started asking the question, "WHY?" She began searching for the cause of a particular health challenge. This first led her to an in-depth study of nutrition and weight control. Karol was later made aware of the importance of exercise and the role it plays in our well-being. This resulted in her, her husband and partners pioneering the mini-trampoline industry; manufacturing and distributing them world-wide. The subject of her first book addresses the benefits of rebound exercise. This book, *Looking Good Feeling Great,* was published in 1983.

Eventually, however, it became apparent to Karol that physical health was inextricably linked to emotional and even spiritual health. Recognizing this, Ms. Truman bacame involved in the ever-deepening study of the Laws of Cause and Effect—the principles that govern trans-formational healing and growth. Along with extensive and exhaustive research and study, she has also participated in numerous conferences, classes, seminars and workshops.

FEELINGS BURIED ALIVE NEVER DIE . . . is a partial compila-tion of the answers she found to the "WHYS."

In her most recent book, *Healing Feelings . . . From Your Heart,* Karol shares the wealth of knowledge and experience gained from her Feelings . . . Seminars, and from the thousands of individuals she has counseled since publication of *Feelings Buried Alive Never Die . . . .*

ORDER FORM

Description		Price	Quantity	Total
Books				$
	Feelings Buried Alive Never Die... (English)	$17.95		$
	Feelings Buried Alive Never Die... (Spanish)	$17.95		$
	Healing Feelings... From Your Heart	$17.95		$
	Looking Good Feeling Great (Rebound Exercise)	$9.95		$
Scripting Tools				
	Laminated "SCRIPT" Card	$2.00		$
	New Updated Laminated "SCRIPT" Card	$2.00		$
	Laminated Feelings Reference Guide (40-3x5 cards)	$14.00		$
	Unlaminated Feelings Reference Guide (40-3x5 cards)	$10.00		$
	Mobile App for Scripting	$8.99		$
CD's				
	Feelings Buried Alive Never Die...	$39.95		$
	Healing Feelings... From Your Heart	$39.95		$
	Infinite Abundance (Scripting for Abundance)	$9.95		$
	Why Weight?	$9.95		$
	10 Healing Feelings Newsletters (Audio CD)	$7.95		$
	Re-Turning (Karol & Dan Truman's music)	$7.95		$
	Songs from the Heart (Delmont Truman)	$9.95		$
	Subtotal			$
	Shipping ($3.95 for 1 item and $1 per item thereafter)			$
	Utah Residents add 6.25% Sales Tax			$
	TOTAL (Prices Listed in US $)			$

Make checks payable to: Olympus Distributing, P.O. Box 4218, St. George, UT 84771

SHIP TO

Name:_____ Email: _____

Address:_____

City:_____ State:_____ Zip:_____ Phone #_____

Prices subject to change without notice. Please allow 2-3 weeks for delivery
Credit Card Orders Call 1-800-531-3180
For product descriptions or more information please visit our web site at
www.HealingFeelings.com
Call 1-800-531-3180
Fax 435-723-6644